GROWING UP WRITING

TIMES **T** BOOKS

RANDOM HOUSE

GROWING UP WRITING

TEACHING CHILDREN TO WRITE, THINK, AND LEARN

ARLENE SILBERMAN

Copyright © 1989 by Arlene Silberman
All rights reserved under International and
Pan-American Copyright Conventions. Published in the
United States by Times Books, a division of Random
House, Inc., New York, and simultaneously in Canada
by Random House of Canada Limited, Toronto.

Library of Congress Cataloging-in-Publication Data

Silberman, Arlene.
    Growing up writing: teaching children to write, think,
and learn/by Arlene Silberman.—1st ed.
        p.   cm.
    Bibliography: p.
    Includes index.
    ISBN 0-8129-1823-1
    1. Language arts—United States.   2. English
language—Composition and exercises—Study and
teaching.   I. Title.
LB1576.S43   1989
372.6—dc20   88-40492
                                                   CIP

Manufactured in the United States of America
9 8 7 6 5 4 3 2
First Edition

To Charles,

whose life,
like his writing,
is infused with strength
and gentleness,

this book is dedicated
with love and full devotion.

ACKNOWLEDGMENTS

It is customary for an author to express intellectual debts at the outset, and to reserve a few words of personal appreciation after everyone else has been properly thanked. A writer, especially a woman writer, who reverses the usual order may risk appearing unprofessional. I choose to run that risk.

My husband, Charles E. Silberman, widely known as an author, scholar, and journalist, has long been my personal mentor. Working together with me when he wrote *Crisis in the Classroom* and I directed the research staff, and separately when I wrote *Growing Up Writing* while he researched a book now in process, Charles has offered guidance but never imposed it. I am deeply grateful for his generosity and his restraint.

I am also indebted to James Gray, founder and director of the Bay Area Writing Project and its offshoot, the National Writing Project (NWP). He changed the tone and content of this book by showing me how thousands of teachers, regardless of subject area and grade level, are learning to teach each other new ways of making writing central to thinking and learning. This book and I owe much to his fresh ideas and to the vast amount of time that he gave me.

All of Jim Gray's associates were helpful, but a full measure of gratitude is due Mary Ann Smith, director of the Bay Area Writing Project; Peggy Swoger, a member of the NWP National Advisory Board; and Sam Watson, director of the NWP Southeast region. My own teaching would have benefited if I had met them earlier in my career. Other NWP leaders who gave special help include Sheridan Blau, Joseph Check, Dixie Dellinger, Donald Gellehr, Marian Mohr, Sondra Perl, Richard Sterling, and Bob Weiss.

Donald Graves's name appears in virtually every chapter, for he shared his time at every stage of my work. No one can write knowledgeably about new ways of looking at writing without reading Don's books and articles, nor can anyone leave the University of New Hampshire without being wiser for the time spent with him and his colleagues: Jane Hansen, Donald Murray, Tom Newkirk, and, in the summer program, Nancie Atwell and Mary Ellen Giacobbe. I am grateful for the help they and education historian Robert Conners gave me.

I am also indebted to Lucy McCormick Calkins, director of the Writing Project at Teachers College, Columbia University, for enabling me to spend time in New York City class rooms, where I saw writing reform struggling to be born, and for responding to the many questions I brought back from my visits. In time, her confidence in new ways of teaching writing became mine. Lucy and her colleague, Shelley Harwayne, enriched the book further by arranging for me to meet writing specialists whom they have prepared, as well as parent advocate Deborah Gordon Litt, of Montgomery County, Maryland, who gave most generously of her time.

Old and new associates have contributed greatly to this book. I have known Theodore R. Sizer for over twenty years, but his Coalition for Essential Schools showed me that there is still "something new under the sun." Also new to me were Jenee Gossard's approach to writing across the curriculum, Leslee Reed's development of dialogue journals, and Tom Romano's use of writing process with teenagers. I am grateful that Patricia F. Carini, Vito Perrone, and Anne M. Bussis, colleagues of long standing, have bolstered values that have come under attack recently. Robert Boynton, publisher of Boynton/Cook books, and Charles Suhor, executive deputy director of the National Council of Teachers of English, bolstered them further. I am also grateful for the interest shown by Harold Berlak, Glenda L. Bissex, Lil Brannon, Courtney Cazden, James Davis, Dixie Goswami, Cecelia M. Kingston, Jana Staton, Patricia L. Stock, and Dolores Vion.

During most of the time I was writing this book, Leanna Landsmann, an associate for two decades, was editor in chief and publisher of *Instructor* magazine. As such, she introduced me to members of the publication's Teacher Board, who responded to questionnaires I sent them. She and the teachers themselves have earned my appreciation, but one member of the board deserves special mention. The teaching approaches and children's material that Judy Meagher shared with me have become an important part of Chapter 4, as has original writing that Wisconsin and Massachusetts students have graciously permitted me to use.

Teachers not connected with *Instructor* have also helped me see how students can learn to express their ideas. I want to express collective appreciation and thank a few individuals: Lois Brandts, Joanie Chancer, Susan DiMaina, Bonnie Geer, Jean Gibran, Bernadette Glaze, Cynthia Holton, Mary Kollar, Eleanor Kron, Ray Lawson, Lin McKay, Terry Moher, Kay Nolan, Laurie Pessah, Gail Segal, Jay Sugarman, Beth Webb, and Kym Zanmiller.

I am also indebted to Mary Fowles and Roberta Camp of the Educational Testing Service, who showed me that instruction and assessment are intertwined, and to Patricia Belanoff, associate director of the Writing Program at the State University of New York at Stony Brook, who explained the value of portfolio evaluation. Further thanks are due Ina V. S. Mullis, who gave me preliminary data on National Assessment of Educational Progress tests of writing, and Rexford Brown, director of communications and senior policy analyst for the Education Commission of the States, who shared his thinking and writing. Six California specialists in writing assessment were particularly helpful: Beth Breneman, Charles Cooper, Sarah W. Freedman, Arthur N. Applebee, Judith A. Langer, and Sandra Murphy.

The two chapters that focus on parents as educators and

parents as activists owe much to associates of many years: J. William Rioux, executive director of the National Committee for Citizens in Education (NCCE), and Don Davies, founder and president of the Institute for Responsive Education. Ruth Green, executive director of the New York League for the Hard of Hearing, and Diane Brackett, director of the League's communication therapy, enriched this section further by helping me appreciate the importance of early language development.

I also want to single out for appreciation Harriet Barlow, director of the Blue Mountain Center, a colony for writers and artists, who are awarded four-week fellowships in order to live in blissful rural seclusion and work uninterruptedly. The award I received furthered my work by providing an opportunity that every serious writer cherishes.

My sister, Bernice Goldberg, served as an indefatigable clipping service in southern states, and my assistant, Doris Preisick, worked long nights and weekends serving as a copy editor, photocopier, and compiler of more drafts of the book than either she or I cares to remember.

These acknowledgments would be incomplete without thanking my agent, Julian Bach, who believed in the importance of this book when it was still a fledgling idea and who provided critical support throughout. He and his associate Ann Rittenberg gave uncommon editorial guidance until the manuscript was delivered into the skillful hands of my two editors, Elisabeth Scharlatt and Ruth Fecych. As the book took final shape, my debt of gratitude to associate publisher Sandee Brawarsky also became increasingly evident. It has been a joy to work with so many caring people.

Finally, I would like to express my collective appreciation to all the unnamed individuals whose help made *Growing Up Writing* possible.

—Arlene Silberman
New York, N.Y.
August 1989

■CONTENTS

INTRODUCTION

You've seen them everywhere: chatterbox children who become tongue-tied on paper; talkative teenagers who monopolize the telephone, but insist they can't write. Spoken thoughts come freely in the school yard, but written ones are labored in the classroom. Why the difference? Preschoolers scribble imaginary letters in snow or sand and string real letters together to invent words. They glory in learning to write their names, in seeing their letters proclaim "Laura" or "Noah." By age four some children demonstrate what world-famous educator Dr. Maria Montessori called an "explosion of writing." When they set off for kindergarten or first grade, often with notebook and pencil case in hand, they are usually eager to write. But that eagerness diminishes when they find their ideas and language being pushed aside. By age five or six, children who have never heard novelist Morris West's observation that language is "a hollow vessel which can be filled with wine, or water, or poison," already sense that the vessel will be filled with poison when it comes to writing. And older students know beyond doubt that safety lies in trying to avoid that poison. Consequently, the very adolescents who jabber in the hallway and prattle in the cafeteria often shy away from expressing written ideas.

I spent three years and traveled 22,000 miles across the United States observing schools, and I believe that today's students are at risk. The danger lies in their becoming part of the "I hate to write" generation, sons and daughters of "I hate to write" parents, and grandchildren of the "I hate to write" generation before that. But I have also seen exciting new elementary and secondary school programs where students are discovering the power of communicating their own opinions and the joy of sharing their own experiences. And in these programs I've seen solutions to the writing problem. The strategies that are already working in inner-city classrooms and rural communities, in suburban districts and medium-sized towns form the heart of this book. They leave no doubt that the sorry methods of the past 125 years can be replaced with new approaches that are well within reach.

I am addressing this book, therefore, to people who can make a difference: parents whose input should extend beyond Open School Night, students who are old enough to understand why writing is important, and teachers who are in a position to make any change succeed or fail—but who are often ignored by policymakers. I am also addressing policymakers themselves: local school board members, superintendents and assistant superintendents, principals, and other administrators, as well as state legislators and governors. Not to be forgotten among influential people are the designers of national and state-wide tests. Together, we can introduce and encourage solutions to the writing problem that has been the Achilles heel of American education. While lasting change cannot be rushed, it is certainly time to begin.

Ever since the end of the Civil War, students have been regularly penalized for errors in basic skills—spelling, punctuation, grammar, and usage—but rarely rewarded for fluency or grace in expressing well-developed ideas. Stripped of intellectual challenge, writing has been reduced to little more than skill-and-drill exercises that still dominate our schools. Without question, a mastery of mechanics can help make a writer's intentions clear. But excessive emphasis on so-called basics overlooks what is really basic: *the ability to use language to organize thinking, enrich writing, and foster learning* in every subject across the curriculum. Unfortunately, the currently popular "back-to-basics" battle cry demeans the most far-reaching basics in its call for a "return" to the kind of narrow training that most of our schools have never left. That narrowness has already trivialized the vitality of writing and turned classrooms into barren places.

Wringing hands over elementary and secondary schools that are wedded to the status quo is an exercise in frustration, but celebrating solutions to the writing problem gives reason for hope. More reassuring still is the clear evidence of successful reform. To understand how a new generation of classrooms is being transformed, look first to thousands of teachers from Maine to Hawaii who are responsible for the metamorphosis. Dissatisfied with initial training that had neither explained why writing is important nor shown them how to teach it, veterans of ten, twenty, even thirty years' standing have been seeking a second chance to find out what they had missed. Consequently, they enroll by the thousands in a variety of summer programs and after-school workshops that contrast dramatically with conventional "methods" courses.

These programs offer a number of practices for teachers to adapt to their needs, depending somewhat on subject and grade level. At least as important as these classroom-tested techniques, however, is the conviction that teachers need to spend time writing for themselves and for others. The belief is well founded. As teachers plan what they want to say and work through ways to convey it, they discover a central truth that professional writers know and that students need to be taught: the best writing is often a gradual process, not a hurried product. To apply this insight, teachers often discard the conventional overnight assignment. Instead they learn how to show pupils ways to develop well-crafted compositions.

After years of going through the motions of reviewing skill-and-drill exercises, newly energized veteran teachers are now determined to have the "second R" receive the same status as the first. They will always value reading—as well they should—because it gives students opportunities to delve into other people's thoughts. But recent advocates of writing have come to see that this long-neglected discipline enables students to discover their own ideas and give voice to them—a voice that others can share. Clearly, both kinds of literacy are important, but one has dominated the other for so long that teachers who expect to convince parents, students, administrators, and school board members of the need to right the imbalance face no small task. However, the new generation of classrooms attests to the power of unwavering commitment and persistence.

To see the impact of writing practices that are beginning to win favor, this book will introduce you to representative teachers and students across the country. An eleventh-grade social studies teacher in the largest school district in North Carolina may seem to have little in common with an elementary school teacher who instructs every child in a rural school in the backwoods of Alaska or with a football coach in a college in Minnesota. And they all may seem removed from a California teacher of English as a second language, a junior high school reading teacher in Maine, and nationwide instructors of algebra, Latin, beauty culture, English, biology, industrial arts, and Spanish. But "writing across the curriculum," as another major innovation is known, now offers a way to teach every subject, from arithmetic to zoology—a way that stimulates thinking, learning, and communication. In later chapters you will discover how new ways of teaching writing animate the classrooms and locker rooms of elementary, junior high, and senior high schools. Indeed, the liveliest ideas in the curriculum are taking shape in the also-ran discipline that teachers didn't learn to teach, students didn't learn to master, and testers didn't learn to assess until recently.

While new ways of teaching writing are still not fully accepted, new ways of evaluating student achievement face even greater resistance. As a result, large-scale standardized tests, typically mandated by school districts or entire states, reduce teaching and learning to a kind of rote drill. There is no denying that in these cases most teachers follow the practice of "teaching to the test." But there is good news in testing, too. For the first time in the history of writing assessments, states like California and Rhode Island have begun to measure achievement by using evaluations that raise a central question: does the test show if students are learning what teachers are teaching? The best tests, in other words, reflect the best teaching practices, making assessment and instruction part of a single whole. As a result, an increasing number of students can finally demonstrate their writing skill by using methods they learned in school, rather than by having to select the "least worst" answer to multiple-choice alternatives.

Regardless of which of the most promising new approaches to teaching and testing endures, this much is certain: language will always be the nucleus of learning, for it underlines listening, talking, writing, and reading. Since parents are the only teachers of language a newborn knows and the most critical teachers thereafter, the strategies that mothers and fathers embark on to heighten the world of words in their child's early years leave a lifelong imprint. But the role of parent-educator does not end when youngsters enter school. Consequently, *Growing Up Writing* spells out effective techniques to use during a child's infant and toddler years, and equips parents further with proven ideas for elementary, junior high, and senior high school.

To be most effective—especially when it comes to making writing a centerpiece of the curriculum—parents and professional educators would do well to view each other as colleagues, not as adversaries; as partners, not as people with a superior-inferior relationship. Such a stance requires a giant change in established roles. Popular overtures for "parent involvement," as the current term puts it, demonstrate the difficulties and the opportunities. As one public school educator pointed out, "Sometimes you need someone who is considered an outsider to say, 'Wait a minute, let's try something different. It's time for a change.'"

The time is now; the need is urgent. And the beneficiaries may be a sensitive new generation that is able to use language to think clearly, write gracefully, and express feelings fluently.

GROWING UP WRITING

WHERE WE ARE NOW

No one deliberately tries to dampen students' enthusiasm for writing, but this much is clear: without major reform, unintended consequences that begin in the first few months of first grade and worsen during the next twelve years are likely to last a lifetime. The destruction starts innocently enough, for early childhood specialists intend to nurture young minds, not suppress them. But to get five- and six-year-old children off to a "good start," even these well-meaning teachers make the mistake of emphasizing early basic skills at the expense of encouraging ideas.

Speaking for many, a teacher explained, "If I allow my first-graders to write stories using some of the words that come naturally to them in everyday conversation, I'm afraid they won't learn the importance of proper spelling." To prevent that outcome—and to unwittingly guarantee that students' writing will be stilted and limited—she follows the custom of permitting children to use only the words on a prescribed list. These restrictions reduce a child's speaking vocabulary of between 2,000 and 2,500 words to a scant 400, and drain students' writing of original ideas. Once confined to a narrow number of words that are not of their own choosing, even irrepressible first-grade youngsters lose interest in expressing individual thinking. As a result, teachers who want to help their first-grade class develop writing skills actually hinder students' ability.

With this beginning, it doesn't take long for active minds that had been filled with ideas to turn into passive mentalities that appear to need to be told what to write. By third grade "story starters" abound. "When I grow up . . . ," "The happiest day in my life . . . ," "If my three wishes came true . . . ," and hundreds more artificial motivators fail to motivate. Photographs and pictures are no better. I have seen circus scenes, mountain scenes, seashore scenes, snow scenes, autumn leaves, frisky puppies, sleepy kittens, newborn babies, and wizened old men, to name a few—all designed to stimulate ideas in children who once brought their own thoughts to school. "Instead of thinking honestly and deeply about why students have learned to dislike writing," teacher of teachers Lucy McCormick Calkins observes, "we rush about, pushing, luring, encouraging, motivating, stimulating, bribing, requiring. . . ."

The cost of damming up what students want to say becomes even clearer in fourth grade. Beverly Bimes, former National Teacher of the Year, saw the evidence when she reviewed the dreary paragraphs that a large-scale national sample of nine-year-old students had produced. "It's hard to imagine that one of a child's first instincts is to want to write," she said, "but we know that children attempt to write before they even think about reading. What have we done to this natural desire in our children?" the distressed Ms. Bimes wondered. While teachers of her stature have shown that restoring students' desire and ability is possible, they also know it is wiser to avoid squelching that eagerness in the first place. And they know it can be done.

Beverly Bimes's question raises other issues that are central to school experience—indeed, to life experience. What have we done, for example, to destroy an early curiosity to explore new ideas (which leaves teachers complaining about pupils' lack of motivation, and employers criticizing insufficient initiative)? Why have we convinced elementary school students and high school graduates alike that they have nothing to say, that their experiences and feelings are not interesting to others, that their thinking is unimportant, their memories not worth sharing? How have we done such a thorough job of silencing the distinctive sound of individual voices on paper? And, underlying all questions, why have we squandered assets that we should have treasured—and then subscribed to the belief that professional writers are the only people who can express themselves capably?

Finding the answers to these questions will take detective work, but Donald H. Graves, the University of New Hampshire's expert in teaching writing, already has described their consequences. "When writing, Americans too often feel like the man who has been invited to a party of distinguished guests," the internationally renowned author and lecturer has observed. "Being a person of modest station, he attends with great reluctance and discomfort. He has but one aim—to be properly attired, demonstrate correct manners, say as little as possible, and leave early." Certainly, the brief papers that students produce under duress fit that description. Ill at ease with written words that are expected to meet someone else's standards, otherwise colorful communicators succumb to the fear that their own natural language will not be accepted in the classroom.

Don Rothman, director of the Central California Writing Project and lecturer in Writing and Literature at the University of California, Santa Cruz, captured the dilemma of the dinner party when he recalled a nightmare he had when he was in graduate school, studying the works of John Milton. In his frightening dream a figure sitting high on a throne alternated between being Milton and Rothman's father. When Don approached the throne, the paternal and awesome figure he looked up to handed the young man a list of words and cautioned, "When you speak to me, you must only use the words on this list. If you use any other words, you will be punished."

As Rothman looked over the list of words that were not his, he knew he could not accept the stipulation that his father and John Milton had laid down. Growing increasingly anxious, he finally screamed out, "It's a good thing this is a dream! If language were this kind of prison, I'd go crazy." For many pupils who fear punishment when the words they put on paper are subject to what Rothman calls "inspection and correction," written language *is* a prison—and is likely to remain so unless we do something to prevent the reaction. This book is about that "something." After facing our failed methods, it will concentrate on new strategies that are already working.

Why, one wonders, do the same students who learned reading and 'rithmetic (later to become literature and mathematics) virtually strangle on writing? Why does a blank piece of paper serve as a gag that chokes off communication? One of the most obvious answers is that most schools do not teach students how to write in the first place. They teach the importance of tidy margins and neat penmanship. The most attractive papers get displayed on a bulletin board, complete with gold stars or smiling faces. They teach spelling, too, and test it so regularly that elementary school students have been found to view the subject as the most important part of language arts.

But language arts also include correct punctuation, grammar, and usage—"basic skills" that Harvard University recognized as an important part of literate writing more than a century ago (see Chapter 2) but that most schools subsequently have defined as virtually the sum total of writing. To encourage easier recall grade schools employ simple "pomes" *("I* before *e,* except after *c,* or when sounded like *a* as in *neighbor* or *weigh")* and litanies ("A noun is the name of a person, place, or thing"). But long before children understand the actual meaning of this doggerel—if, indeed, they ever do—they grasp the underlying message that extols the importance of mechanics over writing.

Though the post-Sputnik years hailed an electrifying new era in space and technology when science fiction sprang to life, children continued to labor over traditional fill-in-the-blank workbooks (no erasures, smudges, or crossing out allowed). In fact, two of the writing assignments that I recall students in my son's class toiling over the day that astronauts Edwin Aldrin Jr. and Neil Armstrong walked on the moon were "Farming in Norway" and "Mining in Iceland," unless the farming was in Iceland and the mining was in Norway. Clearly, teachers who selected topics that captured neither the drama of that moment nor a vision of the future did not recognize the opportunity that writing offered.

How could they? The plain fact is that most teachers don't know how to teach writing because most colleges and universities have not taught them. Reading and math form the bulwarks of the elementary school curriculum in every teachers college, and literature is esteemed when preparing secondary school teachers. But writing gets short shrift throughout. Indeed, a 1978 report that Don Graves prepared for the Ford Foundation found that departments of education in thirty-six universities offered elementary school teachers 220 courses in reading, children's literature, and language arts, but only two courses—less than 1 percent—in the teaching of writing. "I know the lack of method courses for teaching writing is a disgrace," a victim of this preparation remarked, "but it sometimes feels like a blessing in disguise. I'm still struggling to free myself from language arts training that taught me to be a detective searching for errors," she explained, "instead of a teacher searching for ideas."

Of all the elementary school methods courses that Don Graves analyzed, 75 percent were devoted to the teaching of reading—mostly from basal readers. A few courses, thirty in all, were devoted to children's literature. Fortified with graded texts and workbooks, elementary school teachers value classrooms in which two-thirds of the students—be they "blue birds" and "robins" or "oaks" and "pines"—do silent work at their seats, while the remaining birds or trees read softly with the teacher. The ability to use language freely and write readily doesn't enter the picture. "The irony of talk in schools," Christopher Thaiss, associate director of the Northern Virginia Writing Project, has pointed out, "is that probably more ink has been spilled and more arguments in the teachers' lounge have been generated over how to quell talk than how to encourage it." The net result? Silent students produce pallid writing.

Secondary school teachers are also oppressed by flawed teacher training. English majors find their college writing instruction limited to freshman courses. Indeed, the teaching of writing receives such a low priority that these courses are typically taught by graduate students (known as "teaching assistants") and very junior faculty members, who suffer a loss in their fragile status' by virtue of having to teach composition. The remainder of the English major is usually devoted to literature. "With this kind of university background," the Ford Foundation report noted, "it is not surprising that most high school teachers would much rather teach literature than have anything to do with writing."

Teachers on every level, from the primary grades through secondary school, are also prepared to drill the parts of speech, the reasons for capital letter, commas, periods, paragraphs, and increasingly complex conventions. Pressure from home, local school districts, state governors, legislatures, and departments of education combine to make certain that fundamentals such as these are not neglected. But no comparable pressure or teacher training exists to emphasize the importance of language and writing. As a result of lopsided training and skewed values, school systems have had to resort to hiring teachers who have learned neither how to teach writing nor how to write themselves. Consequently, secondary school teachers typically proceed as if English consisted of nothing but literature and mechanics, while elementary school teachers replace writing with "language arts," that hybrid concoction of reading, occasional yawn-producing writing assignments, and the so-called basic skills we're always going back to.

Textbook publishers feed into the strong demand for this kind of emphasis. In a current secondary school series titled, like many, *Grammar and Composition*—a frank admission of priorities—seventh-grade students are given 252 exercises in grammar, usage, mechanics, vocabulary, spelling, and study skills and 104 rather dreary exercises in composition. Eighth-grade students are inundated with 378 exercises in the same basic skills, and 103 banal exercises in composition. Ninth grade is more damning still, with 375 exercises in basic skills and 93 in composition. Even by the time a student is a senior in high school, grammar, usage, mechanics, vocabulary, spelling, and study skills dominate writing, with 286 exercises in basic skills overwhelming 145 unchallenging exercises in composition.

All of this is not to suggest that schools refrain from teaching sentence structure, parts of speech, and syntax— although much could be delayed and even more bypassed altogether without significant loss. Rather, students should be expected to *do* something with these mechanics. As matters now stand, pupils memorize rules in isolation, much as they memorize state capitals. And pupils forget isolated rules for the same reason they forget state capitals: neither is meaningful. Instruction about the past perfect and subjunctive tenses is no more likely to take hold than instruction on whether the statehouse of Alaska is located in Anchorage, Nome, or Juneau.

Writing, on the other hand, carries meaning. Unlike rote memorization, it expresses intelligence and imagination. It collects memories, stores feelings, and enables students to discuss beliefs and biases. Writing also records ideas that stem from talking, reflecting, researching. And it compels writers to organize their thinking more clearly than they do in everyday speech, for an empty page leaves no room for "you knows," the adolescent enemy of communication. We tend to minimize the importance of writing, perhaps because it is the everyday stuff of marketing lists and telephone messages, but skillful prose brings the sound of a writer's voice to a letter, an essay, an answer to a question raised on an application form. Yet *The New York Times* reported that college admissions officers find that each year's responses are getting "blander, safer—more polished, but less inspired— and just plain dull."

Only an estimated 2 percent of the record number of high-achieving high school seniors—some eighteen thousand in all—who recently applied to the University of Virginia were able to compose essays that furthered their chances of acceptance significantly; in more cases, the essay was so bad it hurt candidates' chances, and in most cases, the essays sounded so much alike that they had little effect one way or the other. Cornell University confirmed the writing dilemma. So did Brown. And Stanford. And Colgate. Applicants to these selective colleges and universities wrote correctly, leaving no reason to call for "back to basics." But their subjects and verbs provided the scaffolding for sentences that said nothing of interest.

This kind of writing is predictable, for the occasional essay assignments that most students have grown accustomed to discussing for homework are seldom designed to demonstrate the quality of their thinking. Quite the contrary. The old standby, "What I Did Last Summer," originated in huge college lecture halls in the 1890s, when overworked composition instructors sought trivial topics that could be quickly scanned and graded to serve a single purpose: mechanical correctness. It is said, for example, that Harvard University's Barrett Wendell had to comment on 22,230 papers a year, in addition to critiquing longer fortnightly themes in depth. His counterparts at the University of Iowa and Yale's Sheffield School of Science were no less burdened. With paper loads like these, the practice of assigning college composition topics that required minimal thought was readily rationalized. Before long, however, the single-minded focus on mechanical correctness resulted in these topics coming to dominate secondary school English classes, where the same rationale did not apply, and then trickling down to the elementary school level as well.

But the "What I Did Last Summer" genre is so far removed from meaningful experiences for contemporary students that it destroys children's natural desire to write about real concerns. Feelings of loneliness are meaningful, when youngsters are uprooted from the house they have always known, from neighbors, friends, and teachers to venture into the unfamiliar because Dad or Mom has been transferred or promoted. Fear is real when parents' marriages end in divorce. So is confusion. ("We don't love each other anymore, but we'll always love you.") Visitation rights, remarriages, the integration of newly extended families introduce painful experiences. It is hardly surprising that the celebration of a birthday may cause a child's formerly secure loyalties to waver, or that the gratitude associated with a traditional Thanksgiving dinner may be replaced with tension and turmoil. What is surprising, however, is that schools typically overlook the opportunities that writing can provide students who could come to grips with real concerns, instead of having to feign interest in the irrelevant pap that is assigned to them. Farming in Norway, indeed!

Older students may also be troubled by more global issues: overpopulation, famine, the threat of worldwide nuclear destruction, the rampant spread of AIDS, the ravaging of the environment. Once adolescents succeed in getting their thoughts on paper, they may discover the difference between what they believe and what they need to find out about. But important discoveries are not likely to come easily, because writing has been trivialized for so many. In fact, when Dr. Arthur Applebee and a team of researchers from Stanford University and the University of California at Berkeley conducted a three-year study of American high schools, they found that only 12 percent of the exercises in composition textbooks required writing even a paragraph; most writing consisted of short answers, fill in the blanks, and word choices. Clearly, students who view having to compose so much as a single paragraph as onerous are not equipped to express their thinking about complex issues. Nor are they likely to be able to explore new ideas when 97 percent of their extended writing exercises is limited to tests of previous knowledge. Indeed, the small minority who dare to be venturesome are likely to find that the basic-skills mentality that overpowers most classrooms appreciates error-free papers more than discussions of serious moment.

If I had nothing but bleak news to report, however, there would be little point in writing this book. But I'm glad to report that in every state among the fifty, some schools or at least some classrooms have shaken off the failed methods of the nineteenth century and prepared to enter the twenty-first by introducing exciting reforms that are already working well and call for celebration.

Even faculty members who used to reward error-free assignments above all else are valuing the distinctiveness that illuminates individual style and encouraging students to convey unique experiences. "I didn't know it was all right to sound like *me,*" a high school freshman exclaimed, "because I had been taught since grade school that nobody really cared about my opinions or interests." Then she began a family reminiscence by saying, "I'll never forget the day Uncle Herm came for a one-day visit—and stayed for a month. Who would have thought he could have packed all his belongings in a paper bag!" It was only when Jill's classmates told her that the beginning made them want to know who Uncle Herm was, why he came, and what he brought with him, that she decided to discard the old "rules" that had convinced her she "couldn't write."

Clearly, teachers like Jill's are making major differences in the techniques they are using. By welcoming the sound of students' voices, showing interest in the topics that pupils select, and responding to classmates' reactions to one another's work, teachers are finding new ways to encourage student writers. And pupils who wrote awkwardly are awakening to opportunities in ways that I have yet to see in a "What I Did Last Summer" classroom. Their hard-earned achievements are remarkable, their joy in writing unmistakable. In fact, I was so impressed by the best classrooms I saw (and so distressed by the rest) that I decided to look at some of the assumptions that conventional thinking has accepted as sacrosanct.

What happens, innovators want to know, when parents, teachers, administrators, and students free themselves from practices that have been bequeathed by one generation to the next, as if they were a treasured legacy not to be tampered with?

What happens when the tradition of valuing penmanship, spelling, punctuation, grammar, and usage is respected, as it should be, but not revered—and a writer's ability to transmit thoughts and feelings receives foremost priority?

What happens when writing is valued as much as reading from kindergarten right through high school graduation?

What happens when students discover that writing holds the key to learning every subject from arithmetic to zoology, instead of being the sole province of English and language arts?

What happens when students are no longer limited to completing assignments for their teacher's satisfaction, when they are encouraged to shape ideas to meet their own standards and interest a variety of readers?

These questions were unasked until a few years ago. Today

there are answers. But there are roadblocks, too. Past mistakes still have the strong support of advocates who rally around the curious slogan of "back to basics"—ignoring the fact that, by and large, our schools have always clung to the fundamentals. True, progressive education provided a brief departure from tradition, but, even in its heyday over half a century ago, the movement reached only a comparative handful of schools. Then its excesses overshadowed its merits and, to the regret of some and the relief of others, progressivism disappeared from view.

More recently, short-lived "open education" or the "open classroom" emerged as a reaction against the grim and joyless atmosphere of many classrooms and provided the only other major departure from tradition. But if parents and educators who still believe that writing is merely an amalgam of correct mechanics worry that writing reform could lead to a return to the "open classroom," I can say without qualification that there is nothing to fear. The purpose of the open classroom was destroyed beyond restoration (and beyond recognition) by overzealous early practitioners who rushed to endorse the proposed reform before they understood what it was about. Meaning well, but responding simplistically, they confused the openness of space with the openness of inquiry. As walls of plaster and sheetrock came tumbling down, the serious view of schooling that underlay the open classroom philosophy crumbled in record time, making this reform even more short-lived than progressive education. Aside from these two relatively small interruptions, a strong emphasis on basic skills has characterized the American classroom since its inception. Contemporary proponents who attribute the downfall of writing to an alleged slackening off of rigor overlook the real reasons for our writing dilemma.

It is headline grabbing, of course, to parade gross errors in spelling and usage before a troubled public and pretend that "Johnny" and "Jane" could write if only their knowledge of basic skills had not declined so sharply. Headline grabbing and false. Data from nationwide tests demonstrate that students' grasp of basic skills has not declined. Seventy-five percent of the 55,000 fourth-, eighth-, and eleventh-grade students who took the most recent National Assessment of Educational Progress (NAEP) Writing Achievement test displayed a general understanding of grammar, punctuation, and spelling. Indeed, mistakes have proven to be no more prevalent now than in 1969, when NAEP initiated its testing. Consequently, NAEP has classified three out of four students in its sample as "writing haves" in the area of basic skills. Surely, anyone who cares about correct conventions should be pleased.

But the same NAEP tests show that there is insufficient cause for rejoicing, because knowing the rules about writing has not helped the "haves" to write well. For the most part, they are unable to formulate ideas and organize them clearly, much less to express themselves with verve and style. Even the staunchest champions of "back to basics" would be hard put to pretend that the insistence on error-free compositions that begins in first grade, and is reinforced year after year, carries over into writing ability. Contrary to popular assumption, writing has never been very good in the United States, and it is still poor. How poor it is became clear with publication of NAEP's data. Allowing for the fact that these writing assessments are not altogether reliable (see Chapter 6), the results are still startling: the proportion of students able to write adequately or better ranged between a scant 3 percent and 38 percent, depending on the particular assignment.

While some critics find fault with NAEP's writing assessments and, therefore, question the significance of the results, there is no disagreement with the observation that Theodore Sizer made in his book *Horace's Compromise,* that "writing is the litmus paper of thought." Formerly headmaster of Phillips Academy, Andover, and dean of the Graduate

School of Education at Harvard University, and presently both chairman of the education department of Brown University and founder of the nationwide Coalition of Essential Schools, Dr. Sizer knows that the litmus test applies throughout life. Yet to the despair of Fortune 500 corporations, prestigious law firms, and the "Big Eight" accounting firms, even select men and women with graduate degrees from renowned universities are unable to express their thoughts in writing. If they are stymied, you may be certain that inner-city high school students and dropouts are so impaired that they cannot compete for any job that requires even a minimal ability to write.

Gene I. Maeroff, a senior fellow at the Carnegie Foundation for the Advancement of Teaching, captured the plight of a ninth-grade English class in Chicago whose students are still writing on a level that suburban lower elementary school students have long surpassed. How many members of this struggling ninth-grade class will drop out before graduation is a moot question; how many will become articulate if they remain in school is even more problematic. Asked to write briefly about the reasons for selecting a particular occupation, one student replied:

> I would like to Be a judge and put Bad people in jail and judge make a lot of money to just like the foot ball player even More and I am glad that it is judges in the World to put the people in jail.

This vignette that Maeroff reported in an article in the *Phi Delta Kappan* gives ample reason for not overlooking the importance of mechanics in clear writing—and for not forgetting about the significance of organized thinking, either.

Given the extent of the writing problem and the failure of the back-to-basics approach, a group of Young and not-so-young Turks (most of whom have had between ten and twenty-five years of teaching experience) has chosen to go forward to new basics. Memorizing isolated rules that govern the English language, they point out, is less effective than learning correct mechanics in context through frequent writing. And skill-and-drill exercises, they emphasize, will never develop thinking. Playwright Edward Albee expressed the reformers' viewpoint when he said, "I write to find out what I'm thinking about." In a similar vein novelist E. M. Forster asked, "How can I tell what I think until I see what I say?" These men of letters were not being facetious; rather, they had identified a central truth about the connection between writing and thinking.

Students of every age are beginning to discover the same truth as they struggle to sort out their own ideas and feelings. There is a stir in the air of classrooms that have abandoned the conventional practice of assigning identical writing topics, collecting them on a fixed date, correcting mechanical mistakes, and requiring papers to be copied over—all in rapid order. Consequently, students who used to write as minimally as possible, in order to prevent their words from drowning in a sea of red ink, are straining to use their intelligence to formulate ideas clearly and express them fully. These writers dare to expose their partially developed thinking without fear of being embarrassed and openly ask for advice when they are "stuck." The reason for their unusual school behavior is clear: they have teachers who have encouraged them to take on the challenge of planning, drafting, revising, and correcting ambitious writing. No one ever said that these steps—all parts of what is included when writing is recognized as a painstaking process—are quick and easy. But they can be uniquely rewarding.

The process in some elementary and secondary school classrooms, begins with "prewriting" or "rehearsal," a step that provides time for writers to read, research, interview, and think about what they want to say. Although students postpone the actual act of writing during this planning phase, they are not dawdling. Far from it. Indeed, Pulitzer

Prize–winning writer and University of New Hampshire professor Donald Murray estimates that he spends 80 percent of his time rehearsing before he begins the first of a series of drafts and revisions of his own writing. Anyone unaccustomed to careful planning would do well to read Murray's book *Write to Learn,* in which he shows students the various ways he went about piecing together family history, anecdotes, and memories of his Scottish grandmother before he felt able to begin writing the first draft of his remembrance of her.

Like Donald Murray, students who have come to view writing as a process know they will need to draft and redraft their work many times over before it even approaches its final form. And they have discovered that the hastily written paper they used to submit in time to get full credit on their grade was really a draft—not the finished product they had thought it was. By the time students received their teacher's comments, however, it was too late for them to make any changes. Despite the futility of these after-the-fact observations, the notion of a teacher's suggesting ideas and raising questions while a student's work is in progress remains unheard of in conventional classrooms. And the thought of having other students join their teacher in a conference with the writer still sounds outlandish to traditional minds. But these conferences are essential to innovative classrooms where writers are encouraged to consider other opinions as they revise their work.

Revision, in the true sense of *re-*vision, is at the heart of writing that is seen as a process. Unlike "copying over," which disheartened students view as punishment for having failed to meet their teacher's expectations, revision gives freshly motivated writers opportunities to consider how best to satisfy their own expectations. To demonstrate the difference, the late Mina Shaughnessy, author of *Errors & Expectations,* sympathetically recalled the day one of the college students in her basic English course concluded that Richard

Wright couldn't have been much of a writer because he made so many "mistakes." The so-called errors were Wright's revisions on a manuscript page of *Native Son*.

Consider the difference between that viewpoint and the revisions that Jill's class proposed during a conference. "We don't really have a clear picture of what Uncle Herm looked like," a fellow student told Jill. "Sometimes I see him as a stooped old man leaning on a cane, and other times he comes across as a war hero, walking in straight strides." "Maybe it would help if we knew when you saw him last," another classmate said. "Had he changed much? How did you feel about seeing him? Did your feelings change?" "And how did he feel about the visit?" another commentator asked. "Did his feelings change?" "Where would he have gone if he hadn't turned to you? Did it take a lot of courage for him to appear on your family's doorstep?"

Following the custom of linking literature and writing, a questioner asked, "Was Uncle Herm something like the Hired Man in Robert Frost's poem 'The Death of the Hired Man'?—the part that says that home is where you have to go when you have no place else and where they have to take you in?" The questions poured out, exceeding the number that a teacher would probably have raised at the end of a "finished" profile—and obviously exceeding the number that Jill could have answered if the die was cast once she had already submitted her paper for a grade. "The main thing is, Jill," a classmate explained, "that we really want you to tell us more. You've caught our interest, and you sound more like you do after school than how you usually sound in English class. Besides, if you keep going," she promised, "we'll help you fix your mistakes up at the end." Unaccustomed to finding her writing admired, Jill was eager to revise more drafts and read them to thirty-three fellow students and her teacher for further suggestions.

The rules that govern proper English also occupy a special place when writing is taught as a process, but, as every professional writer knows, copy editing becomes important in the last draft, not in the first. Misspelled words or run-on sentences are not corrected when authors are trying to formulate their initial thoughts. Neither, however, are books published before a copy editor goes over them, word by word, line by line. The same emphasis applies in schools that view writing as a process. Here, however, students serve as junior copy editors for each other, and their teacher serves as senior editor. By recognizing the ultimate importance of correct form and giving initial attention to expressing ideas, teachers and students put the importance of both in perspective.

Even the youngest scribes are beginning to take it for granted that they will need to "cut and paste" (or revise on a word processor) first, taking a paragraph from an early draft, a new lead from a later one, and a strong, descriptive phrase from a revised copy. I have seen youngsters write as many as six or seven drafts, most of which build on previous ones. By the time student writers have finally finished cycles of drafting-conferring-revising-and-drafting again, correct mechanics matter to them, less because proper form will please the teacher (which it will) and more because correct conventions will add to the readers' understanding and enjoyment. "Readers," incidentally, is a plural word, because the final product is "published" in books for the class library, in the school newspaper or literary magazine—even in regional competitions.

Important as this new approach to writing is, however, it would be deceptive to suggest that we are now riding the crest of a wave of reform that has swept over the schoolhouse. But it would also be misleading to suggest that the major changes that are taking place are insignificant. From the Atlantic to the nation's heartland to the Pacific, the process of writing is steadily attracting strong advocates who recognize the value of gradual steps that lead up to a finished product. Indeed, the current concern may not be that the process is spreading too slowly, but that it may be embraced too quickly by enthusiasts who risk undermining a reform they do not understand. Unless care is exercised, therefore, a process whose value lies in its flexibility may be distorted into another lock-step drill: prewriting on Monday, first draft on Tuesday, conference on Wednesday, revision on Thursday, and copyediting on Friday.

Another promising innovation that you will encounter in forward-looking schools removes writing from the exclusive domain of English or language arts teachers and extends it to history classrooms and art studios, to foreign languages and computer labs—indeed, to every aspect of elementary and secondary school instruction. A wide range of teachers has long known that a student who says, "I know what it means, but I can't explain it," *doesn't* know "what it means." In recent years, however, teachers across the curriculum have found that students faced with the discipline of committing ideas to paper learn to clarify their understanding. As a result, the familiar faculty protest that writing is "none of my business" is becoming outdated. Thinking clearly is everybody's business.

This insight has led to a growing appreciation of what is called "writing across the curriculum." To give you concrete examples of what this means, I have modified two illustrations from a book appropriately called *Learning to Write/ Writing to Learn* by John S. Mayher, Nancy Lester, and Gordon M. Pradl.

> *Math:* The object of this math assignment is to understand the Pythagorean theorem in geometry. The task is loosely based on the television series "60 Minutes."
>
> Mike Wallace has been assigned to report on the startling discovery that the Greek mathematician Pythagoras has made. Write a transcript of the interview between Wallace and Pythagoras that explains the mathematician's finding to a world that had not heard of the Pythagorean theorem before.

The "Writing to Learn" that students produced was intended to show if they understood the theorem that had been presented in class or if they had merely memorized the formula. And the "Learning to Write" required that students abandon their own voice in order to capture the style of a contemporary reporter and an ancient scholar. Also new was the experience of keeping an audience of millions of television viewers in mind, rather than writing only for the teacher.

> *Science:* The object of this assignment, "Mr. Wizard Revisited," is to get older students to distinguish among the states of matter—solid, liquid, and gas—in a way that younger students can understand.
>
> You have been selected to give sixth-grade pupils at "George Washington Elementary School" directions for conducting an experiment on the states of matter. Keeping the age of your audience in mind, write a draft of your talk. When it is completed, the sixth-graders will melt a chunk of ice, heat the liquid that results, and observe what happens. If you find that your directions were misleading, you will try to identify whatever caused the confusion and revise your presentation before you use it with a comparable group in another school.

Successful students will show that they have such a clear understanding of how to convert solid matter to liquid to gas that they can explain the procedure to a young audience. Should their explanation not be adequate, students will take the same pains with revision in a science class that they do in English.

High school history and writing can also reinforce each other in unusual ways. It took an inventive American history teacher to have her sophomore students write a condolence letter that a general in the Confederate or Union army might have sent to the mother of a slain son. The general explained to the grieving parent why the cause was worthy, the battle critical. By getting the army officer's voice on paper and viewing the bereaved parent as the audience, students learned to write in a new way—and to understand opposite viewpoints that fueled the Civil War.

Lacking the perspective that comes with time and distance, it is sometimes difficult to predict which of the other new practices I have seen may be captivating fads and which may make a lasting impact. Will students who keep "learning logs" in North Carolina, "process journals" in the state of Washington, and "dialogue journals" in California become better writers? Clearer thinkers? More efficient learners? The answers are not yet clear, but you will see that the practice of daily writing is gaining favor in innovative elementary and secondary school classrooms. While no one can predict the future, seventh-grade teacher Rose Reissman knows the past and has resisted its hold on the present. After nineteen years of teaching, she says, "English isn't just grammar and spelling. Writing is the thread that fuses everything."

■2
THE "GOOD OLD DAYS"

"Teachers must do something on Monday morning," Mina Shaughnessy has written, "and this reality forces them either to do what *their* teachers did on Monday morning or to invent English composition anew. . . ." Recalling the Monday morning English classes that I taught, I know how tempting it was to repeat the practices of Mrs. Flouten, Miss Jordan, and Dr. Logie, who had probably resurrected the lesson plans of *their* teachers, who in all likelihood had relied on memories of *their* teachers as models. Indeed, in 1893 the *Atlantic Monthly* traced this pattern back to the mid-1870s. One generation of teachers after another has typically viewed "good writing" as "correct writing," nothing more, and worthwhile topics as teacher assignments, nothing else. While obedient students have tried to adhere to these standards for over a century, their writing has given little cause for pride or satisfaction. These sorry results led me to examine the way writing has been taught during all these years—and to look for something better.

As I crisscrossed the country, observing classrooms for this book, I expected to find "something better"; I thought that times had finally changed, for many schools certainly *looked* different. Once outside of large city public schools, it was not unusual to see movable desks and chairs in place of row on row of heavy wooden desks and attached seats nailed to the floor; for that matter, the floors of elementary schools were often covered with carpet. And the most appealing classrooms I saw, regardless of the grade level, were brightly lighted and comfortably ventilated. (No hissing steam heat in January or blazing sun in June! No homemade, accordion-pleated paper fans that inventive students used to make to circulate the air.) The new amenities were undeniably pleasant, but underneath the trappings I saw the old school camouflaged in modern dress.

I T E M: A pleasant high school teacher whose Deep South heritage perfumes her speech like magnolia blossoms softly reprimands a seventeen-year-old male, whose southern experience is limited to the segregated side of the city where he, his four brothers, and his three sisters live in cramped quarters with their mother and her current lover.

"You know that I do not approve of street language," she reminds Jason. (He doesn't remind her that he spends most of his free time in the streets.) "And I certainly will not accept writing that is too explicit about sex." ("Explicit" is not part of Jason's everyday vocabulary, but the sex that Ms. Q. finds abhorrent is a daily fact of life in his neighborhood.)

Turning to me later, she explains, "My students know how to embarrass me, and they refuse to take my feelings into consideration. I grew up at a time when gentility was important, but now . . . ," she shakes her head, "I have to drill manners into their heads and teach writing at the same time. It's a pity because Jason really writes quite well, but of course I have to reject his work."

I T E M: A junior high school teacher shares a tender love story a student wrote, a story marred by a red scar slashed

across the words "made love." In their place, the teacher/
censor has written "kissed."

"Did you talk to Nan about your reasons for thinking that
a change of words might be desirable?" I asked.

"Certainly not. There are standards of good taste that do
not require discussion. An adolescent in a suburban community like this should know what her parents expect—and
what I accept. Besides, Nan may not even know what it
means to make love. In her mind that may be what kissing
is all about."

"Then writing offers a way to learn, doesn't it," I ventured,
"if there is discussion instead of deletion?"

Losing patience, the teacher finished what could have
been an exchange of ideas by stating flatly, "Everyone has to
do things in his or her own way, and my way is to state what
I want. After all, I am the teacher."

I T E M: A ten-year-old student is so eager to have an original
book published that she sends me her only copy. Beginning
with material for the dust jacket, the author enclosed her
snapshot and text that concludes, "She started writeing at
age six, but this is her first published book and the best book
she ever wrote so far." The "best book" was dedicated: "for
my family and the memory of my three dead cats, Secret
Sasha and Marshmallow."

"My teacher said I'm missing commas and I made a spelling mistake and I didn't follow directions, so she gave me an
'F,'" the would-be author wrote me. "I thought my tall tale
was funny, but she said we're only supposed to take a story
from our reader and exagerade it, not make up our own
ideas. But I still don't see why using my imaginashun is
wrong, do you?"

How do you explain to a fifth-grader, a junior high school
student, and a seventeen-year-old named Jason that, despite
the modern technology that they see in their classrooms,

teachers still do what *their* teachers have done? Quite understandably, students don't realize that the state-of-the-art computers that appear to be heralding Schools of the Future are often providing more efficient ways of perpetuating Schools of the Past. Not knowing that word processors can enable writers to prepare drafts of compositions and revise them more readily than had been possible before, students simply accept the way these electronic brains are used, misused, or not used at all. Some word processors lie dormant, either because there are too few of them to service an entire class or because they intimidate teachers reared in another age; other machines usually served one purpose: drilling and reviewing basic skills, from the primary grades to college. Herbert Kohl, teacher and author, may not have exaggerated by much when he called computers the world's most expensive flash cards. Wrongly used, they can be. Despite the new apparatus, therefore, Monday mornings in the electronic era seldom differed from those in the gaslight age.

I T E M: "If I'm running behind on my 'adjective unit' by mid-March or early April," a West Coast first-grade teacher confides, "I can speed things up by turning to the computer." To show how she force-fed adjectives to six-year-olds, Ms. T. held up duplicated copies of a page full of Easter bunnies and chicks. "How many of you would like to learn about AD-JEC-TIVES today?" She smiled brightly. Not many. Undaunted, Ms. T. put her mimeographed copies of bunnies and chicks face down on her desk. "Well, then, how many of you would like to learn about AD-JEC-TIVES on a COM-PU-TER?" Twenty-eight hands waved madly. ("They *love* the computer," Ms. T. whispered.) Two days later, the results of student "inspired" examples of a part of speech that was new to them appeared on individual monitors: "The bunny is big." "The chicken is little." "The bunny is white." "The chicken is yellow." ("Look how well the children are learning to write," their teacher said.)

ITEM: "What I like best about computers," a middle-school teacher acknowledges, "is the work they save me. I don't know how else I could guarantee perfect writing." Walking around the room, she points out that spelling mistakes have flashed on some screens, faulty grammar on others, and punctuation errors on a few. But no screen shows signs of students' straining to express their thoughts and revise their writing. In this classroom the adage about not judging a book by its cover needs a contemporary counterpart: don't judge a writing program by its equipment.

Despite these findings, however, I've also had the good fortune of seeing how some teachers are bringing fresh life to writing instruction. The clearest way to recognize the distinctiveness of these new programs is to compare their practices (see chapters 3, 4, and 5) with conventional methods that still dominate the teaching of writing.

So alike are the style and substance of most writing instruction that classrooms often appear to be replicas of one another. Somehow, the local flavor that makes communities distinctive rarely penetrates the schoolhouse door. Indeed, I heard the same "teacher's voice" regardless of regional dialect and saw student reactions that I remembered from my own school days. Neither time nor place had made the impact that a logical person might expect. At the heart of the similarity is the issue of control. And no one craves control more than teachers who cling to their fragile hold on the bottom of the power structure and exercise authority in the only place they can: their own classroom. There they regulate student behavior and performance. That, of course, is what their own teachers had monitored.

ITEM: An eighth-grade English teacher claps her hands, signaling that she wants silence. Two writers continue to confer with each other in whispered tones. "Ladies and gentlemen, that was *not* applause." The writers end their conference. She assigns a one-page composition due the next day. "Raise your hands if you have any questions." Students ask the inevitable ones: "Does spelling count?" "Will you take points off if the paper is late?" "What if we're sick?" "What if we bring a note from home?" "From the doctor?" "What if there's a death in the family?" Aside from the death of a parent or sibling, almost nothing seems to take precedence over the deadline.

ITEM: A language-arts instructor demonstrates what she later says she views as the most important professional accomplishment she has mastered in her seventeen years of teaching: the ability to maintain consistent rules and discipline. "I want absolute quiet," she tells her sixth-grade class, "and I *mean* it." She certainly did. The only voice in the room was the teacher's, announcing the next assignment. "I want you to copy the ten vocabulary words on the board and write a definition for each. You will have to do this in junior high school, so you had better start practicing now." A raised hand. "We've been practicing since first grade," the student reminds her. "It doesn't matter; you need to practice *more* for junior high."

Junior high is a threatening place for sixth-grade teachers who fear that their graduates won't do well—and for students who fear the unknown. "You won't be allowed to use such sloppy handwriting in junior high," an anxious teacher cautions. "Simple spelling mistakes will not be tolerated in junior high," another warns. "You had better not write run-on sentences in junior high," says a third. It's sometimes hard to know who is more distressed: teachers or students.

Senior high is worse. A school that in a working-class community, for example, had a yearly quota of 681 new words for its sophomore classes! What students were to do with their newly acquired vocabulary was unclear. It was common knowledge that, at best, the ditto sheets teachers were required to use prepared students for mindless questions on state-mandated examinations. At worst, the ditto sheets numbed the brain. But I've yet to see vocabulary taught in this way enrich writing. How could it, when skill and drill are uppermost from the statehouse to the schoolhouse?

The resulting distorted perspective begins to take a toll in the earliest grades.

I T E M: Children enter a second-grade classroom in a newly designed school in a large southeastern city the morning after the catastrophic explosion of the space shuttle *Challenger*. The subdued voices of students make it clear that they are as obsessed by the disaster as most adults are.

"Did you *see* it?" one child asks a friend.

"I watched it four times on TV," a classmate volunteers.

"My *daddy* cried," another says, "and I never saw him cry before. Not even when he lost his finger in the machine that picks up leaves in the backyard, and he was *bleeding!*"

"I had a bad dream," a little boy interrupts. "I thought I was an astronaut, and . . ."

Before he can tell what happened in his nightmare, the bell rings, and the young mourners are told to take out their language arts workbooks, turn to page 81, and "get down to business." The opportunity to write about the thoughts and feelings that the inferno aroused in these shaken children is lost. This morning, capitalization is "business"; writing is not.

Standing in the second-grade classroom, I recalled students in the previous generation who were expected to continue writing Thanksgiving stories about pilgrims and Indians the day after President Kennedy was assassinated. Having heard the fatal rifle shots on television, however, and seen their slain president's widow in her blood-soaked clothes, students were hardly interested in conventional topics that the lesson plan provided. Teachers, on the other hand, were usually too committed to that plan to realize that students needed to express their pain and sorrow. But a fifth-grade student who later won a district-wide writing prize found a way to incorporate her feelings with a standard Thanksgiving assignment. "If you think a turkey is afraid at this time of year," she wrote, "you don't know what fear is. I'm TERRORFIED [her spelling] when I think of my country without President Kennedy."

Times change, but most schools don't. Today's grandparents remember having had to take examinations the day after the death of Franklin Delano Roosevelt, the only president they had ever known. Weeping for the father figure she had lost, one high school student completed an English grammar test and wrote at the end, "Why couldn't we have written a letter to Mrs. Roosevelt today and let the test wait?" I recall the question well, for I was the student who asked it.

THE GREAT GRAMMAR MYSTERY

Erasmus, one of the major figures of the Renaissance, encountered comparable misguided instruction almost five centuries ago. "I have no patience with the stupidity of the average teacher of grammar who wastes precious years in hammering rules into children's heads," he said, mincing no words. Montaigne's patience also was tried. Fluent in Latin by age six through the efforts of a tutor who spoke to him in no other language, Montaigne learned "without book, without grammar or rules, without whipping, and without tears"—until he went to school, where artificial instruction destroyed his fluency. Rousseau argued in favor of having children model their language on adult speech, not on the prevailing emphasis on grammar. And John Locke said the conversational way of learning a language "is to be preferred as the most expedite, proper, and natural." But the insights of these intellectual giants did not affect the grammar teachers I observed.

I T E M: "It's amazing," a perplexed eighth-grade teacher commented, furrowing her brow, "but even the brightest students forget the fundamentals almost as soon as they move from one page in the workbook to the next. I can't figure out why my A students can write a thoughtful book report on *I Know Why the Caged Bird Sings,* but get a D or even an F on a short-answer test that only requires their recognizing a few prepositions. You would almost think that students saw no connection between writing and grammar."

Precisely. Many teachers don't see the connection either. Nor do the publishers of the only grammar textbook series for grades six through twelve that has racked up sales of some thirty million copies since it was issued in 1946. This forbidding old standby has had more face-lifts than an aging Hollywood star, but its isolated rules still make the futility of narrow grammar instruction abundantly clear. True, these textbooks now suggest a commitment to writing as well as to formal grammar; but, also true, the content so exaggerates the importance of errors that cosmetic changes are insufficient.

Theodore Sizer captured that futility in his book *Horace's Compromise* when Horace, who is a composite of conscientious English teachers, tries to get his ninth-grade students to recognize an adverb. Betty can't identify any in the first sentence. Bill can't help her. Phil's memory is better; he announces that an adverb modifies a verb—but he doesn't have any idea what "modify" means. Finally, Taffy recognizes "darkly" as the adverb in the sentence, "Heathcliff was a darkly brooding character"—but she doesn't know why it is an adverb. First, she says it modifies "character." When that doesn't work, she suggests that it modifies "Heathcliff." Clearly, she has confused adjectives and adverbs. By a process of elimination, she pounces on "brooding" as the word that is being modified, but she thinks "brooding" is a verb. Sentence by sentence, the class dismembers a paragraph from the textbook, searching for adverbs without success. Small wonder that over fifty years of scholarly research have strongly suggested that teaching isolated lessons in formal grammar is of questionable usefulness. To recognize the truth of Erasmus's complaint about the folly of hammering rules into children's heads, consider the evidence:

I T E M: A handful of students in the cafeteria of a better-than-average high school hatches a conspiracy over lunch. "Why don't we hand in the skimpiest composition we can get away with?" the ringleader proposes. "Mr. J. didn't say how long it had to be, and this way we could cut down on the number of 'awks' and 'frags.' " [N.B. teacher parlance for awkward writing and incomplete sentences.] A companion in outwitting the system agrees with the strategy. "Great idea! Old man J. isn't interested in my ideas, anyway."

I T E M: "I don't know why I have to teach the same grammar that eighth-grade teachers claim they have taught, and seventh-grade teachers say they taught before that," a veteran ninth-grade teacher complains. "What really riles me," she continues, "is that I know the tenth-grade teachers will want to know why I didn't do my job this year. Every teacher covers the ground outlined in a 'Scope and Sequence' chart, but I'd call it 'Hope and Frequence'; there's not much hope left, but there's plenty of 'frequence.' "

Whenever I eavesdropped in hallways and parking lots, I overheard some students—often in the honors English section of an academic high school—who thought they were demonstrating their superiority when they said to one another, "Between you and I. . . ." And I overheard others who camouflaged their wobbly command of English grammar by inserting "myself" when they were not certain whether

"I" or "me" was the correct word. "Maryanne and myself are going to have our graduation pictures taken this afternoon," an Uncertain One said. "Do you want to come with us?"

The products of three or four years of high school English speak a strange and ungrammatical language. Have they never been taught about the subject and the object of a verb? Mounds of ditto work sheets bear witness that students have, indeed, been taught; their use of language testifies to the fact that they have not learned. Doesn't this mean they need more drill? If you think so, try listening to their older sisters and brothers or to their American-born parents and grandparents. When two previous generations of students who have been thoroughly grilled and drilled in English grammar make the same mistakes as the Uncertain Ones, is there any reason to believe that repetition will have a magical quality now that it never had before?

Any sensible person would say there is not; yet a display of the grammar books that leading textbook publishers produce and that thousands of school districts buy at great cost requires an exhibit hall that covers entire city blocks at annual teachers' conventions. Since writing is the current attraction (if not the current fad), while grammar is the mainstay, the new titles feature both selling points. Three publishers call their series *Grammar and Composition;* reversing the order, a fourth titles its newest series *Composition and Grammar;* and a fifth sets itself apart by calling its secondary school series *Grammar and Writing.* Optimists believe that writing is going to enter the curriculum as it never has before. Maybe so, but realists know that traditionally taught formal grammar is not about to leave.

Many back-to-basics schools even supplement textbooks with locally developed grammar work sheets. "No child is going to leave my classroom without knowing his grammar," one teacher who subscribes to the old-school mentality said grimly. Perhaps no one did, in June—but September was another story. Consider these notes from a number of college graduates:

Dear Aunt Jane and Uncle Herb:
Thank you for your generous wedding gift. We're glad that one of you were there and hope to see both of you if your ever in Arizona.

Love Al and Sal

Dear Friends,
Your kind note of condolence was much appreciated. Thank you for telling me that Bills bowling team is going to award a medal for sportsmanship in his memory to a student.

Sincerely,
Ann

Dear Cousins:
After failing the phys ed exam, my teacher "advised" me to work out in the gym during spring vacation and try again. They're goes our camping trip.

Furious Fred

Anyone who cares about the way language is spoken and written cannot pretend that the rules of standard grammar and generally accepted usage are relics that are hardly worth teaching. To the contrary, in the long run they are important and are worth teaching well. But that doesn't mean beginning by ramming bunnies and chicks into the heads of six-year-olds, as the computer-happy first-grade teacher did when she got to her "adjective unit" in mid-March. It means encouraging more writing and reading at every grade level. Young writers and readers learn what a sentence is, before they understand the meaning of "A noun is the name of a person, place, or thing." Nouns and verbs are part of every writer's repertoire; adjectives and adverbs are like paint to an artist, like clay to a sculptor. Sooner or later, writers and readers will be ready to understand formal

English grammar, but most classrooms insist on sooner rather than later.

RIGIDITY AND "REFORM"

Consider the plight of a large West Coast school that is required to meet the fixed demands of an urban school district, despite the fact that the non-English-speaking students who enter first grade speak nine different languages. Unrealistic as local policy is for children of so many origins, the central office has established identical expectations for youngsters from every country in this miniature United Nations. "Trying to satisfy the powers that be at headquarters and still be true to my own beliefs about how children learn best puts me in the position of doing a constant balancing act," the harried principal confided. "Maybe this school needs a gymnast instead of an educator at the head."

To show what he was talking about, Dr. P. deposited a sheaf of papers on the table. "Take a look at some of the 'Standards of Achievement' that I'm supposed to impose on my teachers, and that they're supposed to impose on our children, beginning in the first grade. When you thumb through these norms," the troubled principal said, "you'll see that administrators in this school district have learned nothing from history. When Irish children, Italian-Americans, Poles, and Slavs had to meet similar uniform standards, students often dropped out of school by age ten or twelve. And who could blame them? If we use the same methods and set the same standards today, I'm afraid we're going to lose the very students who need the most help from school."

The "Standards of Achievement" to which Dr. P. referred revealed that by the end of first grade, even students who are still struggling to speak and understand a new language have to:

- form correct upper- and lower-case manuscript letters
- copy correctly a letter, invitation, thank-you note
- spell words from speller or grade-level list
- use a period and question mark, and recognize an exclamation point
- use capitals at the beginning of a sentence and for names
- use a capital letter for the pronoun "I"

"Don't misunderstand me," the gymnast-principal said, "I'm as concerned as the next person about correct spelling and penmanship, but there is no reason to think that practices that failed with earlier groups will succeed with immigrants from Spanish-speaking countries and black Americans who have moved from the South to the North." Dr. P. explained that he believes the large number of Asian immigrants who form the majority of the school's population will succeed where others fail, just as earlier generations of Jewish, Japanese, and Greek Americans were able to do, but he objected to seeing children penalized for coming from ethnic groups that value individual achievement less. "And I can't see for the life of me why back to basics is being hailed as a new 'reform,' " he scoffed. "The only thing that's new now is the color of our students' skins and the nature of the job market."

Descended from Lithuanian grandparents, Dr. P. was fascinated by the history of immigration. He told me that between 1880 and 1920, 23.5 million immigrants, mostly from southern and eastern Europe, flooded American shores. In fact in 1909, 71.5 percent of the children attending school in New York City had foreign-born parents; in Chicago, the percentage was 67.3, in Boston, 63.5. And schools in Philadelphia, Cleveland, Omaha, and Detroit reported population mixtures that included as many as thirty-six different nationalities. New York City Superintendent of Schools William Henry Maxwell was so overwhelmed by what he called "the influx of vast hordes of people from abroad," that he openly labeled newcomers "alien in language, alien in modes of thought, and alien in tradition."

But possession of limited writing skills in the nineteenth century, when 80 percent of the labor force was employed in unskilled jobs, was not a major problem. Being similarly limited in the year 1900 was still not seriously disabling, because unskilled jobs accounted for 60 percent of the total. However, in 1980 that total had dropped to a scant 6 percent, and as the United States hurries into the twenty-first century, individuals with the ability to communicate increasingly complex ideas will be in greater demand than ever. Therefore, the frequently heard call to pursue basic skills with undiminished zeal, while paying scant attention to writing as a mode of thinking, is a prescription for disaster.

It is no exaggeration to say that disaster actually mounts with the second-grade Standards of Achievement that Dr. P.'s urban, West Coast school district has imposed on students, teachers, and principals. Seven-year-old children, many of them still struggling to wrap their tongues around the English language, were expected to be "proficient" in eleven areas of language arts. Foreshadowing the emphasis that clouds writing throughout the elementary grades, six standards fall under the rubric of grammar and mechanics, three under spelling, one under handwriting—and one under composition. Clearly, school board members and administrators had paid scant attention to the connection between writing and thinking. Instead, they were calling for the relentless pursuit of basic skills—and parents and taxpayers usually applauded the effort. Though these advocates are getting what they think they want, it may be that they, like the ugly frog who was granted three wishes, will discover that they are also getting something they never bargained for.

Not every principal lives in fear of regulations that may be imposed by the district office, however; halfway across the continent, Ms. T. devised her own solution to the so-called writing crisis. "I simply doubled the amount of time in the schedule for language arts," she said with considerable pride. As a result, eight-year-olds spend forty-five minutes a day on skill and drill, have a brief recess, and then spend another forty-five minutes on more skill and drill.

"Students are allowed to write after they have mastered the basic skills," Ms. T. stated, "and not before." Might the students develop mastery through writing? The principal was shocked by this foolish question. "That's like asking if they might learn to like spinach through eating ice cream."

The image of writing as spinach returned when I visited a stern, midwestern elementary school that had "punishment tables" placed down a long corridor. Each semicircular table faced the wall and was positioned sufficiently far from the next so as to isolate offenders from each other. Youngsters who had misbehaved were assigned to these punishment tables to repent for whatever the offense might be by writing a hundred times, "I will not ——— again." If the crime was severe enough or if a child was a repeat offender, the one hundred "I will nots" were increased to five hundred. Writing as spinach! If there was anything more calculated to leave children with a permanent distaste for writing, one would be hard pressed to think of what it might be.

I T E M: A ten-year-old sat in the detention room of his school in the Deep South counting, "Seventy-six, seventy-seven, seventy-eight. . . ." Catching my eye, he explained, "I only have to write a hundred of them today; next week, if I'm lucky, I may not have to write any at all." When I asked, "What's 'them'?" he replied, "Oh, you know. Them is an 'I will not.' " I pressed the culprit further. "When I write, I try not to begin every sentence the same way," I said. "Oh, but this isn't *real* writing," he explained. "This is just supposed to teach me a lesson." After reading the same "I will not" seventy-eight times, I assumed the lesson was, "I will not chew gum in class." But I was mistaken. The young culprit explained the lesson without wasting a word: "School writing stinks."

Searching for a study in contrasts, I visited a prestigious private school that prides itself on its writing program. Eight-year-old Jared was hunched over a piece of paper that was blank, except for the smudges left by some frantic erasing. Since his teacher had introduced me to the class as a "real writer," Jared felt free to ask my help. "I have a great story I want to tell, but I'm stuck. I want to write about five goldfish who live in a bowl with their mother, but they're sad because there isn't any room for their father." When I tried to assure Jared that he seemed to be ready to write because he had already thought about what he wanted to say, he shook his head from side to side. "You don't understand. For homework last night, I had to do a page in my workbook with three kinds of 'theres.' I got all mixed up with 't-h-e-i-r' and 't-h-e-y-'r-e' and 't-h-e-r-e.' And we're not allowed to use homework words in a story unless we can spell them right." Perhaps Jared's school had gained an undeserved reputation simply because it was expensive.

To see how representative public schools teach writing, I turned to a batch of questionnaires I had sent members of the Teacher Board of *Instructor* magazine. Despite an overload of paperwork, this group of teachers and principals had responded generously to three pages of questions. Unfortunately, most of their answers were reminiscent of the "old school." A kindergarten teacher in a small town in a large southwestern state, for example, replied that she groups children by ability and concentrates on teaching kids complete sentences, agreement of subject and predicate, correct verb forms, and punctuation. The vice principal of a New England school, who has taught third, fourth, and fifth grades, reported that in her school writing begins with the basics: grammar, punctuation, spelling, and sentence structure. Could that kind of emphasis be the reason that a teacher in a Rocky Mountain suburban school system noted that even young children dislike writing? Although she blamed their parents, the impact of her emphasis on "fundamentals" is open to question. So is the requirement that three main ideas must support the topic she assigns. In a similar vein, a first-grade teacher with fifteen years of experience in a midwestern school system said that since teachers have become more aware of "weaknesses," they have been placing additional emphasis on writing skills.

A Pacific Coast principal's response reflected the opinions and practices of seventeen classroom teachers and several other support teachers who discussed the questionnaire at a staff meeting. She said the teachers agreed that writing is much more important than before, but when she got them to be specific, they were really talking about correct mechanics. "I see a lot of push to get children to write," she said, "but I see little follow-through on thought process. Writing is, alas, an isolated area." As an afterthought this principal noted, "One school in our district has a pilot writing project, but it is mostly gimmickry."

One by one, the members of the Teacher Board described writing programs that are virtually interchangeable. Although the answers were similar, a teacher from a school district in a border state that is stressing basic skills sounded more despairing than her colleagues. She considered the statewide emphasis on fundamentals "a giant step backward" that had already taken a toll on her school. "One of the best teachers we ever had resigned after having taught here for sixteen years," Ms. R. said. "A new teacher with fresh ideas also resigned, and a third teacher was hospitalized with a nervous breakdown. If she couldn't take the stress, how will our kids handle the incessant drilling and testing?" Even this animated member of *Instructor*'s Teacher Advisory Board feared that she might no longer be able to infuse spirit into her fourth-grade classroom—despite her twenty years of experience.

Since most elementary schools fail to give students a genuinely "good start," it seemed even more unlikely that high schools would free students from stultifying traditions. Nonetheless, some of the most exciting reforms in teaching and learning had been spearheaded half a century ago by thirty public and private U.S. high schools that participated in the Progressive Education Association's "Eight Year Study." Therefore, I didn't want to rule out the possibility that present-day reforms might also exist in secondary school writing programs.

In its preliminary observations, the Eight Year Study could have been describing many contemporary high school classrooms. Students, it noted, did not often drive ahead under their own power, pursuing ideas that really meant something to them. Instead, they were so busy doing teacher-assigned work that they had neither the time nor the initiative to delve further on their own and become independent, self-directed learners. Yet the Eight Year Study found solutions to what had looked like an insoluble situation—solutions that produced remarkable results. It seems the high school curriculum had become fossilized, in part, because of requirements that colleges imposed on its applicants. To encourage secondary school inventiveness, three hundred colleges and universities agreed to set aside the usual subject and unit requirements for admission during an experimental eight-year period and accept any student whom the principals of thirty high schools recommended.

Freed from constraints, all that remained was for each school to design its own curriculum. But that proved to be quite an "all." As one principal admitted, *"I fear we have come to love our chains* [emphasis added]." I was to think of that remark many times as I visited high school English programs that are already free to initiate writing programs but that cling to the familiar literature and a rehash of grammar and usage. Despite the fear of change in most contemporary secondary schools, the record shows that graduates of the thirty high schools in the Eight Year Study had acquitted themselves well in college. Indeed, in a comparison study of 1,475 matched pairs, the study's college follow-up staff had found, among other things, that the experimental students:

- were judged to be more precise, more objective, and more systematic in their thinking
- were more often judged to possess a high degree of intellectual curiosity and drive
- earned a slightly higher total grade-point average
- received slightly more academic honors
- more often demonstrated a high degree of resourcefulness in meeting new situations

The findings filled an entire volume (one of five that comprised the full report of the Eight Year Study), but the basic point was that departing from the conventional curriculum did not hurt these students; it helped them. It seemed altogether reasonable, therefore, that present-day writing programs that encourage students to drive ahead under their own power on projects that really mean something to them (in contrast to working only on teacher-assigned subjects) might achieve comparable results. With that in mind, I set out to visit self-described "innovative" writing programs.

The chairperson of the English Department of a Middle Atlantic high school urged me to observe classes there, because she believed the new methods she had supported were making a major impact on student writing. Most of the teachers in the department, for example, were beginning each class by having students spend ten to fifteen minutes keeping a journal. "I can't think of a better way to get teenagers writing than to give them time to express their personal thoughts and feelings," Dr. M. said. "Adolescents often think nothing matters quite so much as their own world." True enough, but if Dr. M. had spent time in the classes she admired, she would have discovered that students were assigned topics Monday through Thursday, and were told to avoid introducing any "personal thoughts and feelings." In fact, the pronoun "I" was not permitted. Although Friday's entries could be on any subject that students chose, the personal and the impersonal were graded with the same red ink. "Journal writing in this school is baloney," a sophomore said. "The only thing I've learned is what the word *farce* means. We keep journals for the teacher's approval, not to put our thinking on paper."

Ignoring the student-teacher confidentiality of most secondary school journals, this angry young man and six of his friends pointed out entries that, sometimes directly, sometimes indirectly, revealed their personal feelings about sex, rejection, fear, and death. The notebooks were clearly not "dialogue" or "response" journals where students have a written conversation with their teacher. By no stretch of the imagination did the entries contain a mutual exchange of ideas between turbulent adolescents and a sensitive teacher. Instead these painfully arrived-at thoughts and feelings were reduced to a grade, as if the journal were a daily test where there was only one right answer. Even more destructive were the accompanying caustic comments. Sarcasm, evidently, was an accepted style here. "These kids view paper and pencil as if the combination were their mortal enemy," a literature teacher said, red pencil in hand.

"Palmer High" is another college preparatory school that is concerned about the quality of writing, I visited there with the intention of paying particular attention to courses for gifted students. On the wall of every English classroom, an identical chart commanded immediate attention. At the top was an inverted triangle; under that, three circles were drawn, one beneath the other; finally, another triangle pointed upward. In an instant, I recognized a portrayal of the old "five-paragraph essay": a topic paragraph, three paragraphs with supporting examples, and a concluding paragraph to summarize the preceding four. Silently I recalled the college admissions officer who said he can recite applicants' essays in his sleep: The debating team (the football squad, the newspaper) taught me leadership. Second paragraph: It helped me organize my time. Two more paragraphs follow, fleshing out the opening thought. Then comes the last paragraph: "To summarize, the debating team. . . ." The only people who have been free of this rigid structure are, to quote Jared's teacher, "real writers."

I T E M: Aaron Stander, director of Michigan's Oakland Writing Project (one of 165 National Writing Project teacher training sites) begins each five-week Summer Institute by holding up a hundred-dollar bill and offering it to any teacher who can find a five-paragraph essay in *Time, Newsweek, The New Yorker, Harper's, The Atlantic,* or any other magazine. "I have yet to lose my money," he said.

Rigidities were most pronounced in a high school that I chose to observe because of its much touted "humanities program." I'm still not sure what that is supposed to mean, but one thing seemed clear: writing was so pruned here that precious little flowering occurred, although a high-level administrator guided me into five classes for gifted students. Since the majority of graduates do not go on to college and 35 percent earn a certificate rather than a diploma, I finally asked to see a broader range of classes.

"I'm going to take you to the most well-organized teacher first," he whispered, as we entered a ninth-grade English class (for gifted students). Ms. L. is so well organized that she always shows visitors her lesson plans for two months at a time. "I devote the first day of each week to word-study drills and to a review of statewide standardized tests," she explained while her class was doing "seat work," "and the last day of the week to spelling." Later, she offered a candid, teacher's-eye view of the classroom in that school system. "Let's face it, if my kids don't score well, they look bad—and

so do I. So we've got to get to cracking on first things first."
Writing, evidently, is not a "first thing."

Spelling is. Every Friday morning in classrooms all over
the United States, twenty words are tested. Indeed, spelling
assumes such a dominant place in the teaching of basic skills
that I found myself reminded time and again of a family
legend that claims that my grandmother took spelling so
seriously that two days before she died in her ninety-fifth
year she was still bemoaning the fact that she had misspelled
"scissors" in a fifth-grade spelling bee. My mother, a great-
grandmother seven times over, also remembered spelling as
the only part of writing that really mattered. "I was lucky it
did," she said, "because compositions would have ruined my
reputation. I was obedient, not original." (Mother had forgotten that originality wasn't always welcomed in her youth,
any more than it is now.) In her eighty-eighth year, my
"lucky" mother could not write a thank-you note or express
her sympathy when a friend was bereaved, but her marketing list testified to her ability to spell "cinnamon," "broc-
coli," and "cauliflower."

I certainly don't mean to dismiss the value of spelling
correctly, or of proper punctuation, legible penmanship, and
accepted usage, because until these matters become almost
second nature, the need to keep checking on mechanics
prevents a student from thinking. But an obsession with any
of the conventions reduces writing to a game of Trivial Pursuit. After all, the entire purpose of correct form is to clarify
what the writer wants to say. Punctuation, for example, in
Mina Shaughnessy's words, "provides a map for one who
must otherwise drive blindly past the by-ways, intersections,
and detours of a writer's thought." Without commas, readers
would not know where to pause; without periods, they
would not know where to stop.

These signals—and at least ten others—are part of the
process of composition, for writers cannot make sentences
clear unless they mark them to indicate excitement, dia-

logue, questions, asides, and such. To place conventions on a pedestal that is totally removed from writing, therefore, is to lose sight of the reasons for rules in the first place, as Teachers College professor Lucy McCormick Calkins has demonstrated in a comparison study of third-grade students in Atkinson, New Hampshire. Youngsters who had learned punctuation in order to clarify their own writing could explain an average of more than eight punctuation marks; children across the hall, however, who had formal drills and exercises in punctuation but who rarely wrote, could explain fewer than four marks.

Similarly, the Atkinson study found that one-third of a first-grade class used quotation marks in their writing; yet, in most curriculum plans, quotation marks are not introduced until fourth grade, at the earliest. Why the difference? In their writing, first-graders used a great deal of dialogue. Realizing that they would want readers to recognize conversation when it appeared, teacher Mary Ellen Giacobbe showed six-year-olds how using quotation marks would set off speech from the rest of the text. Since writers want to communicate clearly, some very young students were ready to grasp an advanced concept, when it was taught as an outgrowth of what they were trying to say. Yet fourth-grade students often struggle with the same punctuation when it is taught as one more fragment of mechanics.

THE NINETEENTH CENTURY REVISITED

The overwhelming majority of English teachers have accepted the idea that an obsession with narrow skill and drill is the only way to overcome the common errors that students continue to make. The act of writing, in faculty eyes, is a problem, not a solution, and the failure of years of rote memorization simply means that students need more of the methods that didn't work in the first place.

ITEM: "We're facing a real writing crisis now," said a high school teacher with thirty-three years' experience, "and we can't solve it unless we're prepared to swallow some unpleasant medicine. If you talk to the other members of the English department, you'll find that they agree." I did—and all fourteen teachers seemed to know what the prescription entailed. Certainly, no one in this Rocky Mountain high school asked what "unpleasant medicine" meant.

ITEM: Opinion in the faculty lounge of a New England high school was also unanimous. "When sophomores and juniors still don't know the difference between 'to' and 'too' or 'who's' and 'whose,' teachers have to take a now-or-never stance and *pound* the rules into students' heads," an English teacher said, speaking for all. "We really have no choice," she concluded. "We certainly can't let our seniors receive high school diplomas, writing as poorly as they do in their junior year."

The illiteracy that teachers bemoan began shortly after the Civil War. And the real "writing crisis" was first recognized at Harvard in 1873. It was then that university president Charles W. Eliot complained about students' poor writing, singling out "bad spelling, incorrectness as well as inelegance of expression, [and] ignorance of the simplest rules of punctuation in writing. . . ." The following year Harvard instituted its first written entrance examinations in English composition—and *more than half of the candidates failed to pass.* In fact, a recent study of the results indicated that, distressing as writing often is in today's public schools and community colleges, it is still more competent than what Harvard uncovered in 1874.

The reason for the great university's nineteenth-century "writing crisis" and our contemporary dilemma are similar: new populations of students lack the background needed to meet the demands of the classroom, even when the demands are limited to clear penmanship and correct spelling, punctuation, grammar, and usage. Educational turmoil, in other words, is a product of social turmoil.

Turmoil at Harvard? Yes, indeed. Over the course of more than two centuries since the university was founded in 1636, it had provided an aristocratic education for young men of inherited wealth and social position who disdained commerce and industry. To prepare for the ministry or the law these young Brahmins pursued classical studies, analyzing the writing of Aristotle, the oratory of Cicero. But a radically different student body began converging on the college after the North's victory in the Civil War ushered in a period of economic growth unlike anything the United States had experienced before. Sons of "captains of industry" who had amassed vast fortunes despite their limited schooling, the new breed of Harvard students grew to manhood surrounded by the opulence of "the gilded age" but unprepared for higher education. Nonetheless, the new industrialists and financiers who had achieved upward economic mobility were determined that their sons provide the social mobility that their families lacked, and saw an elite college education as the way to acquire the desired status.

In stark contrast, the black and Hispanic populations that form a significant part of contemporary schools (but a small part of our colleges and universities) have grown up in the midst of poverty. Like the sons of earlier industrialists, today's "underclass" is unprepared to meet even modest demands of literacy, but is motivated by different goals. The upward economic mobility that nineteenth-century capitalists already claimed is still an elusive achievement for most black and Hispanic families; upward social mobility is also a fantasy for large numbers of dropouts. Even minority students who manage to get admitted to college are only half as likely as Caucasian classmates to remain long enough to get their degree.

Designs for Change, an educational research and advocacy organization, tracked 39,500 Chicago ninth-graders and found that 21,000 of this group failed to complete high school within the public school system. Only 8 percent of the original group of black and Hispanic ninth-grade students both graduated and read at or above the national average.

I T E M: "Allow me to offer a familiar moment of school talk," Dr. Michelle Fine says, tongue in cheek, at a conference of Chief State School Officers. "At the first Parent Teacher Association meeting, Mr. Stein, the principal of a comprehensive public high school in New York City, announced, 'Welcome to ———— High School. We are proud that eighty percent of our graduates go on to college.' " Of course, Dr. Fine pointed out, "only twenty percent of any entering ninth grade ever graduates."

Nineteenth-century statistics tell a different story: the number of students between the ages of eighteen and twenty-one that attended college more than doubled between 1870 and 1880—going from 52,000 to 116,000—and more than tripled by 1890, when enrollments reached 157,000. "Successful people clamored for admission to more prestigious circles," historian John Higham has explained. "Social climbing ceased to be a simple and modest expectation. It became a genuine social problem." The resulting upheaval posed a new kind of educational problem as well, when, as a scholarly account reports, the captains of industry arranged to have their sons "carefully tutored by hired intellectuals and shipped to Harvard, Yale, and Princeton to be finished off." But the careful tutoring wasn't careful enough. Consequently, professors who had been accustomed to teaching Harvard gentlemen the oratory and writing of Aristotle and Cicero were distressed, even ashamed, and certainly unprepared to find themselves teaching the first influx of college-level remedial writing courses. In a single generation, from the 1870s to the 1890s, Harvard's abstract ideals changed to pragmatic goals, in keeping with the needs of a changing society and a changing student body.

Unfamiliar with college students of this sort, Harvard's faculty, understandably enough, faulted inferior secondary school preparation, but it faulted the preparation for the wrong reasons. Instead of realizing that students were barely able to express their ideas because they needed far more practice in writing compositions than they had experienced, professors placed the blame on insufficient drill in formal grammar. To compensate, Harvard enshrined the very basics that reformers now urge us to go "back to," the basics that have haunted us for over a century and that have never produced admirable writing.

A composition "training" course was mandated for all Harvard freshmen. Skill-and-drill exercises were to be repeated as often as necessary until, according to plan, rules would finally take hold and students would produce error-free writing. And error-free writing, no matter how superficial, no matter how mechanical, was considered admirable. With falsely conceived pedagogy (if, indeed, one can so dignify training), freshmen composition was destined to fail. And, judging by subsequent student writing, fail it did. Undeterred by these results, however, and impressed by Harvard's reputation, other colleges foisted similar training on their freshmen. Predictably, secondary schools, not wanting their college candidates to lose out in the race for admission, adopted the same pattern.

For two decades, Harvard's Board of Overseers objected to skill-and-drill training, not because the board took a different view of what constituted good writing, but because it resented Harvard's having to compensate for inferior student preparation. "It is obviously absurd that the college—the institution of higher education—should be called upon to turn aside from its proper functions," the 1892 Committee on Rhetoric and Composition lashed out, "and devote its means and the time of its instructors to the task of imparting elementary instruction which should be given . . . in [grade] schools." The Board of Overseers received similar reports in 1895 and 1897.

However, neither the Board of Overseers nor many other nineteenth-century critics dared allow themselves to see the most critical issue: despite all of Harvard's training, students had neither mastered the mechanics that the University valued nor learned to write intelligent prose. Then in the May 1893 issue of *The Atlantic Monthly,* J. J. Greenough faced some hard truths. Refusing to be mesmerized by the prestige of what was arguably the foremost Ivy League institution, he called attention to "the inability of students admitted to Harvard College to write English clearly and correctly." The frequent written exercises that schools required, Greenough pointed out, served no purpose. "With all this practice in writing," he demanded, "why do we not get better results?"

But the Harvard model did not provide "all this practice in writing," as it does now. "Basics" provided practice in error avoidance and rule worship, rather than practice in learning to write—and writing to learn. It is not surprising, then, that Greenough's observations have an amazingly contemporary tone insofar as most kindergarten-through-twelfth-grade teaching is concerned. He pointed to "a narrowness in the range of the modern [student's] ideas," to "a lack of clearness in those ideas," and to "an increased inability to read the printed page understandingly." Greenough also noted that:

- High school students read nothing solid in literature or history.
- The students attended schools where the work was too easy.
- The students put too much emphasis on athletics and not enough on academics.
- The students engaged in social lives that had become too advanced.

- The students came from homes that did not stimulate "verbal proficiency."
- The students reflected the impact of living in an "era that placed too much value on practical pursuits."

I T E M: If he were writing now, Greenough also might express concern about the amount of time students spend watching television. Surely there is no more popular explanation for our present writing dilemma.

Since students with similar limitations also applied to Yale, Princeton, and Columbia, these prestigious colleges began to judge candidates' writing by requiring them to compose entrance examination essays on the works of "standard authors." Fallout from what the University of Michigan's Fred Newton Scott termed a "feudal" model inevitably followed: the "standard authors" whom colleges chose dictated the books that secondary schools had to teach.

The revolt against the dictatorial power of certain college entrance examinations wound up contributing to college and high school English teachers' banding together in 1911 to form the National Council of Teachers of English (NCTE). Scott became the first and only two-term president. And in the first issue of the council's publication, the *English Journal*, William D. Lewis, a Philadelphia high school principal, denounced another indication of Harvard's heavy hand. The university, Lewis complained, "thinks it necessary to send out to the [high] schools a pamphlet stating the most flagrant errors among its freshmen." By pointing out the areas in English that the university felt schools should concentrate on, Lewis protested, Harvard was exerting control over the writing programs of the high schools.

Actually, the tension between colleges and secondary schools stemmed from two clearly different missions. As Henry S. Pritchett, president of the Carnegie Foundation for the Advancement of Teaching, explained in 1910, high schools were expected to prepare great masses of students for citizenship in a democracy and a small number—perhaps 5 percent—for college. But as "the great masses" expanded, so did the college-bound population. The scant 5 percent of the high school population that was prepared for college in 1910 has multiplied six times over. Yet the years that marked the beginning of the twentieth century and those at the end have a common failing: at neither time have college-bound students or job-seeking high school graduates been able to write acceptably. Basic skills have served both groups poorly.

THE GREAT MISTAKE:
SEPARATING WRITING FROM THINKING

After years spent in classrooms where content is less important than correctness, most students are ill-equipped to compose a compelling paragraph, much less a complete paper. To avoid having to express their own thinking, they often prefer an assigned topic, no matter how dreary it may be. "I hate having to think up my own ideas" is as typical a refrain now as it was in years past. One would expect that today's more outspoken adolescents would want to express their own opinions about controversial issues, just as younger children might want to write about experiences that are close to them. After all, the era of "children should be seen but not heard" has long vanished. But even the sons and daughters of the sixties generation seem to recognize that school has its own rules—rules that had best be followed.

I learned that lesson in my sophomore year in high school, when I wrote a book report, stating the reasons why I disliked Nathaniel Hawthorne's *The House of the Seven Gables.* Although I thought students were supposed to think independently in my school, I learned that independence was punished and the student humiliated. Standing in front of the room and displaying my paper with a scarlet *F* on it for the entire class to see, my teacher thundered my name. "Young lady, who are *you* to criticize Nathaniel Hawthorne? It would be like *my* criticizing God."

I T E M: Richard Marius, director of Harvard University's excellent Expository Writing program, tells of speaking with a graduate of Harvard's class of 1950 who still winces when he recalls his writing teacher. Though now middle-aged and clearly successful, the former student cannot forget the teacher's destructiveness. "I tried my best, but I could never do anything to his satisfaction." The crowning blow, not the least softened by the intervening years, Marius reports, was the writing instructor's insistence on reading the student's work to the class while interjecting sarcastic comments.

Although memories of this sort abound, it was not until quite recently that two scholars, C. H. Knoblauch and Lil Brannon, identified the underlying issue. Typically, they pointed out, students produce assignments, not in order to be heard, but in order to give teachers something to judge on the basis of *their agenda.* Since the teacher's agenda is usually the only one that matters, students have to puzzle out what the instructor wants—what in Knoblauch and Brannon's term constitutes the "Ideal Text."

"To the extent that the teacher's expectations are not satisfied," they explain, "authority over the writing is stolen from the writer by means of comments, oral or written, that represent the teacher's agenda, whatever the writer's intentions may initially have been." That agenda distorts communication, when teachers, who alone know what Ideal Text they have in mind, display little interest in understanding anything that differs from it.

To test their hypothesis, the two scholars devised an experiment in which they asked forty teachers to comment as they normally would on an essay a student had written.

The work in question was designed to be the closing argument by the prosecuting attorney in the Lindbergh trial. In presenting the most convincing statement, the student explained to Knoblauch and Brannon, he [the gender is not reported] wanted to create sympathy for the Lindberghs and revulsion for the accused. Consequently, he had studied the trial transcripts and had tried to capture the voice and tone as well as the persuasive grounds of the prosecuting attorney's statement without reproducing the exact words.

None of the forty teachers responding to the writing had the benefit of the student's explanation of intent—and none of the teachers expressed interest in finding out what that might have been. Instead, most decided that the writing was too emotional for their more restrained Ideal Text, and, therefore, reflected an immature, undeveloped rhetorical sense. The remaining teachers also saw the writing as a departure from a carefully reasoned Ideal Text, but they viewed the emotional appeal as a clever spoof. Although the teachers' conclusions differed, their responses were identical in one respect: no one had asked what the *student's* agenda might have been. Why was the writing so flowery? Had the writer considered other approaches and discarded them? If so, what was the underlying reasoning? If not, why did he go directly to the florid style? Had the teachers asked any of these questions, they would have discovered that the student had done a superb job of avoiding plagiarism while presenting the passionate tone that the prosecuting attorney had used.

The theory of the Ideal Text helps explain why students in every generation have thought that their teachers were dictators. From my sophomore-year experience with a Nathaniel Hawthorne book report, I learned that it was better to avoid original thinking than to provoke such powerful wrath. For my remaining years in high school, I chose to second-guess my teachers. My writing suffered—but my marks improved. Contemporary teachers are less prone to rule the room with undue imperiousness, but there's no denying that well-intentioned teachers-turned-stylists still red-pencil students' writing style with a heavy hand.

"Do not use the first person," one teacher-stylist may decree. "Do not use contractions," another directs. "Your writing is too colloquial," a third criticizes. Yet students do not expect an explanation of these sweeping statements, nor do they anticipate having an opportunity to explain why they made the choices they did. Quite unconsciously, a conventional teacher takes control over each student's writing, and without asking questions most students simply accept a teacher's judgments, never understanding what evoked approval or disapproval. Most important of all, teachers take control over each student's thinking. And make no mistake about it, writing *is* thinking. Or it should be.

The way schools view writing, therefore, reflects the way they view learning and teaching, inquiry and risk taking, development and mastery. Indeed, writing in every area of the curriculum provides an accurate gauge of the health of the entire school. The health of many of the nation's schools is not good. But others are acquiring fresh vigor as a growing number of teachers help each other develop innovative strategies for linking writing, thinking, and learning. The results of these forward-looking techniques give cause for hope and celebration.

3

WHEN TEACHERS
TEACH TEACHERS

"Jim Gray has probably convinced more teachers that there are new and better ways to teach writing than anyone I know," commented Donald Graves, an early pied piper of writing reform for teachers of young children. "Certainly, among reformers Jim is the only person whose reach extends across all subjects from kindergarten to graduate school."

Jim may also be the only reformer whose casual disregard for appearance is matched with meticulous concern for developing an orderly plan to transform the teaching of writing at home and abroad. The discrepancy is startling. Gray's office on the University of California's Berkeley campus is sometimes overrun with books and papers, but there is nothing disorganized about the founder of the pioneering Bay Area Writing Project (BAWP) and the National Writing Project (NWP), with its 165 offshoots. Baggy sweaters and a crowded desk are minor matters for a man who has devoted the last fifteen years to proving that veteran teachers with no preparation in writing instruction can gain the expertise and confidence to address, rather than evade, the teaching of writing.

Jim Gray evokes a widespread following because he puts a premium on what is working, on learning from what he calls "success models"—and on rejecting "deficit models" that aim to patch up what has failed. If successful programs are hard to find, he develops his own. The Bay Area Writing Project, for example, had been on Jim's drawing board during the early seventies and was already in operation in the summer of 1974, a year and a half before *Newsweek* magazine alerted, indeed alarmed, the nation with its dramatic cover story, "Why Johnny Can't Write." Jim Gray's teaching experience has convinced him that Johnny *can* write, though he knows that over 40 percent of Berkeley's first-year students—all drawn from the top 12.5 percent of high school graduates—recently have had to take "Subject A," a remedial course that comes before the university's freshman composition class. He also knows that writing difficulties are not a new issue for Berkeley freshman—or for freshmen in any other college. (The highest percentage of Berkeley students required to take Subject A dates back to 1936.) "Of course, old problems don't free us from facing the clamor over current ones," Jim says, "and old 'solutions' didn't provide the answers that heated articles and overheated discussions now demand."

"Remedies" that view teachers as damaged goods in need of immediate repair have long aroused Jim's ire and have spurred him on in new directions. "Look at the results of conventional one-shot 'in-service' or staff-development programs that school districts rely on. Do you think that so-called experts who are paid handsomely to overcome teachers' 'weaknesses' really *serve* or *develop* the faculty that has to attend these training sessions after working hours?" Jim Gray clearly doesn't. In fact, a key principle of what was to become the Bay Area Writing Project emerged when he first questioned whether outside "authorities," many of whom had never taught in a school classroom, know more than what some teachers have taught themselves.

"Any rescue measure that is too little, too negative, and altogether devoid of common sense is bound to miscarry," Jim Gray says. "There's no way that an application of Band-Aids can cure years of neglect." Indeed, if there is a state license that requires English teachers to take so much as a single course in writing instruction, Jim says he has yet to see it. At best, English majors are well read in British and American literature. And elementary school teachers are expected to teach the three R's, although they studied only two—with an emphasis on reading. The results of these policies are clear. "At the end of four years of training," Jim observes, "most teachers can't teach students how to write, because no one has taught them the techniques they would need. For that matter, most teachers don't know how to write, either."

The solution to the dilemma, in Jim Gray's view, is obvious: since few teachers have any way of learning the first thing about writing instruction *before* they get their license, the majority need a plan to give them a thorough grounding *after* the fact. But the solution that is obvious to Jim Gray was not apparent to other educators when he initiated the Bay Area Writing Project. No such plan existed, no trained staff was available. "If any but a handful of teachers who worked closely with me in the early 1970s knew about the program that I had on the drawing board for counties in the San Francisco Bay area, I think I would have been run out of town," Jim says. "Remember, the national furor over the so-called writing crisis was reaching its peak, and public confidence in teachers had neared an all-time low. They were blamed for students' shaky grasp of basic skills, limited vocabulary, declining test scores, inferior writing—you name it."

Despite the widespread teacher-as-scapegoat mentality, Jim Gray knew that some teachers had devised successful techniques to overcome their lack of preparation in writing instruction. Consequently, he invited twenty-five exceptional men and women who had developed proven classroom strategies to become "fellows" in a summer institute on Berkeley's campus, where they were expected to demonstrate their methods to one another. They came from different schools and colleges in the Bay Area, and they taught different subjects, but they had one thing in common: all twenty-five had found effective ways to teach writing. And Jim Gray was persuaded that these accomplished teachers were best equipped to bring expertise to the Bay Area Writing Project.

If BAWP had been designed as a small five-week summer program, its impact would have been limited. But from the outset Jim Gray had planned to prepare graduates of the summer institute to become "teacher consultants," equipped to lead in-service writing workshops for colleagues who elected to take advantage of a ten-week-long series of training sessions from September to June. By going to nearby school districts that paid for the programs, a small network could give several hundred teachers the assistance in writing instruction they had never received. Jim believed, quite correctly, that teachers would find learning from fellow teachers a heady experience. He was also right in thinking that he could build a unique university-school partnership that departed from the tradition of having university faculty on top of the heap, secondary school teachers on the bottom, and elementary school teachers excluded altogether. Every fellow in a summer institute learned strategies for teaching writing from every other fellow.

BAWP might have remained a Bay Area project as Jim Gray had intended, were it not for the national reaction to the claim that Johnny can't write. Suddenly educators were looking for programs that were doing something to change the teaching of writing. But the only innovative program anywhere seemed to be the Bay Area Writing Project. Consequently, university faculty and school representatives began visiting BAWP with an eye to setting up programs in their own parts of the country. An initial flurry of interest showed signs of becoming an avalanche, and the project that began with twenty-five summer fellows expanded into the National Writing Project, which now reaches over 87,000 teachers a year.*

Seventeen more projects have mushroomed into the California Writing Project, nine into North Carolina's, another seven into Virginia's. In all, branches have developed in forty-six states, the District of Columbia, Puerto Rico, and nine other countries (Canada, England, Australia, New Zealand, Germany, Sweden, Finland, Norway, and, most recently, Greece†). "Our work keeps expanding," Jim says, "because we have tapped into the energy and ability of an obvious—and overlooked—resource: first-rate teachers." (Since no one person can oversee such a mammoth undertaking, Jim's "we" includes project directors and codirectors for 165 sites, plus ten regional directors.) Together with thousands of teacher consultants, they are disproving the old saw that "Writing is a gift that can't be taught." Clear, fresh writing *can* be taught, and teachers *can* learn to teach it.

Anyone who visits the summer institutes will see how it's done. Each morning on Berkeley's campus and on NWP campuses that follow the same basic model, summer fellows take turns demonstrating effective methods so that colleagues can consider knowledge about writing instruction that has come from actual experience. Although one of the great strengths of BAWP and NWP is an open-minded stance to whatever teaching produces quality student writing, in Jim Gray's words, "Cream rises to the top." Without being doctrinaire, teachers typically celebrate the best teaching practices and adapt them for further use. A high

---

*This overall figure includes teachers who participate in summer institutes, sustained school-year programs, and single Saturday workshops.

†The network of sites also serves American teachers who teach in Department of Defense Dependent Schools and U.S. Independent Schools throughout the Pacific rim, in Brazil, Panama, the Caribbean, and the Middle East as well as at bases throughout Europe and Japan.

school teacher of romantic poetry may seek ideas from a specialist in learning disabilities, a kindergarten teacher may exchange thoughts with a college instructor. From such collaboration emerges the unique atmosphere of mutual respect that Jim Gray has long believed possible, indeed essential, in order for teachers to see the importance of writing instruction at every level.

Jim also believes that anyone who subscribes to the idea that "Those who can, do; Those who can't, teach" couldn't be more mistaken. "I'd say that those who *can't write, can't teach writing,*" he insists. "That's why the Bay Area plan has always combined *teaching* writing and *doing* writing." To "do" writing, summer fellows divide into small "response groups" that meet three afternoons a week to discuss and edit the major writing assignments that participants are expected to prepare outside of class. Initially, even successful writing teachers may find they are "stuck" for ideas, embarrassed by the risk of looking foolish when they show their work to peers, and resentful of others' suggestions. In other words, they are likely to experience the feelings their students experience.

In time, however, teachers feel so strengthened by group support and suggestions that they usually seek ways to introduce response groups into their own classrooms. The summer fellows and project directors maintain that this strong emphasis on teacher writing has proven to be one of the most valuable parts of an institute. From all quarters, I heard the same basic statement: "I would not have had as complete an understanding of teaching writing if I had only examined the best practices and discussed them." Even the most talented writing instructors I talked with said that they could not have taught their classes the importance of drafting and revising, conferring with each other and revising again, until the teachers themselves had experienced the struggle—and ultimate success—of being able to express what they had in mind. Jim Gray is not surprised by their discovery. "Revision," he says, "is what writing is all about."

Learning from each other's teaching strategies and "doing writing" are important, but it is not until the institute weds the worlds of research and practice that teachers benefit from the findings of studies with which they are not familiar. "The difference between what we knew about teaching students to write in the fifties and now," international authority Mary K. Healy explains, "is as great as the difference in medicine between bleeding people and laser surgery." Before long, even skeptical teachers are won over as they delve into studies that seek out the reasons why some methods of teaching writing are successful and others fail. In fact, the link between research and teaching is so compelling that many teachers draft plans for studies they can conduct in their own classrooms as they become "teacher-researchers."

In one way or another, participants whom I first met in a summer institute on Berkeley's campus and went on to observe in programs in fourteen states have benefited from preparation that is based on a common set of principles:

- Since writing problems affect both universities and schools, they can best be solved through cooperatively planned university-school programs.
- Student writing can be improved by improving the teaching of writing, and *the best teacher of teachers is another teacher.*
- Students who learn to write fluently also learn to organize their thinking, reflect on their experiences, and express their feelings.
- Change can best be accomplished by those who work in the schools, not by transient consultants who appear briefly.
- "Teacher-proof" materials that are supposed to "work" so long as teachers do exactly as they are told are formulas for failure.
- Programs designed to improve the teaching of writing

should include teachers at all grade levels and from all
subject areas.

- Teachers of writing must write themselves.
- Classroom practice and research together have generated an important body of knowledge on the teaching of
writing.
- Practicing teachers can conduct useful research studies in
their own classrooms.
- No single "right" approach to the teaching of writing is
appropriate for every teacher and every student.

Teachers from the Bay Area and National Writing projects
know that "the best teacher of teachers is another teacher,"
just as people coping with other issues find that friends and
neighbors can help each other deal with common concerns:
day care for children or constant care for the elderly, death
or divorce, alcohol or drug abuse, colicky infants, late toilet
trainers. "There's nothing quite so helpful," a troubled parent explains, "as hearing an experienced mother say, 'Here's
what worked for me.' " But those five words are denied most
teachers. An acknowledgment of teaching success tends to
be considered arrogant, a search for help shameful, and an
exchange of strategies almost impossible. Ironically, the
most practical source of help can be as close as the teacher
next door or down the hall, but even nearby teachers are
usually out of reach.

And the distance doesn't narrow in most faculty lounges,
where teachers who relax over a cup of coffee are often too
guarded to share educational practices. Separated from colleagues much of the day, they trade pent-up frustrations,
exchange school gossip, and chat about weekends, sports,
films, even the weather. But the closest they come to a discussion of techniques that had succeeded or failed is an occasional suggestion for an elementary school bulletin board
display or a new ditto sheet. Talking about teaching experiences seems to be too threatening for comfort.

An extensive study of teacher behavior found that the average teacher observes someone else's classroom *only once every three years.* Observation, the researchers explained, is equated with evaluation, and evaluation can be risky business. "I have never heard a teacher say, 'I have a problem,' " a teacher told the researchers. "You just don't do it. You solve the problem on your own, or you pretend that you don't have one. You never open up to anyone about anything important." After hearing one account after another of this sort, the scholars wrote, "For most teachers in most schools, teaching is indeed a lonely enterprise. With so many people engaged in so common a mission in so compact a space and time, it is perhaps the greatest irony—and the greatest tragedy of teaching—that so much is carried on in self-imposed and professionally sanctioned isolation."

Tragic, yes, but understandable. "If I feared that my best efforts were more open to criticism than to assistance, I'd want to hide from view to avoid possible loss of face, too," Jim Gray observes. "When classrooms become virtually sealed off territory with an invisible Do Not Disturb sign safeguarding privacy, teachers gain the security of not having to reveal failures publicly—even though they pay the price of isolation and loneliness. It is a terribly high price, but most teachers view exposure as more costly than concealment."

Though the reasons for seclusion are understandable, research shows that teachers are best able to learn new techniques when they actually see them practiced. And that's exactly what takes place in every BAWP and NWP summer institute and after-school workshop. The contrast between the "Here's what works for me" approach that Jim Gray and his colleagues have cultivated and the solitariness of most classrooms is dramatic. Some of the indelible memories of their first year of teaching that veteran teachers have recalled in the *English Journal* (December 1986) illustrate their lonely introduction to the classroom. "It was a painful, lonely year," an English teacher, later on the faculty of Windsor High School in Connecticut, acknowledged. "I learned that few people want to listen to the questions and concerns of an idealistic, naïve rookie. If I wanted to survive in the 'egg-crate school system,' I would have to do it alone." Looking back over a span of twenty-five years, the survivor said, "During that first year, my isolation in the classroom was a fact I never questioned."

"Teachers who have enrolled in BAWP or NWP summer institutes or in after-school workshops are questioning isolation now," Jim says with evident pleasure, "because they know that loneliness does not have to be the lot of a teacher. If the Bay Area model does nothing else, I hope it will free teachers to exchange ideas and techniques with each other—without fear of stepping out of line or looking foolish." Jim's hope is no small ambition. Witness the veteran faculty member, now on the staff of Orange High School, California, who still believes she will never be able to forget the lack of support she had to overcome in her first year of teaching. "From the teacher whose journalism class I inherited, I learned to be truly on my own," she reminisced. The neophyte was left dangling when the experienced teacher told her, "I'm not going to help you with the class, because no one helped me when I started."

Taking his cue from the poet Robert Frost, Jim Gray's premise has consistently been that good fences don't make good neighbors—or good teachers. "Until barriers finally crumble," he explains, "teachers can't discover what it means to enter a professional world where colleagues learn from the support they give and receive." True to Gray's original plan, therefore, English and language arts teachers, math and science teachers, even music teachers all learn new techniques by seeing them practiced and hearing them discussed in BAWP and NWP programs. "Writing stimulates thinking and learning in *every* subject," says Gray.

In keeping with this approach, South Carolina's Charleston Area Writing Project operated a summer institute to which it invited a kindergarten teacher and a physical education teacher, a college Spanish professor and a debate coach, a special education teacher, an array of English teachers on every level, and a director of elementary education from a school district's administration office. An institute in Hawaii had a similar configuration when it included a principal, a dean, and teachers in four content areas in addition to English. The Boston Writing Project enrolled two full-time tenured college faculty members, along with part-time composition instructors, and the mix jelled, as expected.

Jim Gray takes particular pleasure in recalling experiences that demonstrate ways in which summer fellows from markedly different fields have discovered the role that writing can play. "Take the time a head football coach was so fired up by what he had learned at a Minnesota Writing Project that he drove straight to the home of the president and talked about new ideas almost nonstop for an hour and a half. You might think that kind of enthusiasm would be short-lived, but in the fall, he had his football players writing journal entries in the locker room before every game. University athletes don't usually warm up with pencil and paper—but coaches don't typically enroll in writing programs, either."

The anecdote that seems to be inscribed in the annals of BAWP accomplishments concerns a project-prepared biology teacher who spent the fall semester incorporating a great deal of writing in his teaching, while a colleague taught the subject in the traditional way. At the end of the semester they gave their classes the same test and, to the disappointment of the BAWP-trained teacher, students achieved similar results. When Jim recalls this experience, he pauses for the listener to mull over the seeming defeat. "But the story didn't end there," he says triumphantly. "Six months later the biology teachers retested their classes. The group that had taken the traditional biology course had lost nearly fifty percent of their earlier learning, while the other students had retained as much as they had six months earlier!"

Not content with extending his reach beyond the usual teachers of writing, Jim Gray has never wavered from his original decision to puncture education's "top-down" caste system in which teachers' expertise is untapped, while university faculty brings its knowledge of various disciplines "down" to the secondary school level—and ignores elementary school teachers altogether. "It's no coincidence," Gray notes, "that the standard expression is to study 'under' professors, not to study 'with' them, for these words reflect the mischief that occurs when knowledge of a discipline is thought to be the same thing as knowledge about how to teach that discipline. A Ph.D. degree honors scholarship and research, not teaching, while classroom experience— unhonored as it is—puts the focus on students' learning."

Jim has always seen instructors on every level as peers who would benefit from joining together in a common program where they would bring their strengths to each other. Unshaken by warnings that professors would never consent to work alongside of elementary school teachers—or that such a mixture would intimidate the "lowly" while the "lofty" dominated—Gray held fast to his vision of a joint university/ school summer institute. "Successful teachers who can demonstrate the results of sound practice," he predicted at the outset, "will be respected by other teachers, who have a natural interest in discovering what can happen when writing is well taught."

To portray NWP's egalitarian spirit, teachers and professors at the Charlotte branch of the University of North Carolina wrote and produced a spoof called *Ourtown, USA.* Poking fun at education's discrimination in most "ourtowns," elementary school teachers bowed before secondary school teachers, who kowtowed before college and university faculty. "We like to laugh at ourselves," narrator/project director Sam Watson said. "But we are serious about the ways in which our coming together as a community of learners is affecting our teaching and our professional lives."

The kinds of teaching and learning that BAWP and NWP offshoots value have won over the minds of thousands of doubting Thomases, although certainly not all. In January 1987, *The New York Times* reported that a state board of education suggested that insufficient credit is given to neatness and punctuation. Indeed, the chair of the task force that was appointed to review outcomes observed that student writers of "pretty papers" got no rewards. "Now," the chair was quoted as claiming, "we're saying that if a student can write good sentences that don't say anything, it may not be good writing, but it is competent writing."

When a state's education system proposes giving credit for appearance as opposed to content, Jim Gray feels the urgency of accommodating the growing number of university/ school partnerships that want to join the national network. But he recognizes financial realities as well as philosophical ones. Funding BAWP-NWP sites presents problems; retaining the original BAWP model program presents none. "Why should it?" Jim Gray challenges questioners and admirers. "We've never relied on 'teacher-proof' materials or a bag of tricks; we've always rejected what Sam Watson calls 'a gimmick-of-the-week' or an authority to transmit the mythical One Right Way to teach." From the outset, BAWP has counted on informed teachers who know what they're doing—and why they're doing it. The original Bay Area Writing Project, in other words, is still stable because it continues to celebrate good teaching and good writing in every subject and on every grade.

To put an NWP branch within relatively easy reach of most school districts, Jim Gray would like to establish 250 projects in all, at a cost of $30,000 per site—with the national office contributing half the amount, and the local unit paying the other half. Realistically, however, Jim knows that he is not likely to have the means to initiate more than five new projects a year. "Berkeley's chancellor was able to come up with the thirteen thousand we needed for BAWP's first year," Jim recalls, "but no single source can provide the over eight million dollars that our sites need now." This financial insecurity is reflected in reports project directors have sent Jim Gray*:

> We have enthusiasm, dedication, skills, knowledge, and verbal support. We do not have enough money!
> —Wisconsin Writing Project

> Foundations believe our colleges should be able to finance the program ourselves since it has been so successful.
> —Twin Cities Area Writing Project

> We want to avoid being wiped out if we lose our funding. Consequently there is no permanent staff member except the director; most work is contributed on a voluntary basis.
> —Sun Belt Writing Project

"Can you imagine what could happen," Jim Gray asks, "if half the money that schools spend on entrepreneurial consultants who appear for a day—never to be seen again— were spent on *teacher-consultants* who remain on the scene and bring proven, classroom-tested practices to their colleagues?"

A biased viewpoint? Not at all. Ask the teachers themselves. In every large-scale survey, they almost unanimously dismiss the gains from visiting "experts." Or read the report that NWP's program officer at the National Endowment for the Humanities sent Gray to say that the project "has been by far the most effective and 'cost-effective' project in the history of the Endowment's support for elementary and secondary education programs." And listen to James Squire,

---

*Fluctuating support comes from university campuses that host summer institutes, school districts that are served by BAWP and NWP sites, eleven states, and local foundations. In addition, BAWP administers national foundation grants and a network of gifts from individual and institutional sponsors.

former executive director of the National Council of Teachers of English, who said, "If I were an administrator, I'd want to get every teacher in my school out to a Writing Project; I wouldn't consider hiring anyone who hadn't been trained by it."

One of the most satisfying—and frustrating—signs of recognition came from former U.S. secretary of education William J. Bennett, who wrote Jim Gray, commending the method his projects use to recognize "outstanding teachers, bring these teachers together to demonstrate effective teaching practices, and to introduce them to new methods—and then train these teachers to teach other teachers." Believing that the significance of writing is not always recognized, Secretary Bennett went on to say, "Writing is fundamental to learning. *Clear writing and its counterpart, clear thinking, are vital tools for individual and national growth* [emphasis added]. Your project gives some of the most dedicated and capable teachers the vital nourishment they need."

Although Secretary Bennett made no mention of the financial nourishment that the writing projects need, the letter clearly recognized the importance of writing. In 1988, though, Secretary Bennett prescribed a model four-year high school English curriculum that did not reflect the priorities he had conveyed to Jim Gray. The new sequence that he advocated focused on:

- Introduction to literature
- American literature
- British literature
- Introduction to world literature

Conspicuous by its absence was any commitment to the very writing that the secretary had viewed as essential to learning and individual growth.

More important than curriculum reform that is imposed

on classrooms and fails dismally is the uncommon faith in teachers' ability that the BAWP model first advanced and the distinguished Carnegie Task Force on Teaching as a Profession has recently recognized. In its book *A Nation Prepared: Teachers for the 21st Century*, the task force observed that schools "operate as if consultants, school-district experts, textbook authors, trainers, and distant officials possess more relevant expertise than teachers in the schools." Rejecting that approach, the Carnegie Task Force put its confidence in the "determined, intelligent, and capable teachers" who people our schools.

Similarly, task force member and longtime president of the largest teachers' union, Mary Hatwood Futrell, recently advised business leaders, "Don't come to us and say, 'This is the plan.' If you do, the education community will resist. But if you come and say, 'We will work with you to help determine what the plan should be,' you will have one hundred percent cooperation."

In keeping with a new regard for teachers, James A. Adams, superintendent of the Indianapolis Public Schools, has freed the staff to develop the entire curriculum of the Key School, whose applicants outnumber available space. And the Minnesota state board of education voted to permit the Taylor Falls School District—a one-school system with 340 students—to elect a team of teachers to help make decisions with the superintendent on curriculum, staff development, discipline, and budget. If the experiment with teacher leadership works out, other Minnesota school districts will probably be able to follow suit.

Some of the ground rules that dozens of university/school collaborations are establishing are also encouraging, although limited. Taking cues from NWP, for example, James R. Vivian, director of the Yale–New Haven Teachers Institute, made certain that the university did not impose a plan on the school. Instead, secondary school teachers have decided on the topics they want to explore, and the word *course* is not used, lest it detract from the idea of colleagues collaborating with each other. With mutual understanding, the joint efforts have won kudos from most of the fifty-six professors and 229 "fellows" who have participated since 1978. "I've been able to grow beyond my environment, which is room 105," a New Haven teacher said—not realizing that he had put his finger on an issue that has troubled Jim Gray for over fifteen years: teacher isolation. "I'm enthusiastic about what I teach, and the students pick this up."

Looking at all that has followed the first BAWP summer, it is clear that Jim Gray was ahead of his time when he and a handful of associates devised a plan to influence, even to transform, the professional lives of thousands of teachers in five intense weeks. Witness the verve and spirit of teachers' voices when they recalled their experiences:

> I came with a spark, an idea that worked (in my classroom). I go away with a tank full of fuel.
> —Connecticut Writing Project participant

> The work has been intense, exhausting, often troublesome, and often exhilarating. The impact of the project is the way it touches the nerve endings of everyone it reaches.
> —Southern Nevada Writing Project participant

> When good teachers come together and share their thoughts and feelings with one another through writing, a sort of magic occurs.
> —Northern California Writing Project director

The magic endures, since summer institutes only mark the beginning of career-long opportunities for teachers to share "Here's what worked for me" lessons and ideas in a growing circle of professional associates. Indeed, if institutes did signify the end of the metamorphosis that teachers experience, Jim Gray would be seriously disappointed. A new teacher consultant from California's Great Valley Writing Project captured the wonder of her summer experience when she wrote Jim Gray, "I left the last day of the class stuffed with ideas, eager to return to the classroom, a newborn teacher consultant, equipped with new friends and professional contacts, and sad to see it over . . . but then I found out it really wasn't!" Her reaction is widely shared, for teacher consultants discover that summer institutes don't end in the usual sense of the term. At their best, they point to new directions on a professional journey.

Donald Gellehr exemplifies the best long-term impact, for he encourages teacher consultants who have the zeal to remain connected to the outstanding Northern Virginia Writing Project that he directs. Despite the responsibilities that come from working closely with Jim Gray and serving as professor of English at George Mason University in Fairfax, Virginia, Don has a special commitment to his own writing project. The success of the site, he believes, has been a direct result of continuity. "We keep at it, morning, noon, and night. We don't let up—period. It isn't because we're tenacious," he explains, "it's because we have seen that you can't predict when teachers will be ready to change—so we have to be there regularly to show that we are sincere about giving anyone the assistance that's needed—when it's needed."

In Don's view it is relatively easy to run a summer institute for short periods, but harder to orchestrate ongoing activities that keep teacher consultants involved: courses in research and theory, writing groups, conferences and special programs. But, again, he persists. "That's how teachers grow as professionals," he explains, "that's how their schools take writing seriously, and that's how students begin to improve as writers and learners."

Similarly, the director of South Carolina's Charleston Area Writing Project reports, "Through our continuity breakfasts and meetings, we've been able to preserve the enthusiasm and camaraderie which developed in each institute." Likewise, seventy-five teacher consultants returned to the University of North Carolina/Charlotte Writing Project for the stimulation of an annual day of sharing ideas and learning together once again. Experienced teacher consultants from the Los Angeles area formed their own ten-day institute to develop a curriculum portfolio for teaching bilingual students to write. And the New York City Writing Project started a training group for teacher consultants who wanted to observe courses for developing colleagues and discuss the art of teaching teachers. While a survey has indicated that no two NWP sites seem to maintain ties in quite the same way, there is a common bond that links teacher consultants in every site. No longer "just" teachers of children and adolescents, they are teachers of teachers. Instead of sitting passively in the audience of a mandated staff development program, while outside "experts" lecture, teacher consultants *are* the experts—for they know what fellow teachers also need to know. "Imagine the impact on their sense of being professionals when school districts hire *them,* instead of automatically turning to professors of education!" Jim Gray exclaims.

Gail Segal has experienced that professional gratification ever since she was "BAWPD" in 1978 and began conducting in-service workshops in schools in different parts of California. During the preceding seven years of her teaching career, she had been required to listen to "experts" whose classroom experience was rusty at best, while her own grasp of the interests and learning styles of students counted for little, if anything. However, once she finished her five weeks at the Bay Area Writing Project in Berkeley and emerged as a teacher consultant, she enjoyed full status as a teacher of teachers. Ms. Segal still teaches eighth grade at the Ross School in Marin County, but her horizons now extend beyond one classroom, one school, one district.

"I'm starting to see substantial changes in the questions asked, wherever I go," she said, sounding like the seasoned educator she has become. "Teachers want me to help them use writing as a learning tool. I hear more questions that ask, 'How can I incorporate writing in teaching social studies?' or 'Can I *really* use writing to teach science?' Shaking her head in a mixture of amazement and admiration, Gail Segal said, "I never thought I would see a mini-revolution in a decade. But there's no doubt about it. Teachers are teaching teachers now and writing occupies a pivotal place in learning."

Research findings confirm Ms. Segal's impressions of the impact teacher consultants are having. As early as 1979/80, and again in 1980/81, a study in the Chicago area assessed the impact of an NWP site on a total of some 3,500 students. The results showed that students of NWP-prepared teachers made over twice as much improvement from pre- to post-testing as did students in the control groups, who had begun each year with essentially the same pretest scores.

The results were even more dramatic in a 1977–1982 study of seven sites: New Jersey; Missouri; Edmonds, Washington; Denver; Los Angeles; the Chicago area; and the San Francisco Bay Area. The smallest difference in improvement between NWP students and a comparison group showed a rate of 2.3 years; the largest, a rate of 9 years; and the writing of 4,200 city high school students with BAWP-trained teachers showed seven and a half times the improvement of pupils with other teachers. After reviewing the data, Professor Michael Scriven, then teaching at the University of San Francisco, reported that the National Writing Project "appears to be the best large-scale effort to improve composition instruction now in operation in this country, and certainly the best on which substantial data are available."

The Scriven report is preserved in Jim Gray's files along with a letter from Paul Diederich, a scholarly evaluator well known for his career with the Educational Testing Service. Wrote Dr. Diederich: "I now believe that the Bay Area Writing Project really has started a movement that is sweeping the country. . . . I am pretty sure that this is one of those ideas that will last—like Langdell's invention of the case method of teaching law about 1870." Sounding a similar note, the cautious Council for Basic Education called the NWP "perhaps the most successful and certainly the most far-reaching of all the recent initiatives to improve the condition of writing in American schools."

The journal *English Education* explained part of the reason for success when it said that teachers are viewed as professionals who have contributions to make to the improvement of their fellows. Professor Sarah W. Freedman of the University of California at Berkeley added to the explanation when she found that a group of NWP-trained teachers required student writing primarily to foster independent thinking, while a comparison group of teachers required writing primarily to have students practice mechanics. To complete the explanation for success, the National Council of Teachers of English recently passed an unusual resolution commending NWP for demonstrating "sound practices in the teaching of writing," and for providing leadership in demonstrating the significance of a public school–university collaboration in teaching writing.

These accomplishments have resulted in the National Writing Project's being inundated with increased requests for services. NWP's professional time and administrative hours are taxed to the limit when scholars from the Union of South Africa make several visits, when a representative from the Israeli Ministry of Education comes for a day and stays for the summer (and sets up an Israeli version of BAWP-NWP upon returning home), and when educators from Quebec and Puerto Rico show similar interest. But in Jim Gray's view, the National Writing Project is—and should be—a national showcase, and he is prepared to stretch himself as far as necessary. And that means that no school district should hesitate about writing him.

Project directors and codirectors are similarly stretched, for they get little released time, if any. "I am doing the project while teaching four courses per semester," one director wrote Jim. "I'm not sure I can do much about this, but I feel stretched a bit thin." And another asked, "Where do we find the time and energy to serve teachers and visitors, mount new programs, and look for money?" Jim Gray is rarely negative, but he acknowledges that the university pattern of valuing research and publishing but devaluing service takes a terrible toll on project directors, who spend uncounted and unrecognized hours operating a site. "Without question," he observes, "these are hours that college professors could otherwise devote to traditional scholarship and to climbing the academic ladder. I'm almost tempted to say that anyone who chooses to devote large amounts of time as a project director does so at his or her own risk."

BAWP is not the only workable design, however. Witness some other important writing programs that Jim has influenced, but that have emerged independently. Tom Newkirk, for example, put his finger on the impact that the Bay Area model and its offshoots have had on his thinking and on the widely respected New Hampshire Writing Program that he directs. "Jim Gray really opened our eyes," Tom said. "Until he came along, we made the mistake of not recognizing the importance of classroom teachers. I'm not even sure that we really appreciated the significance of having writing teachers do their own writing. The plan we put into place was not intended to be a replica of BAWP's, but we certainly recognize our roots."

It would be hard not to. The New Hampshire Writing Program is a summer mecca for a hundred or more teachers from kindergarten through ninth grade who flock to the University of New Hampshire (UNH) campus for an intense three-week session devoted to improving their skills as writers and teachers of writing. Despite the program's location, approximately 80 percent of the teachers who are accepted come from out-of-state or Canadian schools. Indeed, teachers from your child's school may be enrolled, no matter where you live. Unfortunately, though, year after year qualified candidates are turned away because they apply too late. By keeping his program small, Tom Newkirk gets to know every participant, and the faculty is able to concentrate on each person's growth as a teacher and as a writer, the dual goals of the New Hampshire program.

None of the faculty that guides this program is far removed from his or her own classroom experience. Four of the six staff members are gifted classroom teachers who for the most part have returned each summer since the program began in 1980; the other two, who were recruited from the university faculty, had been classroom teachers themselves. Even a UNH star such as Don Graves, who gives an occasional lecture (if you can call Don's style "lecturing") was a teacher and principal. The combination of BAWP's influence and Tom Newkirk's modifications has produced a blend of talented teachers and former teachers of writing who give their best to summer residents seeking to enrich their own skills when they return to their classrooms each fall.

Convinced that a writing program that works in a small-town New England setting can be redesigned for teachers in other parts of the country, Professor Lucy McCormick Calkins developed a summer plan at Teachers College, Columbia University. Magnetic speaker and captivating writer that she is, Dr. Calkins lures some six hundred teachers who endure the city's steamy heat because they are eager to become writers and teachers of writing. Lucy's widely read books, *Lessons from a Child* and *The Art of Teaching Writing,* have made her a strong attraction and the faculty of writers that she has assembled is another drawing card that distinguishes the Teachers College writing program. No matter how large the enrollment is, however, teachers divide into groups of twenty each afternoon in order to write and respond to one another's writing.

In addition to her work with the summer workshop, Lucy Calkins derives great satisfaction from the ongoing assistance that she provides New York City elementary school teachers in eighteen districts year in and year out. Recognizing that most teachers have been denied the opportunity to learn to teach writing, Lucy goes into classrooms where she and the teachers try to figure out what techniques seem to work and what seem not to—a mighty challenge when thirty-eight children speaking fifteen different native tongues are learning together. "Despite these obstacles, my staff and I have found some superb teaching," she said, "and we've found an exciting by-product, too. Writing teachers formed networks to help each other develop further." Answering the question I was about to ask, she said, "I have seen them skip lunch hours in order to work together and forgo planning periods for the same reason. I'm not even surprised anymore when I see teachers lingering after school or when I learn that they have given up part of their weekends for writing sessions." Equally remarkable, Lucy Calkins has seen 150 principals from what she calls "our schools" remain as invigorated at the end of a daylong retreat (there are two each year) as they were when the day was fresh. "What's going on in New York City is really wonderful!" she exults.

Thanks to Lucy's further assistance, what's going on in some of the suburbs of New York City is also wonderful. Forward-looking school districts such as Westport, Connecticut, and Chappaqua, New York, that have long had reading specialists on staff have recently engaged their own *writing* specialists whom Calkins has helped become teachers of teachers and teachers of administrators. Her personal and professional belief that writing can and should be an exciting part of the school day has proven to be catching. Katonah-Lewisboro, New York, for example, signed up so many teachers in the spring of its second year for a staff-development writing program scheduled for the following fall that a later application from an elementary school principal had to be rejected—with apologies from the district's only writing specialist. Blessed with healthy funding, New Canaan, Connecticut, engaged a separate specialist for each elementary school in the district. And, having gotten a head start over most neighboring school systems, New York's Bedford Central School District's writing specialist has reached teachers, parents, supervisors—even members of the school board.

Unlike local programs, the Iowa Writing Project Institute initiated a plan in 1978 to reach classroom teachers on a statewide basis. And reach them it does. In a single summer, director Jim Davis said, the project has conducted twenty-three three-week institutes, with twenty-five participants in each. All told, the project has enrolled some 2,500 teachers in more than half of the state's school districts. Follow-up research has documented that year after year the institutes accomplish two major goals: changing students' negative attitudes about writing and improving the quality of their performance.

The Iowa Writing Project Institute begins each day by providing the intellectual base that Davis believes writing teachers need. Surrounded by a sizable library of handouts and every important work that takes a fresh look at the teaching of writing, teachers explore and discuss books that they have had on their "wish lists"—but have been too busy to read. "The central issue," Jim Davis explained, "is to have participants see how ideas make sense in terms of their school and their classroom." The summer plan typically expects teachers to delve into ways to generate writing, respond to student development, and assess outcomes. Ample time is also provided to consider two major concepts: writing as a process and writing across the curriculum. "Regardless of the issue we're talking about," Davis said, "the leader of the session tries to build on what teachers already know." Then, following in the footsteps of Jim Gray, the program devotes the afternoons to writing workshops. "This is not an

afterthought, mind you, but a central part of our program."
While the Iowa Writing Project Institute concentrates on providing solid groundwork and writing experience for teachers throughout the state, the Program in Writing at The Bread Loaf School of English has taken a different approach. Sponsored by Middlebury College in Vermont, Bread Loaf began by focusing on the needs of isolated secondary school English teachers from rural locations and remote sites nationwide. These school districts are small, to be sure, but over half a million students go to schools in some 4,200 districts with fewer than three hundred students. In fact, added together, the student population in small districts actually exceeds the enrollment in every metropolitan area in the United States except New York City and Los Angeles.

Since Bread Loaf's residents are widely scattered all year long, their coming together in the summer to share ideas with each other and with distinguished American and British university faculty members gains added importance. Further, exchanging writing and responding with teachers of English who tap into Bread Loaf's computer network reduces isolation the rest of the year. "I like to think that we save rural teachers from leaving education," Professor Paul Cubeta, director of the Bread Loaf program, said. "I can't overstate the terrible professional loneliness that teachers from places like Pelican, Alaska, and Fort Wingate, New Mexico, have to overcome every day of the school year. Here they develop new ways of thinking and teaching that can sustain them during those long months when they crave intellectual stimulation."

Dixie Goswami, coordinator of Bread Loaf's Program in Writing and a product of the rural South herself, knows the craving well. Under Paul Cubeta's direction she is also coordinating new projects that a major grant is funding, but Dixie is certain she will not neglect rural high school teachers. Perhaps the biggest departure from what had been an exclusive concern with rural secondary school teachers is a program built around children aged four to fourteen. Appreciating the value of genuine literacy, which includes thinking, speaking, writing, and reading, the program dismisses skill-and-drill exercises that are enshrined in basal readers and workbooks. Instead, students and teachers select activities that they want to research and record in increasing depth. Since their interests frequently center on topics that are close to home, Bread Loaf innovators have termed this new style of teaching and learning "community-based literacy." And by "literacy" they mean a seriousness about language and learning.

At the same time that Bread Loaf decided to extend its reach to the lower grades without sacrificing its program for secondary school teachers, the New Hampshire Writing Program began thinking about extending its reach, too. Although a program for teachers in elementary and junior high schools is still New Hampshire's centerpiece, a component for secondary school teachers is on the drawing board. The challenge is to meld the most invigorating techniques for teachers of younger students with approaches appropriate for high school English teachers. In other words, the leadership of both the New Hampshire Writing Program and Bread Loaf realize that their programs are likely to be more effective if they include teachers from the elementary grades through senior high.

But it would be unrealistic to think that the 2.5 million teachers staffing U.S. classrooms could carve out weeks at a time to enroll in a summer writing program, even if there were enough programs to accommodate these numbers. Some teachers need the income that comes from holding down summer jobs, some have ongoing family obligations, and some, while well motivated, do not yet have the ability to qualify for invitational writing programs. But none of these limitations is insurmountable. Even teachers who can spare only a day or two gravitate to abbreviated writing workshops, sometimes setting out before dawn and driving hundreds of miles. True, they cannot forge bonds with fellow teachers in the way summer interns do over the course of weeks. They cannot experience frequent writing, editing, and research sessions. But they can begin to think of writing in a new way. They can enroll in workshops during the year, they can read books by educators like Donald Graves and Lucy Calkins, they can start writing themselves, and they can perk up their ears when a teacher says, "Here's what worked for me."

Thanks to a coterie of leaders—Jim Gray, Don Graves, Tom Newkirk, and Lucy Calkins; Paul Cubeta, Dixie Goswami, Jim Davis, and more—there is not a state in the nation that does not have at least one good writing program, which results in teachers teaching fellow teachers. As Paul Cubeta put it, "Teachers who have learned a different way of teaching writing are seldom content until they have affected other teachers." The programs are all important, but only one writing project has welcomed teachers from every field and grade level from the outset. Despite the shortage of funding and the rigidity of a system that has resisted reform for well over a century, the original Bay Area Writing Project has extended its reach to become the *only* national writing project—indeed, the only international project. Teachers who no longer hold fast to the view that writing is merely an amalgam of correct spelling, penmanship, punctuation, and grammar are still in the minority, to be sure, but that minority continues to gain adherents. Each year another crop of teachers is learning to listen to students' voices on paper, voices that may take many drafts and revisions before a clear style and point of view emerge—complete with correct writing conventions. The final product takes time that seldom conforms to a rigid schedule, but, as Jim Gray had expected, teachers and students alike are often amazed by the substance and form of their accomplishment.

4

"RINGING BELLS, BLOWING TRUMPETS" IN THE LOWER GRADES

E scaping from the clutch of "the old school" is no mean feat. Parents often blame teachers for not teaching "correctly," which is to say, the way that they themselves had been taught, and teachers who might break the mold if they could, blame principals for making penmanship, spelling, punctuation, and grammar top priorities. Principals shift the blame to assistant superintendents and to the superintendent of schools himself for imposing those constraints on the schools, while superintendents blame their local school boards for tying educators' hands. If members of boards could speak in a single voice, they would protest, "Don't blame us; we have to make certain that our schools do well on the standardized tests that state policymakers require." And elected officials—governors and legislators—insist that *they* have to carry out the expectations of parents. Round and round the circle goes, propelled by the fear that someone is always looking over someone else's shoulder and disapproving. Change is not for the timid or for those who lack vision.

As a result, blue-ribbon panels of "reformers" simply prescribe fortified doses of time-worn solutions to cure education's ills—and give short shrift to writing instruction. But some elementary schools are bucking the past and heralding new solutions to old problems that have plagued the misunderstood second R for over a century. Australian educator Bob Walshe spoke for the *real* reformers when he exclaimed, "The exciting truth about 'The Writing Problem' is that most of the answers we have lacked until recently have been found." Indeed, in Walshe's view the new understandings are so important that he has said, "We should be ringing bells, blowing trumpets." In this chapter you will meet elementary school educators who are doing precisely that.

In the view of these educators, writing is neither spinach nor ice cream, neither rote memorization of conventions and nothing else, nor undisciplined self-expression without careful thought and correct form. They know that writing can be hard work—at times the most difficult and discouraging of all disciplines, at other times the most gratifying. But never, they assert, do moments of exaltation come cheaply. The "Aha!" that can finally emerge, however, is a peak experience, and heights can be scaled at every stage of development, beginning in kindergarten.

Kindergarten? Yes, indeed! Anyone who has watched preschoolers begin to experiment with their first symbols such as /M͡ꓥ and ꀿꓦ knows that even very young children want to write. The early marks they make on pavement and paper, on walls and slate, lead to the discovery of letters, and the stringing together of letters produces the beginning of written words. According to Donald Graves, these activities convince about 90 percent of the youngsters entering school that they can write, while only 15 percent believe they can read.

CHALLENGING THE READING-WRITING SEQUENCE

Despite evidence to the contrary, most conventional educators still hold fast to the unproven conviction that children have to master beginning reading before they can learn to write their first words. But anyone who has seen five- and six-year-old children devising "invented spelling"—which is their own approximation of standard spelling—in order to send messages and write stories will question the accepted reading-writing sequence.

More than half a dozen scholars have documented evidence that inventive spellers employ remarkably similar strategies for recording words that no one taught them to write. They use the same alphabet you and I do, and, at times, come close to figuring out conventional spelling. But at other times, before they make the transition to standard spelling—*and inventive spellers all make the transition*—they drop vowels and consonants and run letters together in rather uniform ways that may confuse parents and traditional teachers. It doesn't take long, however, to become accustomed to reading young children's "invented spelling." As a result, they can write what's on their mind and adults can understand what youngsters are saying well before they would otherwise print their first correctly spelled words.

As children begin to understand the idea of sounding out words, the first step they take in invented spelling is usually to "spell" each word with a single large capital letter, typically the initial consonant. Next, they are likely to use two consonants, usually the first and last letters of the word. In time, they record a consonant in the middle of the word, so that "bird" moves from B to B D to B R D. Short vowels are the last to come, but long vowels come soon after the consonants. "Came," for example, is often spelled K A M or C A M. Just as you can predict this kind of progress, you can also predict that most inventive spellers tend to be deceived by two things: sounds they don't hear and the position of their tongue when they speak. Try saying "and" or "bump" and you'll find that you don't feel these nasal sounds as separate from the consonant coming after them. That's why inventive spellers are prone to spell those words, A D and B U P. And no matter how you strain your ears, you can't possibly hear a silent *e*.

Parents and teachers who are new to invented spelling sometimes wonder whether they may be encouraging bad habits. Will children really learn to put a space between words and sentences? Will children benefit from a system that allows them to write the same word in different ways until they finally settle on conventional spelling? Is there any reason to go along with invented spelling when standard spelling was good enough for us?

Scholarly research and direct experience indicate that there appears to be no reason to believe that invented spelling fosters bad habits. Indeed, the approach is likely to encourage very young children to grasp the basic spelling principle of sounding out words and recording them by beginning to match letters to sounds. Researchers and teachers also explain that children may run words together so long as they remain prereaders, but will separate words when they become familiar with the printed page. If you listen to people talking, you will understand that the boundaries between words are blurred, and inventive spellers are recording the speech they hear, not the words they see.

Serious students of invented spelling believe that inconsistencies serve as developmental landmarks, documenting that children are actually moving closer to correct spelling. As they fine-tune their ability to hear sounds and record them, youngsters are able to begin to write fluently, instead of being inhibited by the search for the correct spelling of a limited number of words. And that fluency provides the reason for giving invented spelling a chance. Standard spelling *wasn't* good enough for those of us whose stilted writing is the aftermath of classrooms where error-free writing was valued over genuine communication.

Paul Bissex was an inventive speller. When he was five years and one month old, he captured his distracted mother's attention by delivering his first printed message.

"R U D F" (Are you deaf?), Paul asked, determined to tear her away from the book that had engrossed her. When his mother promptly responded, Paul began to discover the power of putting his words on paper. Three days later, he typed, "4547781 P A U L S T L E F N M B R" (Paul's telephone number) and "P A U L S B Z R" (Paul's buzzer). After two weeks of invented spelling, Paul presented his mother with this typed message: "E F U K A N O P N K A Z I W I L G E V U A K A N O P E N R." Reading it aloud as he pointed to the appropriate letters and paused between words, Paul said, "If you can open cans, I will give you a can opener." This lengthy sentence is difficult to read at first, but, it is worth the effort when you realize that most five-year-old youngsters have not begun to think of writing as communication.

By the time Paul was five and a half, he wrote and posted a sign over his workbench, which read: "DO NAT DSTRB GNYS AT WRK." Fascinated by the "genius" who did not want to be disturbed, Paul's mother, Glenda L. Bissex, wrote such a detailed case study of how her son learned to write and read that it became a major part of her doctoral dissertation at Harvard University. Dr. Bissex's insights and observations were so important that Harvard University Press chose to publish her book, *GNYS AT WRK: A Child Learns to Write and Read,* in 1980.

Talented teachers build on beginnings that children like Paul Bissex bring with them when they start school. Mary Ellen Giacobbe used to begin the first day of the school year in Atkinson, New Hampshire, by giving her first-graders their own blank books for writing in, each with the author's name on the cover. "It was the rare six-year-old who protested, 'But I can't write,' " she said. *"They* knew they could write something—a picture, a few letters or numbers, their name, even words or a complete sentence—and *my* job was to help them extend those early beginnings." And extend them she did. Donald Graves reports in his book *Writing:*

Teachers and Children at Work that in a single year the twenty-five children in Mary Ellen Giacobbe's first-grade class had composed 1,300 five- to six-page booklets and published 400 of the best for their classmates to read.

Jane Hansen, a colleague of Don Graves's in the University of New Hampshire's outstanding writing program, also shared some her reminiscences as a first-grade teacher with me. "I wish you could have seen the class 'author of the week' sitting in the special 'author's chair,' under a bulletin board that displayed a picture of our celebrity and a list of previously 'published' works." Professor Hansen smiled as she recalled a six-year-old student's reading a work in progress and listening to the reaction of classmates. "Young as they were, the children learned first to talk about what they thought the author was saying. Then they asked questions to help the writer clarify the piece by including more information. With fresh ideas, the child usually began to revise what had been a draft. Writers who saw their finished piece typed and bound in cardboard covers, along with a biographical statement that they supplied, felt the gratification that every published author knows."

Neither Mary Ellen Giacobbe nor Jane Hansen—indeed, no one in the schools portrayed in this chapter—dismisses a child's need to communicate. No one questions whether youngsters who do not spell correctly or form letters as they should be written can express what they want to write. No one scoffs at the importance of respecting early efforts. Instead, teachers value what their students write. "When a thirsty baby says 'botty,' you respond by bringing him his bottle, not by correcting his speech," Judy Meagher, alternately kindergarten and first-grade teacher in Bozeman, Montana, points out. "The same holds true when it comes to early writing. I respond to what my children's meaning is, first, and rejoice in each sign of progress. It helps if you realize that errors aren't failures," she explains. "They are really partial successes."

Judy Meagher has been a teacher and a teaching principal for thirty years—and has never lost her enthusiasm. Though three decades in the classroom could drain any teacher, Judy Meagher is not one of them. "I'm so excited by the way our writing program is taking shape that I no longer want to see the year end," she says. What teacher wouldn't be excited if she knew that students leave her room with plans for summer writing, indeed, with gusto for lifelong writing? Especially gratifying was Ms. Meagher's discovery that her students had the potential to become prolific writers in the first place. "I simply provided materials and opportunities to encourage the children's ability," she said.

The ingredients are found in Whittier School's kindergarten, where writing flourishes. Anyone who expects to see a pleasant room that is limited to the usual housekeeping center, block corner, costume box, and such should also see Judy Meagher's writing centers where "pictionaries" illustrate and spell words and writing tools of every description encourage young scribes. The results of this stimulation are found in authors' files where each youngster has a folder to hold past and current writing. Particularly appealing is the small easel with pictures of sounds that the class discovered together and some of the stories that "invented spelling" and "real spelling" combined to produce.

Ms. Meagher knows that many five-year-old children find delight in "real" schoolwork. Barely into her kindergarten year, Denise wrote, "Mom I No [know] H O W to mac [make] spl [spelling] wds," copied the words "popcorn" and "chocolate" from the dictionary, and added, "I ate milk"—without assistance.

With some help from Ms. Meagher, kindergarten children are able to write class books. One Valentine's Day, the youngsters wrote a heart-shaped volume, *The Things We Love Book*. Some children drew pictures, some wrote the predictable "Mom" and "Dad," and some wrote one sentence after another, spelling words in the "Gnys at Wrk" fashion. A trip to a bakery resulted in another collective book. Undaunted by their inability to write every word, but determined to describe what they had seen, some five-year-old students cleverly interspersed words and pictures. Anyone who believes that young children don't have the skill or the desire to put their thoughts on paper would have a change of mind after reading *The Bakery* or reading efforts like these:

> *I haf a dog*
> *Hs nam is Bvr. [Beaver]*
> He is frndle *[friendly]*
> *My frend has a dog*

> *I like thes Rakon [racoon]*
> *Caz tha [they] clim a tree*
> *Wen tha wt [want] to go to bed*
> *When et is morny [morning]*

> *wusn on [once upon] a time ther was*
> *a Bad prsn hos NaMe Was CLock Be cas He*
> *was Bad He Allwes*
> *paocht [pushed] pepl Dawn And*
> *That is the end.*

With her first-grade students, Judy Meagher avoids the roadblocks that impede children's writing, while establishing standards, nonetheless. "At the beginning of first grade, these children are only a few months older than they were in kindergarten," Ms. Meagher points out. "If I insist on correct spelling, they will be afraid to venture beyond a limited, 'The big dog can jump' or 'I like to run and play.' I know they have much more to say than that, and I want them to be able to express their ideas and feelings. That's why I also accept invented spelling at first."

But Judy Meagher doesn't believe in an "anything goes" classroom, either. "The children know that I celebrate their writing, that I honor their thoughts; but when I teach a first-grade class, students also know that in time I want them to learn that 'magic' is not spelled 'madjick' and that 'school' is not spelled 'skool.' " The solution? Children begin by writing words as they sound to young ears, but as they progress, Ms. Meagher helps them express their ideas by using correct spelling. Since she also introduces invented spelling in the years that she teaches kindergarten, many pint-sized students are accustomed to the idea of writing by the time they reach first grade.

By spelling words her way at first, six-year-old Kari was able to write about her kitten who was "soe cululfol" and "cuddoly" instead of being restricted to a "My cat is nice" composition. Shawna told the story of a "madjick geany" (magic genie). And Westerly drew upon the 134 words he needed to tell his story, 123 GO TO SCHOOL. True, at first he wrote "skool is a plase you lern wut you dote nowe," and his early efforts produced "at school we do not have shoe and tel we have a lekshr serse" (lecture series). But, also true, children in schools that insist on error-free spelling in first grade would not dare try to spell "hard" words like "lecture series" in the first place.

Ms. Meagher surrounds her children with opportunities to communicate in writing. Her "Tell It to the Teacher" file box, for example, contains one example after another of writing with a purpose. Nick and Garrick placed their 5 × 8 cards on Ms. Meagher's desk at exactly the same time, while Elizabeth's "Dere M." message arrived a bit later. Clearly, all three cards demonstrate the same principle: an imaginative teacher can use a discipline problem to encourage writing—without resorting to the "I will not . . ." one hundred times tactic. What's more, the cards serve to demonstrate how Judy Meagher uses her answers to her students' complaints as a natural way of introducing correct spelling, punctuation, penmanship, and grammar. Without resorting to tedious and ineffective exercises, she teaches, in part, by serving as the best possible role model. "I hope I'll never be a drill master," she said. "But I won't overlook the importance of teaching phonics, either."

Some special favorites are as follows:

To.. M. M.
from.. Garrick
Nick is not bein nise
to me at resis.

That is not good. I talked to him
already. Do you think you two can
work on being friends?
Nope.

To.. Misis M.
from.. Nick
Garrick is budgin owt
at reses.

That is too bad. I will visit
with him. O.K.

These first two were placed on the teacher's desk at exactly the same time.

To :
from :

Dere M.
    Travis is Spitin on mie
                   desc.
What do you want me to do, Elizabeth?

    Moov hem.

Judging by the letters of welcome that a group of departing first-graders wrote to incoming kindergartners who did
not know Ms. Meagher, this early primary school teacher
does not have to worry about tipping too far in any direction.
For further confirmation all anyone has to do is talk with
parents who are dazzled by the writing their children have
produced with Ms. Meagher's encouragement. Indeed, several of her successful strategies have been written up in
Instructor magazine so that elementary school teachers in
other parts of the country can adapt the approaches for their
own grade level. In Judy Meagher's classroom, for example,
everyone has a chance to be a "Special Person" for a week
and receive a letter from each of the other twenty-four students. The letters single out something that each writer particularly likes about the "Special Person." At week's end,
they are compiled in a booklet with an individualized cover.
The honored child has a memento to treasure, and the other
students have had an opportunity to hone their rapidly de-

veloping writing skills without having to limit themselves to conventional student-teacher communication.

John Henry Martin is another veteran educator who has frowned on the traditional way of teaching children to read and write. During his more than thirty-five years as a teacher, principal, and superintendent of schools, Dr. Martin saw five- and six-year-old children come to school with an astounding mastery of language. Yet he saw early basal readers and workbooks (reading always came first) limit them to a few hundred reading, spelling, and writing words—while the rest of a child's rich vocabulary and personal experiences remained dormant. Believing that young children can learn to write anything they can say and to read anything they can write, he decided to develop an approach that would use a youngster's entire speaking vocabulary.

Dr. Martin also became convinced that the traditional sequence that requires that children learn to read before they are considered ready to learn to write was altogether illogical. There has always had to be a writer before there could be a reader, he reasoned; no one has ever read blank pages, blank papyrus, or blank walls in caves. Hence in the "Writing to Read" system that he designed, children learn to write the words and sentences they already know how to speak— their *own* words and sentences—and then read what they have written. What's more, youngsters learn a way of spelling correctly that does not expect them to use twenty-six letters in the English alphabet to represent forty-two sounds, a limitation that inevitably produces too many rules, too many exceptions—and too many mistakes.

Dr. Martin put writing before reading for another salient reason: he realized that learning to write requires action, while learning to read is more passive. "Children *want* to learn to read," he and coauthor Ardy Friedberg explain in *Writing to Read: A Parents' Guide to the New, Early Learning Program for Young Children*, "but they *love* to learn to write."

John Henry Martin also has taken strong issue with the traditional belief of early childhood teachers that kindergarten youngsters will be deprived of their childhood if they are burdened with learning how to read and write instead of remaining free to play. Indeed, the formulator of Writing to Read has long insisted that learning is an exciting experience for children of any age. To support his viewpoint, Dr. Martin encourages doubters to look at the delight on the faces of babies who have just taken their first unassisted steps. No one, he told me some twenty-five years ago, can view these toddlers as being "burdened" with learning. Similarly, he indicates in his latest enterprise, five- and six-year-olds who can write notes to be exchanged with classmates or posted on refrigerator doors at home are engaged in a heady experience, not in an arduous task.

To accomplish his goal of teaching kindergarten and first-grade children to write as well as they talk and to read what they have written, Dr. Martin combined computer technology with time-tested knowledge about how youngsters best learn two of the traditional three R's. The resulting Writing to Read system has attracted some admirers, some detractors, and a great deal of attention. In schools that have purchased this program, children spend up to an hour a day in a special center, rotating among six costly, carefully equipped "learning stations":

- *The Computer Station*—equipped with an IBM PCjr personal computer and instructional diskettes that attract the most interest
- *The Writing/Typing/Word Processing Station*—equipped with IBM PCjr personal computers or IBM Selectric typewriters and other writing materials
- *The Work Journal Station*—which goes by a different name but is all too similar to familiar workbooks
- *The Listening Library Station* of taped stories
- *The Multi-Sensory Materials Station*—stocked with unlined paper, soft lead pencils, slate, chalk, clay for rolling

into letters, and a tray lined with black emery paper and filled with sand or rice for tracing letters

- *The Make Words Station*—a version of Scrabble in which a child uses letters on two-inch-square cards to form words that spell out the names of pictures another child presents.

To evaluate the outcomes of Writing to Read IBM provided its own hardware and software for a large-scale national study and engaged the Educational Testing Service (ETS) to compare the results of the new system with conventional methods of teaching language arts. Well satisfied with the findings, IBM purchased *Writing to Read* from John Henry Martin so that the corporation could use its own resources to market the system widely.

No one, of course, has been more pleased with ETS's findings than Dr. Martin himself. Nonetheless, to guard against unreasonable expectations he and his coauthor Ardy Friedberg have since felt the need to caution against an unguarded, overly enthusiastic response to the program alone. Writing to Read, they emphasize, can be only as worthwhile as the quality of the writing instruction that supplements the hour that children spend in a learning center; *no program can do what schools neglect to do.* The Martin/IBM system, in other words, is a way of introducing language arts, not a way of wrapping up writing and reading. In Dr. Martin's own words, "Writing to Read isn't magic." Nor was it ever intended to provide "hurry-up" learning. It has incorporated writing, however, as an essential part of literacy.

Consider the results that have stemmed from Writing to Read in Wausau, Wisconsin. Although the district's preliminary statistics that measure writing improvement are promising, even more impressive is the original work that some children shared when they were in second grade—work that cannot be reduced to charts and measurements. Indeed, a number of the seven- and eight-year-old students were not the least self-conscious about viewing themselves as authors—and for good reason. Connie Roeder, for example, had written eight books; she labored over the twenty-four chapters in *The Mystery of the Haunted House* for two to three months before she achieved hard-won gratification. *Connie Roeder Meets Nancy Drew* was less demanding. "It only took a month and a half," Connie recalled. Even her quickest effort, *The Silver Lion,* took the young mystery writer two to three weeks, but, as she was quick to say, "That one was easy." Easy? Second-graders in most schools, who write three- or four-sentence assignments, would hardly agree with Connie's assessment of her writing at Rib Mountain School.

Nathan Kieffer, a student in Wausau's Longfellow Elementary School, took the same stance as Connie. Nathan's favorite story, "My Pencil," begins:

> Once when I was writing a story at school my lead broke. I went over to the pencil sharpener and started grinding away. Then my pencil started screaming. I took my pencil out of the pencil sharpener and said, "Shut up."

After recounting the trouble the noisy pencil then caused him, Nathan describes a conversation in which the pencil said:

> "Well it herts when my lead breaks but I hate getting sharpened. And when I get small you throw me in the garbage without giving me a funeral."

Nathan wrote some colorful dialogue among his pencil, his mother, and himself, before ending his 364-word story with the pencil's demise:

> When they [his friends] came, we took turns sharpening the pencil. When he was very short we gave him a funeral. Then we threw him in the garbage. I don't think he liked it but he got what he wanted.

In most elementary schools, boys' writing lags behind girls', and both boys' and girls' lag behind that of students like Connie and Nathan. Children who are limited by skill-and-drill exercises cannot spin stories that compare with the funeral of a pencil, a Nancy Drew sequel, or, in the case of the writing that Grant School's Nathan Boettcher sent me, with the adventures of a leprechaun. Instead, banal little "story starters" result in banal little stories, if that. One of the advantages of Writing to Read, however, is that, when well used, it lays the groundwork for an elementary school writing program that builds on the conviction that as children's vocabularies grow and their ideas develop, their writing will also mature.

The Bedford Central School District, located less than an hour from the heart of New York City, provides a case in point. Writing to Read is a preliminary step in the first-to-twelfth-grade "Bedford Writes!" program that writing specialist Dolores Vion has instituted. Having gotten her grounding at the Bay Area Writing Project, where she learned that even five-year-old children delight in writing, Dolores is pleased to find that youngsters who enter the program that she oversees had already become experienced writers in kindergarten. Jackie Mandia, principal of the Bedford Hills Elementary School, is also pleased with the youngsters' early start. "They should call the program 'Writing to Write,' " she told me. "I used to be a language arts specialist, and I've worked with many reading programs. If there is such a thing as one 'best' program, I've never found it, because effectiveness depends on the needs of the child. But Writing to Read is the best *writing* program I have known. Children who otherwise would just about be writing what they call 'baby words' in first grade often have their entire speaking vocabularies at their command." Ms. Mandia likes to think of future implications. "If students and adults pay a price for *not* learning to write fluently when they are young, doesn't it stand to reason that they will benefit from a program that teaches them to write whatever they can say—in *kindergarten?*"

The West Patent Elementary School was selected as the other site for Bedford's Writing to Read installation (there are five elementary schools in the school district) because the principal, Kay Bowen-Smith, also had been a language arts specialist. Although the Bedford Central School District primarily serves a privileged population, she likes to remind visitors, "Our children range from wealth to welfare, but they are all benefiting from the same program." To show the early impact that Writing to Read can have on first-graders when teachers continue to value writing, Ms. Bowen-Smith shared her copy of a largely child-made book called *Squirrels.*

In this collection of reports that kindergarten "graduates" of Writing to Read produced two months after they began first grade, John wrote that squirrels use their tails as parachutes when they jump from branch to branch, Lauren said that squirrels scamper, and Vicki observed that they ruin nature. Lest the reader doubt the accuracy of her statement, Vicki explained, "They eat new born trees." Clearly, Writing to Read had taught these children to write what they can say. "Parachute," "scamper," and "ruin" are not words that new first-graders would otherwise be able to write or read. What's more, they spelled virtually every word correctly! And who can find fault with a new first-grader who writes that squirrels "hubernate" in winter?

As Dr. John Henry Martin emphasized, however, the impact of Writing to Read is only as lasting as the quality of the writing instruction that follows it. The quality has improved since teachers and students from elementary school to college began to discover what professional writers already know: writing, like painting or composing music, is not a product that springs full blown on demand as a finished piece; it is a painstaking process that needs reflection and revision before taking final form. When well practiced, the approach encourages students and teachers to postpone a concern with the end result until they have struggled with the means to that end. When abused, the concept turns into a formula, whose four or five steps, or six or seven, impose an orthodoxy that Donald Graves calls "the only enemy." But a formula makes no sense when you realize that the steps will vary with the individual and the task. Answering a twenty-minute essay question on a test, for example, is entirely different from writing a term paper; indeed, very brief test-taking barely touches on process.

She probably doesn't know it, but when Wausau student Connie Roeder told me about the way she goes about preparing a book, she was describing some key "process" steps that fit her own writing style. "First of all, I spend a lot of time figuring out who my characters are going to be, and planning the chapters I will need for the story I want to tell." Connie didn't talk about "prewriting" or "rehearsal," but she was discussing this phase in her own language: "figuring out" and "planning" were a second-grader's real words. Prewriting came so naturally to Connie, avid reader of mysteries that she is, that the young writer thought she got some of her ideas from books. "I guess I got the rest from inside my head," Connie said. "I'm not sure how I do it, but I have a way of digging inside my memory bank so I never run out of ideas."

"When I've finished planning, I write my first copy," Connie continued (unaware, perhaps, that she was talking about the drafting step), "but I usually have to change parts of it two or three times, or more. I really can't tell how often that will be, because I find that out as I go along," she said matter-of-factly—as if every second-grader took this approach. "I had to rewrite *The Mystery of the Haunted House* five times before I was satisfied with it," Connie said. Nor did this miniature Agatha Christie think there was anything unusual about *her* satisfaction being critical. How could it be otherwise? She took pleasure in writing at home as well as in school, setting her own standards in both cases, and had yet to realize that most pupils write only in school—when they absolutely have to—for their teacher's satisfaction.

Although she continued to use everyday language as she told me about her five rewrites, Connie was really talking about *revision,* that all-important step in the process of writing that is unknown in conventional classrooms—but is second nature for professional writers. Indeed, while renowned men and women of letters differ on how they proceed from the moment they begin a new work until the time they complete it, they agree on one fact: revision is the single aspect of their writing that is absolutely essential. (Many of these writers have discussed their labor fully in interviews spanning the years from 1958 to 1986 that have been collected in a seven-volume series entitled *The Paris Review Interviews Writers at Work.*)

Revision is also central to Dolores Vion's ongoing project, "Bedford Writes!" for she knows that no one has the magic ability to put words on paper perfectly the first time. Central, too, is the conviction that writing is essential to learning and knowing. After the kindergarten exposure to Writing to Read that is similar to Wausau's, therefore, Bedford takes on an unusual commitment to writing-as-process. Teachers using this approach in other school districts may have the encouragement of an occasional principal, but teachers throughout the Bedford Central School District also have the full support of their superintendent of schools, and he in turn has the commitment of the school board that initiated the writing program in the first place and that continues to endorse it. As a result, the looking-over-the-shoulder fear of disapproval that prevents change in most districts is conspicuously absent in Bedford.

Have you ever heard of a school district in which members of the board of education, district administrators, and a group of teachers give up a day in order to be introduced to writing as process—and to experience it by rehearsing (prewriting), drafting, and revising their own writing? That's exactly what the leadership of the Bedford Central School District did in November 1983, before launching its writing program. Nor was process writing limited to this group; from the outset, the presidents of the PTAs have participated in a variety of workshops and Dolores Vion also arranged for special presentations to the general membership of the parents associations in all of the schools. In addition, she established a community writing group for interested citizens.

Of course, it was essential that elementary school teachers receive a grounding in a process approach to writing. Nor has Bedford overlooked English, social science, and science specialists in the middle school and secondary school, for the district believes strongly in writing in every subject. As of this writing, a great many of the district's 150 teachers have participated in mini-workshops, two-day workshops, four-day workshops, in-class demonstrations, one-on-one sessions, and summer programs that focus on writing as a process. Nor is there any sign that "Bedford Writes!" is nearing an end.

The short distance between the rolling hills of the Bedford Central School District and the pavements of the inner city of Brooklyn, New York, cannot be measured in time or mileage. But you can get a clear sense of the difference between the suburban school district and Brooklyn's District 15 when you compare the number of city children who qualify for free-lunch programs with their Westchester counterparts or the proportion of single parents struggling to raise youngsters on scanty welfare payments. Despite the deprivation, however, writing can flourish in inner-city classrooms.

"There wasn't much flourishing in my classroom for the first fifteen years I taught writing," Cynthia Holton recalled. "I thought having row on row of second-graders repeating 'Fuh, fuh, fuh' was the surest way of having them learn the sound of the letter *f*. And since the board of ed's 'graded goals' syllabus was something like the Bible that we teachers were expected to carry with us at all times, I didn't dare depart from the 'buh, fuh, puh' way of teaching—even though I think down deep I always knew that it made no sense."

Traditional as Cynthia Holton was in many respects, her principal would not have chosen her to serve on a panel of ten superior language arts instructors to design a writing program for District 15 if she had not developed a strong reading program and class library, organized book sales, and insisted that drama be part of language arts. Nonetheless, as she met each Monday with nine other "superior teachers," each of whom had been chosen by a school principal, Cynthia Holton used to wonder what she was doing there. "If my principal had picked me for my math ability, I might have understood why. If she had recognized my work as a reading teacher, that would have made sense. But *writing!* I hated to write. I even avoided a composition course in college. When I absolutely *had* to write, I bored my poor professors to death by submitting papers whose only redeeming feature was that they were grammatically correct. That was my way of getting around an awful fear of being wrong."

The first insight that Cynthia Holton gleaned from these Monday sessions was that her students were probably as afraid of being wrong as she had been. Then she came to see that writing can be risk-free in classrooms that don't expect a ready-to-be-handed-in paper the first time round. "Once the burden of instant perfection is lifted," she explained, "a writer can begin with an 'I'll try this and see if it works' approach. The worst that can happen is that the first draft gets off to a false start; the best, that unexpected ideas may surface. But either way, we're still talking about a draft, an early attempt, that will improve with revisions."

Though Cynthia Holton can now assert that a first draft is a far cry from a published work, she needed support and assistance when she first tried to "unlearn" her own student days, teacher training, and experience with graded goals. "If it hadn't been for Lucy Calkins's help and for key people in

District Fifteen's office," she reflects, "I might have gone right on setting *my* deadlines, even if my students needed a different pace. Instead of having brief conferences with individual children from time to time, I might have reserved all of my comments for the class at the end."

Bit by bit, this elementary school teacher, who became a spark plug for change in her own Public School 58 and most recently a teacher trainer for other schools in District 15, volunteers a before-and-after self-evaluation. Before, error-free writing used to be her first consideration. Now she waits until students have gotten their writing in close-to-final form and *then* pays careful attention to writing conventions. "I'm still a stickler for correct English," Ms. Holton says without apology, "but I look for meaning first and search for errors last." Before, this transformed teacher always assigned top-ics. Now, she assigns topics at times and encourages students to develop ideas of their own choosing at other times.

Before, she served as an audience of one. "The kids always wanted to know what *I* wanted, because I was the only person who mattered." No more. Today she and all the chil-dren in the class respond to a writer's work. "In a few min-utes, you'll see the class gather on the rug in the back of the room," Ms. Holton told me the first time I visited her writing workshop. "Today Stephanie will be sitting in the author's chair, reading a piece that she's having a problem finishing. With twenty-five writing 'teachers' realizing that she is writ-ing to attract their interest, not just my comments, I think she'll get the help she needs. They may ask to hear the last draft in order to puzzle out where she is headed. They may ask for more information. And they'll probably suggest new ideas for her to mull over."

Knowing that children can be cruel, I was a bit con-cerned about the twenty-five teachers, until I saw a chart on the wall with a list of comments that Cynthia Holton and her students had compiled. Clearly, a writer receives appreciation first and criticism later. What's more, the comments showed that children take each other's work seriously. They know that anyone who has spent time pre-writing, drafting, and revising a piece of work, deserves their help. And anyone who has the courage to expose her writing warrants their support.

It doesn't take long to recognize some of the obvious differences between a traditional classroom where rows of silent students sit passively, doing the same thing at the same time, and a writing workshop such as Ms. Holton's. So much activity takes place almost simultaneously in Room 207 that Ms. Holton seems to be part teacher, part choreographer. As a writing workshop I observed was getting under way, she was in one corner of the room, listening to Ray, who told her, in a burst of enthusiasm, that he had decided to write a book about robots. "Let's talk about what you know about robots," Ms. Holton suggested, conversationally. "Hmmmm, I guess I don't know much," Ray replied. Avoiding the familiar "teacher's voice," Ms. Holton asked, "Well, how do you think you might find out about them?" Ray decided that he would go to the well-stocked book corner and see what he could learn about robots before he started writing. In Ms. Holton's room he'll learn a lot.

THE LINK BETWEEN
READING AND WRITING

Cynthia Holton has long prided herself on being the excellent reading teacher she is. No one could love books as much as she without having that love permeate the classroom and infuse her teaching. It is not surprising, therefore, that when Cynthia decided in 1982 to introduce her sixth-grade class to writing as a process she saved five of the eight periods for reading. Her students became so excited by writing, however, that by the end of the year she had reversed the ratio and was only spending three periods on reading. "I was terrified of their doing poorly on the reading test," she recalls, "until I realized that I was teaching the same issues through writing. The ability to draw inferences is a perfect example of what I mean," she explained. "Or, regardless of whether you're a writer or a reader, you learn to distinguish between central points and irrelevant information." When the results were in, the link between writing and reading was clearly established. The students scored as well as before, but they wrote beautifully as well.

"If the expression 'whole language instruction' had entered the school vocabulary then, I hadn't heard it," Cynthia Holton recalls, "but I wanted my students to experience the richness of language, so we did a lot of reading, a lot of writing, a lot of talking. Sometimes the writers were professional authors whose books I had chosen for our class library, sometimes the writers were the students themselves. Anyone who was looking for a silent classroom would have been well advised to stay out of that sixth-grade room," Ms. Holton remembers, "because I encouraged the sharing of ideas in every subject, and kids who became comfortable readers and writers didn't need much encouragement to enter into discussions." Cynthia Holton has since found books and articles about the kind of teaching style she valued, not because "whole language instruction was in vogue," but because, in her words, it "simply made sense."

She continued to emphasize writing when she taught a second-grade class. Pointing to a collection of her favorite books, Ms. Holton told her students, *These* are the master teachers. If you have a book you love, read it over and over again and figure out what made it good. Then try to write the way the author did." That's a tall order for inner-city second-graders, but not so tall as to exceed their grasp. Ramona must have read Cynthia Rylant's *When I Was Young in the Mountains* at least a dozen times before she began writing *When I Was Young in the Country with My Grandmother*. By the time Ramona had finished, however, she was a more accomplished writer because of her reading, and a more thoughtful reader because of her writing.

"Most public school children don't read anything except for a basal reader," Ms. Holton said, shuddering, "and that's not literature; it's just a way of teaching children how to read. But it's one thing to know *how* to read and another to *want* to read." By spending at least an hour each day reading a book to the class and talking about it, Ms. Holton makes reading a longed-for activity. But the books she reads are not chosen randomly. "If the kids are beginning to introduce dialogue in their writing, I'll select a favorite story of mine where the dialogue is particularly well done. And we'll discuss what the author did to make the conversation so true to life. If I see that some of my young authors are trying their hand at mysteries or fantasies, I'll read a well-constructed mystery or an imaginative tale." The reading and discussion hour is always focused on students' ventures. And if most of the children don't seem to be doing much venturing at all, their teacher finds books to get them out of their rut. Instead of divorcing reading from writing, she makes a point of using reading to develop writing. And since she chooses books that exemplify the best in children's literature, Cynthia Holton often succeeds in developing a writer's ear and sense of style.

When I read the volumes that her students had written and published for the class library, I saw at once that these young writers are clearly at home with books. Only children who are accustomed to reading would follow the style of a professionally published book, by including a brief biography of the author, a dedication, and a table of contents. "Why should our books be different from other books?" Cynthia Holton asked. "What you saw was just another way in which we link reading and writing. Once you see the connection, it's almost impossible to come up with a single reason for wanting to separate two sides of the same coin. Of course," she admitted, "there was a time when I used to talk a good game about the fusion—and do almost nothing about it."

While Ray burrowed around the book corner to begin prewriting his book, four of his classmates were busy writing entries in journals that reflected their feelings. "We're doing this so that someday when we are famous authors, people will know what we were like when we were seven years old," one of four told me. "We're writers now," he explained, "but we're not famous yet." Meanwhile, Ms. Holton has moved on to have a brief conference with a boy whose drawings were advanced far beyond his years. Although she appreciated the great talent that he may have inherited from his parents, both of whom are artists, Ms. Holton was disturbed that her young student had yet to put words on paper. Kneeling down, as she always does at a conference so that she's at eye level with her student, Ms. Holton tried to interest him in writing. But when he insisted that he wanted to go right on drawing, Mrs. Holton knew she would have to find a way of intervening. "As your publisher," she said, "I no longer have a need for picture books; I need word books now." Nodding, the youngster put away his picture and began to try his hand at writing. In Cynthia Holton's words, "Sometimes we have to find a way of saying, in effect, 'It's time for a change.'"

In the next half hour, she had "kneeling conferences" with six other children. "How's it going, Josie?" Ms. Holton began one conference. "What idea have you come up with now, Chris?" she asked another student. The answers to these simple questions lead the way to what will follow. The conferences are always brief, but they evoke new ideas from some who thought they had nothing more to say, and find focus for others who have so much to say that they are rambling.

While Ms. Holton wended her way around the room, a pair of writers was editing a story that was almost ready for the teacher's review. "I think you're missing commas to set off the name 'Lulu,' " said one. "Only one comma," the other pointed out, "because 'Lulu' ends the sentence." Two tables away, a student was interviewing his seatmate for biographical material. "I can't write a dust jacket," he complained, "unless you tell me more about your writing, Yolanda. Have you written poems before? Is this your first limerick? Where do you get your ideas?" A skilled interviewer, he had learned to ask the questions he would need for his writing.

Anyone who observes a busy writing workshop has to know that this kind of teaching is not easy, but it is so rewarding that at last count twelve teachers out of a staff of forty at P.S. 58 had chosen to develop writing programs that emphasize process before product. Even kindergarten children were beginning to take turns sitting in the author's chair and reading their stories to classmates who cluster together on an oversized rug, where they listen to the author and respond. When the first child begins by saying, "I like the picture of your school," she sets the atmosphere for the flurry of affirmative responses. Although the supportive environment is also apparent in other grades, children gradually learn to ask the author more probing questions. After hearing a story about a pet, a kindergartener might want to know, "Why did you name her Fluffy?"; a first-grade student might ask, "Does your cat ever scratch people?" and a second-grader might point out, "In the beginning you said that your brother was allergic to fur, but you never told us what happened to him after you got Fluffy. Does your brother sneeze around Fluffy?" By third grade, students would probably ask about the species.

Third-grade children also become quite skilled in detecting mechanical errors as they learn to use the *Editor's Checklist* that teacher Bob Hoerberger designed. "Any traditionalist who worries that a process approach ignores the importance of writing conventions can relax," he says.

EDITOR'S CHECKLIST

AUTHOR—EDITOR _____

TITLE _____

CO-EDITOR _____ DATE _____

CHECK FOR	EDITOR	CO-EDITOR	FINAL EDITOR
SPELLING			
PUNCTUATION			
PERIODS			
COMMAS			
QUESTION MARKS			
EXCLAMATION MARKS			
QUOTATION MARKS			
APOSTROPHES			

CAPITAL LETTERS			
SENTENCE STARTERS			
PROPER NAMES			
SPECIAL PLACES			
STREET NAMES			

Elementary school teachers and principals from New York City to Berkeley, California, have developed remarkable writing programs; but the Joseph J. Hurley School in Boston, Massachusetts, offers a feature I haven't seen anywhere else. Located on Worcester Street in Boston's South End, the undistinguished building looks like every turn-of-the-century city school in a decaying neighborhood. This school, however, houses its own up-to-the-minute publishing company, the Worcester Street Press. And, in the tradition of commercial publishers, it has begun honoring its multinational writers at a spring publication party called, "Authors/ Autores." Lining the hallway are multiple copies of volumes such as *Our Class Book: Information, Entertainment, and Persuasion; Poetry; My Neighborhood; Look What's Growing on Worcester Street;* and *Dogs: How to Care for and Identify Them*—all complete with dedications and tables of contents. A handsomely bound original copy of each is on display in the library, where student authors and *autores* beam at some three hundred parents and neighbors who pack the room to beam back at the children. For that shining moment, at least, students are proud of their school—and of themselves. "Anyone who has seen the faces of these kids and their parents knows why I say, 'We've just begun to write'," pledges teacher-writer and guiding spirit Jean Gibran.

Anyone who has seen Ms. Gibran teach and has examined her background and credentials recognizes the reasons for her resolve. Granddaughter of the celebrated author-poet Kahlil Gibran, Jean imbibed the value of writing from earliest childhood. It follows that as a teacher, she became committed to the belief that thinking and writing are the foundation of all curricula. To advance that belief, Ms. Gibran completed summer institute introductory and graduate writing programs at the Boston Writing Project (an NWP branch) and began conducting workshops that teachers in her school flock to. And to Jean Gibran's delight, all of her teacher-students attended the publication party to glory in their children's writing.

Unlike schools I have seen in "South Ends" elsewhere, Joseph J. Hurley uses writing to take children to places never dreamed of; one year, for example, Ms. Gibran's third-grade students discovered what life is like is in Eagle, Alaska, where the closest paved streets are two hundred miles away and the average winter temperature is 50 degrees below zero. The discoveries were made through questions and answers that emerged when the Boston youngsters corresponded with twelve children in Eagle. Richard wanted to know whether there are subways in Eagle, where, according to eight-year-old Alaskan Lena, the population of two hundred adults and children lives in log houses. Ever curious, Richard also asked, "Do you have transformer toys? How do you eat bear? How do you get salmon? Do you have cars?" Do you have computers?" Through Lena's answers, Richard soon learned that computers have, indeed, found their way to Eagle's little backcountry grade school.

Tikeya, who wrote her friend in Eagle, "I tried to get my mother to move to Alaska," had only one question that perplexed her: "How does a Yukon River look?" Thomas was more inquisitive: "Do you have television in Alaska or radios?" Confused by both geography and climate, he also wondered, "Is it always snowing down there?"—until he learned that his nine-year-old counterpart pans for gold in the summer and checks the salmon net in the fall. The letters showed that inner-city youngsters are as isolated in their way as wilderness children are in theirs, but that each can learn from the other, through writing letters.

An exciting writing, reading, and science project that Jean Gibran orchestrated gave another group of third-grade students new appreciation of their own city. Nine months of collaboration between two teachers and over half a dozen out-of-school resources led to twenty-two students' writing and illustrating *The Tree Outside Our Window: A Place Inside Myself,* which recorded the life cycle of an aging linden tree outside their classroom window. But the book went well beyond that. One chapter was devoted to a trip to the Arnold Arboretum, others to planting bulbs in autumn and marigolds in spring, and still others to activities that were the highlights of unlikely months like December and February.

The children's new experiences with soil and water, bulbs

and seeds were the *real* story starters, because they provided a "Guess what!" quality for city dwellers that artificial
stimuli do not. Writing in November, Taisha wanted to share
exciting moments with her readers, from digging a hole for
her anemone bulb and mixing fertilizer, to the "bird up in
the tree that almost hit Raheem and Renee with dodo."

Three months later, the children reveled in imaginative
writing.

> Me and the dirt are having a good time. I went to the
> movies last night. We saw Beverly Hills cops. We have
> parties. At parties we eat cake and ice cream and lots of
> candy. Crocuses have to go to the dentist the day after we
> have a party.
>
> —Michael Moore

> I am a crocus bulb. I am very hot and sleepy under the
> soil. I hope that when spring comes I will be purple, white,
> and yellow. I work for the Plant Crown Society. But for a
> hobby, I just sit in the dirt.
>
> —Tahisha Prater

Unlike other eight-year-olds who may want to become
anything from astronauts to zookeepers, many of the boys
and girls in Jean Gibran's third-grade class seemed to harbor
a single ambition: to become authors. They knew that writing took concentration and hard work, but they also knew
how exciting it had been to write their "Tree" book. At
year's end one student, LaKiesha, wrote Urban Forester Ernest DeRosa:

> Dear Mr. DeRosa:
> We enjoyed your lesson. We learned a lot about trees
> that we didn't know. We learned that we can tell how old
> a tree is by counting the rings. But nobody wants to cut
> down the tree.
>
> Over by the South End I saw a tree growing into a
> fence. The tree is big. It looks like a person getting hurt.

Every time I go over there I don't want to look at it.
It's awful. I don't know how it got there. The tree roots
don't have any room. Brick is in the soil. Everything happens in the city. That tree needs to be in the forest.
Good-bye.

Of course, LaKiesha was expressing concern for the environment, but self-awareness was also taking root. What was
happening to this little girl in the city? Was she getting hurt?
Did she not have enough room? As LaKiesha continues to
write, she is likely to express old feelings as well as new
knowledge.

The Tree Outside Our Window linked writing, art, and
science; correspondence between students in Boston and
Eagle, Alaska, linked social studies and writing. And young
Hurley School children in a Resource Room for students
with learning problems link writing and math. "My mother
gave me my allowance. It was 75 cents," one youngster
wrote. "I bought a bag of chips and a juice. It cost 50 cents.
How much change did I get back?" he challenged his classmates. "I had 7 dozen eggs in each dozen comes 12. How
much do I have altogether?" another youngster asked. Thus,
in one way or another, from kindergarten through fifth
grade, "writing across the curriculum" has enriched the lives
of children in the Joseph J. Hurley School in Boston, Massachusetts.

The same concept also enriched their counterparts in
Eagle, Alaska. To get some sense of Boston, children learned
to read maps that would show location, direction, distance,
and main physical features. Even a zip code directory was
informative. This strange place to which they mailed their
letters was so large that *streets* had different codes! It was a
challenge to address their envelopes correctly. It was also a
challenge to calculate the cost of stamps and postcards. Perhaps the greatest challenge of all, however, was to become
"experts" who could answer their pen pals' questions on wild

life and art activities, on government, local history, and native groups.

WRITING ACROSS THE CURRICULUM

Writing used to be considered the solitary domain of English or language arts teachers; it no longer is. Dr. Toby Fulwiler, a leading proponent of writing across the curriculum, summed up the change in the title of an article he wrote for *The Phi Kappa Phi Journal,* which he called, "Writing Is Everybody's Business."

"Student writing will improve," Toby Fulwiler asserts, "when student learning does; and student learning will improve when students do more writing. That," he concludes, "is what Writing Across the Curriculum is all about." Implied in Dr. Fulwiler's statement lies another virtue that teachers and students are also discovering: nothing clarifies thinking quite so much as having to put ideas in writing. Much to their surprise, students often discover that writing evokes insights, recall, and understanding that had been buried; conversely, the act of writing is the most powerful way for students to discover that concepts they thought they had grasped are in fact still fuzzy. Writing in any subject and on any grade level reveals what students know and what they still need to learn, regardless of whether they are explaining the rules for playing football, a method for long division, or ways to prevent a measles epidemic. Writing across the curriculum knows no bounds. And, as students put new information in their own words, as they connect it with what they already know, they discover the bond between writing and learning.

To underscore the connection between writing and thinking, JoAn McGuire Simmons, editor of *The Shortest Distance to Learning: A Guidebook to Writing Across the Curriculum,* says wryly, "Rodin's *Thinker* may be one of the few who doesn't have a pencil in his hand." Altering Descartes's famous pronouncement, "I think, therefore I am," she suggests that he might have said, "I write, therefore I think." Taking her rearrangement one step further, teachers are coming to appreciate the concept of, "I think, therefore I learn." It is by linking writing, thinking, and learning in every subject on every grade level that writing across the curriculum offers the most promise.

California consultant Jenee Gossard emphasizes that linkage at teacher workshops she conducts. "Writing across the curriculum," she explains, "has the potential of transforming the purpose of writing. If you only use writing to see what students know long enough to succeed on a test, you won't find out what students *think*—how they react to a book, an experiment, a painting, a film, or a new idea in any content area. And that," she underscores, "is a great strength of writing across the curriculum." Ms. Gossard suggests, for example, that in the course of events or following an activity teachers have students respond briefly in writing to questions such as:

- What was the most important (interesting, confusing) part of today's music lesson?
- What do you know about fractions (haiku, nutrition, maps) after today's lesson?
- What do you think I wanted you to discover in last night's homework?

To see award-winning examples of writing across the curriculum, I arranged to view videotapes that Jim Musante made of his third-grade classroom in Moraga, California. One of seventy-one teachers who entered tapes after having been nominated by Bay Area and National Writing Project sites as models of outstanding teaching of writing, Musante was one of four winners.

Each year Jim uses a different historical theme to link

writing with different content areas. One year he chose King Tut (the Tut exhibit was in the neighborhood) and used a sandbox as a dig box for students to explore ancient history by digging up artifacts and researching them. Third-graders became archaeologists, exploring through history and writing about their findings. Another year, he linked writing, reading, science, and history by reliving the history of flight and aviation, going back to the time of Benjamin Franklin, hot-air ballooning, and the first flights into space.

Once Jim Musante transformed the classroom into a medieval castle city in the year 1100, and students became the people living in the castle. As castle astronomers, they wrote reports on the planets in the solar system. As castle residents, they made finger puppets, representing the characters who also lived there. They improvised dialogue, wrote down and revised their scripts, and performed their plays for the whole class. By so doing, their written vocabulary expanded to include words such as: wizard, knight, tower, dragon, majesty, suit of armor, capture, dungeon, and giant.

Ever inventive, Mr. Musante devised another theme that led to students' becoming interested in giants. Youngsters read every story they could on the subject, and talked about plots and characters. They went on to write their own giant stories (using a writing-as-process approach) and published their original work in giant-sized books. Then the class learned techniques for interviewing subjects so that they could write brief biographies of the authors, which they pasted inside the cover of their books. By year's end, Jim Musante reported, "These kids, who had been workbook experts, learned that writing is changing a blank piece of paper with thoughts and ideas of their own."

Students in grades four through six at the Columbus School in Berkeley, California, have devised their own guidelines for scoring the writing samples that their school requires each student to provide three times a year. According to students' standards, papers rate a top grade of three if they meet these criteria: "imaginative title, good paragraphs, spelling is good, good sentence structure, good content, lots of action, good use of words." These children have willingly learned through their own experience that good writing requires a mix of skill with words and ideas and skill with accepted conventions.

These upper elementary school students, whose backgrounds resemble those of their Boston counterparts, have decided that a writing sample warrants a score of 2 if it "has some good ideas, a very good topic sentence, pretty good handwriting, pretty good content, and some spelling errors," but its "title is not creative" and its writing shows "no imagination." According to the students' standards, however, a paper should receive a grade of 1, if it is "boring, does not make much sense, and has sloppy handwriting, no title, bad spelling, poor sentence structure, no title, poor indenting, television talk," and if it "needs details." When you read the criteria that young students have established, you don't have to worry about whether writing as a process and writing mechanics are completely compatible. They are.

In the face of these no-nonsense student guidelines, each week Christine Lim, then principal of Columbus School, took courage in both hands, and posted on a giant bulletin board an early draft and the final copy of her weekly bulletin to parents. "I felt threatened," she admitted, "but I couldn't think of a better way of showing students how writing progresses." Since Chris Lim and every one of the nineteen teachers at Columbus School had been trained by the original Bay Area Writing Project, their emphasis on writing was hardly surprising. Neither were the classroom scenes I encountered. Halloween was a classic example. On the blackboard of a fifth-grade room, I saw two lists: one, with forty-two items, was titled, "What We Know About Witches" and the other, with twenty-seven, was titled, "What We Want to Learn About Witches." My favorite question, "Do they want to be beautiful?" had been asked by a little girl who was trying to shed thirty pounds. "Do they want kingdoms of their own?" a boy who slept in a bed with his brother had wanted to know. Here, as in Boston's Hurley School, children used writing as a way of learning—and as a way of recognizing their own feelings.

Writing is also closely linked with a literature program that has replaced basal readers with multiple copies of over one hundred novels, biographies, and anthologies of stories and folktales. "The books are better than our old readers because you can use your imagination," one sixth-grader commented. "You can see the characters and understand how they feel." Through this exposure, many young writers are able to bring their own characters to life.

I'm learning a lot about things I never knew about," a fifth-grader said. "You can ask more questions and have more discussions because the stories aren't so simple." And a fourth-grade student remarked, "If you don't know what a word is, you can think of the whole story and take a good guess." With their increased knowledge and expanded vocabulary, upper elementary school students like Tereso, Virna, Yodira, and Shamika write stories that make you want to ring bells and blow trumpets in a neighborhood that is more accustomed to the sight of drug dealers and the sound of police sirens. Though change is not for the timid or for those who lack vision, it has already found a place in venturesome classrooms.

5

SIGNS OF CHANGE
IN THE UPPER GRADES

"I feel like a revolving door, not a teacher," the head of a southeastern high school English department told me. "Every time one group of students scrambles to leave the room another group scrambles to enter." No isolated statement, this. Whether fresh out of training or seasoned by years of practice, secondary school teachers have to pursue their profession with similar comings and goings every time the bell signals the end of a 45- or 50-minute period. This arrangement typically results in English teachers' meeting with some 150 students a day, most of whom become faceless names on attendance charts. And teachers who dread the thought of nights and weekends consumed by reading, correcting, and grading 150 papers single-handedly, dare not assign so much as a modest writing task each week to the five or six classes that file in and out of their rooms. "We're already overloaded with too much paperwork," they protest, almost in a single voice. And they are—if they accept ways of teaching writing that don't work.

Theodore Sizer portrayed their distress effectively and sympathetically throughout his book *Horace's Compromise*. "Horace," a composite of many highly regarded secondary school English teachers, believed that students should write "something for criticism," *his* criticism. Indeed, with the best of intentions, he wanted pupils to produce a minimum of a one- or two-page essay "at least twice a week," but even with fewer students than many English teachers (his five classes "only" totaled 120 individuals), he was realistic about the demands of his teaching schedule, other school expectations, and the outside job he needed to hold down for extra income. As a result, he felt he had to pare writing assignments down to no more than one or two paragraphs once a week so that he might have a *little* free time.

But the paperwork that afflicts every English teacher doesn't overpower all. When high school English instructor Guy Doud, of Brainerd, Minnesota, was named National Teacher of the Year, he was teaching *six classes a day with a total enrollment of 165 students*—but hardly a week went by without his classes' doing substantial amounts of writing. "Groups of students read each other's writing three or four times before I even see their papers," he explained, "so most of the rough edges—careless thinking and mechanical mistakes—don't even reach my eyes. I reserve my time for raising substantive issues on some papers." *Some* papers, but not all, for Guy realized that he could not read every essay with the same thoroughness, and still assign all the writing he desired.

Other management techniques also continue to serve him well. To avoid having every student turn in papers at the same time, Mr. Doud staggers his lesson plans. "I may show a film to one class," he says, "discuss literature with another, or help a third class plan its next paper, which usually reflects the reading we have been doing together." Even students who have been concentrating on writing essays rarely submit their work in one fell swoop, because their teacher has assured them that no penalty will be exacted if some writers need more time than others before they feel ready to show him their best effort. The methods Guy Doud has designed for handling his paperwork are important because he believes they provide a way to increase the amount of writing that any teacher can realistically assign. And Guy has found that frequent writing produces "unbelievable improvement!" in the students' work.

Members of his school's English department who have moved in the same direction have met with similar success. "One of our teachers," Guy says, "has been stressing writing for twenty-seven years, and he is still brimming with energy. And paperwork hasn't gotten me down during my fourteen years." Doud thrives on getting to school an hour before classes begin, staying two and a half hours after they end, and taking work home for evening hours that aren't devoted to his family. Clearly, his writing program stimulates Guy Doud as much as it stimulates his students. And similar writing programs are beginning to invigorate a number of teachers outside of Brainerd, too.

While teachers no longer shackled to a failed course of study see that writing enables them to accomplish more of their goals, traditional colleagues consider writing an imposition on schedules that are already choked with weekly reviews of spelling, punctuation, grammar, and usage. Why such opposing viewpoints? The answer lies in the methods that underlie teaching and in the values that give rise to different techniques. Time is a particularly precious commodity in secondary school. Whether that time is wisely spent or squandered, however, is another issue, for differences in educational philosophy separate the "I don't have time to waste on writing" majority that advocates rote memorization from the "I insist on *making* time" minority that claims correct mechanics take hold when students apply them to their own writing.

English teachers who back away from introducing new high school writing programs are also the first to worry about having to "cover" the literature curriculum—the same literature that some teachers are able to combine beautifully with their writing programs. Not coincidentally, teachers in other content areas also complain about having to "cover" their curriculum, be it biology or history, geometry or Spanish, without realizing that writing offers a fresh way of teaching. Given the cover-the-curriculum viewpoint that state education departments often impose, many intimidated instructors regard writing as an interruption except for purposes of testing. Feeling oppressed by still further demands from all sides, they conclude that they will concentrate on what they know best, which certainly excludes the teaching of "real" writing. (Short-answer responses to tests of mechanics and a one-paragraph assignment every six weeks are "real" enough in the lives of most students, but are "unreal" examples of writing.)

Yet some teachers have developed strong writing programs, even though they are subject to the same stresses as others: standardized tests, anxious parents, student conferences, evaluations by a department chair, principals' reviews, occasional visits from the district office, daily peer pressure. Perhaps the greatest stress every high school teacher experiences stems from recognition of the long view: some students have to be prepared for the job market, some for further education, and everyone for life after graduation. That's a tall order.

To find out how writing can actually relieve these multiple demands without adding yet another one, I turned first to Ray Lawson, chair of the English department of Rochester (Michigan) High School. "Let's take that agenda apart, piece by piece," he said. "Think of all the people who will be relieved if high school graduates think clearly and retain what they've learned, and think of the enormous weight that will be lifted if they can write correctly as well. Students and graduates will pass muster with teachers, principals, parents, test makers"—he paused for breath—"employers, college admissions officers, and these days, I would add state legislators." Lawson reserved for the end what he values most.

"And if young men and women can express themselves with fluency and grace, they've got the makings of educated people. Tell me," he asked rhetorically, "can you think of any discipline other than writing that can accomplish all this?"

By his own admission, Ray Lawson has come a long way since he started his teaching career as a strict grammarian in 1942, when, he now claims, no one gave more weekly quizzes than he. An unlikely story. Since grammar was—and still is—one of the easiest parts of the English curriculum to test, it lends itself to nightly quizzes, weekly quizzes, any kind of quiz you can think of. "The trouble was, my students kept failing," Ray recalls, "because I went about teaching grammar the wrong way." Again he was not alone.

To save colleagues from continuing to make the mistakes he did, Ray Lawson led a system-wide committee that devised ways to teach grammar by replacing lessons from a publisher's text with ones drawn from the students' own writing. Instead of relying on a formal assignment on pronouns and antecedents that may seem abstract, for example, a teacher might say, "Sometimes I'm confused about who the 'we' is in your mystery, Bob"—thus making connection between correct grammar and clear expression more relevant. Similarly, by editing their own writing, students can learn and retain an individual grammar lesson. The same kind of editing, the committee pointed out, also teaches desirable usage. "Going through their papers and rewriting all the sentences that begin with 'There is' or 'There are' provides a more lasting lesson," Ray said, "than any textbook can."

By reviewing the curriculum, grade by grade, Ray and his colleagues produced an English-language arts curriculum guide that is available to Rochester's two high schools, three junior highs, and ten elementary schools. "We believe we have overcome the failings that result from teaching isolated rules, at the same time that we have been careful to respect the importance of correct English," Ray Lawson said. Yet, as is true in every school district, some of the chief architects of failure prefer to hold fast to methods that don't work—while other teachers respond eagerly to new ideas.

In Ray's early years of teaching, a silent classroom was regarded as the measure of a good teacher whose class was "under control"—as it often is today. Lawson was a "good teacher" then. Anyone who walks into his four writing classes now, however, will hear the buzz of students sitting in a horseshoe arrangement or around small tables discussing their ideas with each other, first during the prewriting stage of their composing, and later as they share drafts and revisions. There's nothing hard and fast about the procedure, but Ray Lawson clearly views writing as a several-step process—a viewpoint that thirteen members of the English department have learned to adapt in individual ways. They have a mentor, of course, in their department chairman, while Ray Lawson had no one to guide him. How did a teacher like Ray find his own way in the 1940s? How can high school teachers who are still without direction find their way today?

"Sometimes my compass was sheer instinct," Ray muses. "Teachers have to trust themselves, you know." Ray's "compass" pointed to a contradiction between the chatter he heard students exchange in the school yard before the bell rang and the stilted language in the brief writing they did in school. He knew something was wrong when they groaned when they had to stop talking and start writing. It stood to reason, Ray Lawson realized, that students talked about what interested them, but had to write about what interested the teacher. What's more, when they talked to each other, they weren't worried about correct grammar, but when they wrote a school assignment, they knew they would more likely be judged by their mechanical mistakes than by the substance of what they had to say.

Consequently, well before pioneering teachers recognized the importance of writing—and the particular importance of seeing that writing stems from a painstaking process—Ray Lawson set about transforming his classroom. Hardly a day passed without his encouraging writing. Students knew that their teacher's primary interest lay in finding out what they had in mind and wanted to communicate. If they weren't expressing themselves clearly, Ray helped them see that they weren't thinking clearly in the first place. He also led them to discover that the importance of correct writing wasn't just a teacher's whim. It was hard for readers to prepare themselves for a new thought, if one sentence ran into another. Writing that jumped back and forth from one verb tense to another was enough to confuse even the most interested reader—and they didn't come any more interested than Ray Lawson. His students knew that this teacher really cared about *them,* and his supervisors knew this teacher didn't dismiss the expectations of others. As a result, most of Lawson's students wound up writing fluently and correctly, and giving voice to their own individual style. And Ray progressed from being a teacher ahead of his time to becoming a department chairman as well.

Even a teacher who has acquired as clear a sense of direction as Ray, however, finds it reassuring to learn that some colleagues—albeit a minority—have compasses that point the same way. Despite years of accumulated expertise, therefore, in 1981 Ray enrolled in a five-week NWP summer institute, conducted by the Oakland (Michigan) Writing Project. "I couldn't imagine what *we* were going to teach *him,"* project director Aaron Stander recalls, "but I came to see that an institute serves an important function when it provides a support system for teachers as gifted as Ray Lawson. They are reassured to learn that, like Molière's *bourgeois gentilhomme,* they were speaking prose all along, and they return home even more committed to teaching than before—if that's possible."

It *is* possible. Ray Lawson turned down an opportunity to say that more than forty-five years of classroom teaching was enough. In place of his heavy teaching load and chairing a department (the equivalent of at least another course), he could have moved into administration and become coordinator of Secondary English and Social Studies for the Rochester school district. Since advancement in the teaching profession typically means that the best teachers leave the classroom, Ray would have followed a common pattern had he accepted the position. But Ray Lawson is an uncommon teacher; he knew that his place was with his students. Flattered but untempted by the promotion, he has chosen to spend his professional days in the classroom and in the school whose principal looks to him for leadership in making Rochester High School a model for the district. But even a would-be model school has much to overcome. "Many of my students grew up on the system of doing an assignment to get a grade and then holding their breath until the next assignment was announced," he said. "They always hoped there wouldn't be a 'next,' but they always knew it would come. I'd like to change their world."

Rarely does Ray announce group assignments; students usually develop their own interests. Never does he grade writing prematurely; he works with students to help them clarify their thinking first and then to sharpen their writing. "Once they see the light," Ray says with considerable satisfaction, "there's no turning back." And in Ray Lawson's classes, students don't just "see the light"; year after year, he teaches them ways of looking.

Secondary school teachers can also benefit from learning new ways of looking. Ask Terry Moher, who teaches four writing courses and one literature course at Exeter (New Hampshire) High School. Since students in her literature class write original analyses of what they have been reading, this public school English teacher works with one hundred full-time and twenty-five part-time writers every day. Instead of feeling overwhelmed by what some call paperwork, however, Terry Moher is invigorated by teaching writing.

"There's a world of difference," she explained, "between being a paper-pusher and being a professional. I would have quit teaching years ago if I had to spend my life marking quizzes and correcting dreary assignments." There is also a world of difference between writing that is limited to correct mechanics and the definition of writing that is posted over the table and chairs where Terry sits and confers with student-writers. WRITING, the poster reads, IS THE CONTINUOUS STRUGGLE TO DISCOVER WHAT YOU HAVE TO SAY AND HOW TO SAY IT.

"Believe me, teachers who say they are already overwhelmed with paperwork are really bored silly. So are their students," Terry Moher claimed. It took the impact of an intense summer at the New Hampshire Writing Program for this revived writing teacher, who came close to leaving the classroom, to find her niche. "I can't blame anyone who is a paper-pusher for practically screaming, 'No more, no more!' But now that I know the difference between a draft that a student still needs to work on and a carefully crafted paper that is ready for my after-hours attention," the "new" Terry Moher said, "my paperwork has been cut in half, if not more. Best of all, when I read polished work that shows what a student writer can finally accomplish, I know why I wanted to be an English teacher in the first place—and why I intend to remain one."

Undaunted—no, delighted—by the growing number of student writers, Terry carves out class time for frequent mini-conferences with all of her pupils, as they plan and refine their work. (Why didn't I have my students write in class? I wonder. Why didn't I welcome them, one by one, to a seat next to mine? Why didn't I also circulate around the room, pausing at each desk?) "One idea per conference while students are immersed in the process of writing, is more helpful," Terry points out, "than ten ideas on a piece that is already completed." She also relies on the technique of repeating what she understands a student to have said. "Is this what you meant," she asks, "or am I interpreting what you wrote incorrectly?" Brief as her questions sometimes are, she helps students sharpen their thinking, yet she divides her limited time so as to reach everyone. "Reaching everyone is important," she says earnestly. "Unless I pay individual attention, I'm really not teaching."

Any teacher who protests, "But I'm only one person," and wonders, "How am I going to give enough individual class time to everyone?" will find twenty-five or thirty answers sitting behind student desks every day. As Terry Moher explains, by the time she reads a student's writing, it has already been read by other students, commented on, and revised. Even mistakes in spelling, grammar, usage, and word choices have usually been detected and corrected. "In the long run," Terry acknowledges, "I have more papers to read than a teacher who assigns no writing; but the papers are easier to respond to than the ones that face teachers who don't contribute any ideas until the bitter end—and it is *very* bitter."

Despite the advantages that Terry cites, language arts specialist Janice Allen crusaded for eight years to change the way writing was taught in ten secondary schools and twenty-six elementary schools within Ogden, Utah, and its surrounding suburbs. A more easily discouraged educator might have conceded defeat after being scorned time and again. "I discovered what it felt like to be rejected by people I had thought were my friends," she told me, "but I had seen that writing worked beautifully in New Hampshire when it was taught as a process, and I was convinced the approach could work in Utah, too." Since the members of NWP's Utah Writing Project share Janice Allen's conviction, she had the support system that every innovative writing teacher and administrator in that state can count on. "And my students spurred me on," the persistent Ms. Allen said. "In fact, when I was feeling most discouraged, it was their belief in what I was doing that convinced me I had to continue my crusade."

Now colleagues who had formerly shunned Janice Allen are beginning to appreciate the students' point of view, and a long-neglected, but essential part of the curriculum is finding its place under the sun. Change is never easy, but the change I am talking about is worth all the effort your school can muster. It is through being emboldened to take risks that students dare to manipulate language. It is through the response of classmates that students learn to communicate with many audiences. And it is through frequent writing that students discover and shape unformed thoughts that lie dormant in their minds.

Guy Doud gave me a clear sense of the thoughts and concerns that occupy contemporary students' minds when he told me about an open-ended writing assignment. His class had read Jonathan Swift's satire *A Modest Proposal*, which had put forth an outlandish solution to the problem of overpopulation in Ireland. Linking literature and writing as he often does, this small-town Minnesota teacher told his students to write their own *Modest Proposal*. Some found their concerns too serious to satirize. One student, for example, addressed the question of how to end nuclear war, another suggested ways of dealing with illiteracy, hardly trivial thoughts. Adolescents who have fears, and thoughts, and "modest proposals" can express them in writing, given the opportunity.

Doud encountered similar seriousness when his students read George Bernard Shaw's *Man and Superman*. After discussing the section of the play where the Devil speaks to a character named Tanner, students wrote individual reactions; some considered the Devil's viewpoint realistic, some regarded it as unduly cynical, but everyone revealed deepfelt thoughts and feelings. "Students of this age can be too embarrassed to make their personal values heard in the classroom," Guy Doud told me, "but writing offers the benefit of privacy. And responding to Shaw and Swift adds the benefit of being challenged by ideas that are more sophisticated than what the usual teaching guide offers."

Because she has become a widely read writer, Nancie Atwell is probably the best-known proponent of techniques to create what she calls "a literate environment" where even "nonreaders" and "I-hate-to-write" students collaborate with each other and with their teacher. She described some of the strategies she developed in her Boothbay Harbor (Maine) junior high school classroom in "Writing and Reading from the Inside Out" (a chapter in an anthology called *Breaking Ground*), and later expanded on these techniques in her award-winning book, *In the Middle*.

Nancie's students, including eight special education pupils, read an average of thirty-five full-length works, from Blume to Brontë, and exchanged almost three thousand pages of letters with her, following the plan she wrote them in September:

> This folder is a place for you and me to talk about books, reading, authors, and writing. You're to write letters to me, and I'll write letters back to you.
>
> In your letters, talk with me about what you've read. Tell me what you thought and felt and why. Tell me what you liked and didn't like and why. Tell me what these books meant to you and said to you. Ask me questions or for help. And write back to me about my ideas, feelings, and questions.

The use of letters was inspired by the "dialogue journals" that California teacher Leslee Reed had devised in order to have daily written conversations with her elementary school students. Why not, Atwell reasoned, have written conversations to discuss secondary school students' observations about books and writing? Why not, indeed? Look at the impact of that approach on a student Nancie calls Daniel. (Since she is an expert "teacher-researcher" who carefully

records changes in attitude and accomplishment, Nancie Atwell's files bulge with letters and surveys portraying the
growth of "Daniels" of every description.)

Nancie describes his wearing an unvarying outfit: blue
jeans, duck boots, and a chamois shirt over a T-shirt. When
not in school, Daniel was usually found with his dirt bike, a
.22, or his twenty lobster traps. (He planned to become a
lobsterman full-time when he finished school.) Daniel had
never bought a book or borrowed one from the town library, and he read nothing but the magazine *Dirt Bike*—
until his teacher piqued his interest with a new book,
About David [by Susan Beth Pfeffer]. Daniel wrote a brief
letter, saying he liked it "because it made me feil [feel] it
happened to me. it was one of the first books I read that I
enjoyed. Because I don't read much." However, when Ms.
Atwell wrote saying, "I think you'd like *Tex*, by S. E. Hinton. Have you read it?" Daniel replied that he was "too
bissee."

More letters. Few books. Then at grading time Daniel
wrote to protest the unfairness of people getting bad grades
because they "don't like to read or read slow. In my case I
can't find books I like." And he concluded, "I'm just saying
it's not fair!" Ms. Atwell's reply satisfied him:

Dear Daniel,
    I won't give bad grades to people who read slowly. If
you put in the time and use it well, you'll get a good
grade.
    I also won't give bad grades to people who don't like to
read. It depresses me that people sometimes feel that way,
but I won't give someone a bad grade for an opinion that
differs from mine.
    I do give bad grades to people who don't read or don't
use reading time well. In this class, which is called reading,
I'm expecting my students will read.
    I know hundreds of good books, as good as the ones
you've read this year and liked. . . .

In his next note, Daniel thanked Ms. Atwell for "explaining the situation" and said he was going to go to the town library. When that proved unsuccessful he wrote to say, "I will have to go out of town to find a good set of books." In December Ms. Atwell gave Daniel a copy of *Tex,* and he discovered S. E. Hinton—the same author and book Daniel had said he was "too bissee" to read in October. After reading three Hinton books in succession, he was ready—eager—to find books on his own and discuss them with Ms. Atwell. And in January he wrote a five-page paper on camping, using the work of an author he admired to guide him.

By year's end, Daniel had read twelve novels of increasing complexity, had continued writing long, nonfiction narratives, and had begun spending weeks writing lengthy fiction as well, turning to professional writers as role models; in addition he had exchanged thirty-five letters with Ms. Atwell. "I wish Paula Danziger had made the father less like a cartoon character," he wrote, as he began to suggest revisions in published works. Or, "This book got good as I got into it, but I think the author should have tried a different lead." Daniel was reading like the writer he was becoming and writing like the new reader he already was.

Nancie Atwell's Boothbay Harbor classroom was not the same as Guy Doud's in Minnesota, and his is not the same as Terry Moher's in New Hampshire. Terry's in turn differs somewhat from Ray Lawson's in Michigan. For that matter, all the teachers under Ray's direction do not teach identically; their individuality asserts itself, as it should. And the classrooms that Janice Allen has managed to develop in Utah are neither replicas of the ones that inspired her nor imitations of each other. But, since each of these classrooms is treating the teaching of writing as a serious intellectual exercise, each in its own way is beginning to produce successful student writing.

THE FAIRFAX, VIRGINIA, PUBLIC SCHOOL DISTRICT

A model of good writing instruction is taking hold in the mammoth public school district in Fairfax County, Virginia. Like every solid program, it relies on a critical mass of well-prepared teachers. That preparation began in 1979 when social studies teacher Bernadette ("Bernie") Glaze became one of the first Fairfax teachers to participate in the Northern Virginia Writing Project (NVWP) at George Mason University. "This summer institute was in its infancy then," she recalls. "Of course, I had no way of knowing it would become one of the best in the country, but I couldn't wait to enroll. It seemed to me that my history students would benefit from the connections between clear thinking and clear writing—but I needed help in figuring out how to develop the linkage. Besides, even though I believed that my ideas about teaching and learning made sense, I needed to have them validated. I felt like such a loner back then." So secure is Bernadette Glaze now that she won't need to have her ideas validated again, even if she is initially a loner in the school district to which she recently transferred.

Within a few years' time, hundreds of Fairfax teachers completed NVWP's five-week summer institutes, where even veterans of fifteen or twenty years' standing learned for the first time how to write and how to teach writing. And hundreds of other teachers accomplished the same goal after choosing to enroll in after-school courses that the Fairfax County public schools began sponsoring. Here, too, Fairfax found a key to success: a school board, a superintendent of schools, and administrators who support new writing programs—but who don't impose them on teachers. In this environment, former "loner" Bernie Glaze became a spark plug of her district, a teacher of teachers and a teacher of students.

"I learned that the steps my high school juniors take to

develop their writing and the steps that their teachers take are really alike," Bernie observes, "not because anyone is following a formula, but because the process of writing has certain universal characteristics. Do you know anyone who has never crossed out lines? Who has never tossed crumpled-up papers into the basket? Never drawn arrows that lead to balloons in the margin? We were all drafting and revising before anyone coined the words. And, whether we knew it or not, we all viewed writing as a process, because that's exactly what it is. But anyone who expects schools to replace long-entrenched methods that don't work with these process steps that do, will have to exercise patience, patience, and *more* patience."

Neither the after-school credit courses, however, nor NVWP summer institutes fully explains how Fairfax has been able to reach so many teachers. Part of the answer lies in the informal ways in which teachers affect each other's style. Take the impact that Bonnie Geer, ninth-grade English teacher and grade-level team leader at Lake Braddock High School had on her colleagues when she sought an alternative to student writing that was typically directed at the teacher. Rejecting earlier methods, Ms. Geer arranged to have her freshmen write individual books for fourth-grade youngsters in Ravensworth Elementary School. The challenge of prewriting, drafting, and revising books for nine-year-old readers that began one October morning lasted for almost seven months—and its legacy lingers on.

When winter inched into early spring, Lake Braddock's authors sent their latest drafts to Ravensworth's readers, who in turn visited Ms. Geer's classroom in order to meet the authors, extend compliments, ask questions, and make occasional suggestions. The ninth-grade authors were so flattered by their new celebrity status that they didn't object to going through still another revision when necessary. "Besides," Bonnie Geer explained, "the kids had become really competent, secure writers by then, so they weren't unsettled by hearing that "there was too much description at the beginning" or "the clues you wrote helped me figure out the mystery too soon."

To cap the project, the ninth-graders bound the books between covers that they illustrated handsomely and had the satisfaction of seeing their names in the card catalogue of Ravensworth's library. Bonnie's added professional reward came when four ninth-grade teachers told her that they planned a similar project for the following year. "Three of these teachers had not shown much interest in writing as a process before," Bonnie Geer said. "They may have begun to give it serious thought when a hundred and twenty parents came to school to read the books. Or, perhaps, being the professionals that they are, they had to ask themselves whether their students would have spent months working on a single writing project of this sort. I'm pleased to think that I may have been an effective role model," she said, "but I'm also pleased to think that they came to their own conclusions."

The concept of writing for a real audience isn't limited to freshmen at Lake Braddock High School. Sophomores, for example, rewrote Geoffrey Chaucer's *Canterbury Tales* to make the book appealing to sixth-graders. Not content with "merely" rewriting this medieval classic for a young audience, each sophomore assumed the role of a Chaucer character, and the class traveled from school to school producing the drama in costume. The traveling players were the hit of the sixth grade and Chaucer was the hit of high school sophomores. Combining reading, writing, and drama added another dimension to the innovations that have a home in the Fairfax County school district.

Despite these success stories, even the strongest advocates of change realize that they can't rush pell-mell over the sensitivities of colleagues and citizens who are not yet ready to abandon old procedures. The cochairs of the English department of West Potomac High School, for example, know that the last draft a student writes always emphasizes correct grammar, usage, syntax, and sentence structure; these matters are an essential part of the process of writing. But co-chair Lea English also knows that anxious parents and reluctant teachers often worry that mechanics may be neglected by this "newfangled" method. To relieve these concerns, therefore, while still moving forward, Lea promised that writing teams would conduct special workshops in usage, punctuation, grammar, and other traditional areas to supplement the semester of writing that every one of the nineteen members of the English department teaches each year.

"After all," Lea reminded me, "we're asking parents to understand an entirely new system. When they went to school, the final copy—the *only* copy—was all-important and the steps leading up to it were ignored. Now one-third of our students' final grade is based on how their rough drafts took shape, one-third on their final copy, and another third on journal writing. That's quite a jump from the world that parents knew," she said. "If we want mothers and fathers to make such a mental leap, it seems to me that they are entitled to have us meet them halfway." In Lea English's opinion, the success of this forward-looking writing program rests heavily on whether parents understand how and why it differs from teaching that has never worked.

Wherever I spoke to teachers in Fairfax County schools who are championing the idea that writing is a gradual, painstaking process, I heard similar words: "If parents who look for perfection can begin to accept the idea of early drafts—spelling errors, punctuation mistakes, and all—our approach stands a chance," the message went. "We can promise mothers and fathers that papers will be edited for correct mechanics later, but we need them to promise that they will not fuss when we put first things first." The "first things" these teachers emphasize are fluent writing and ample revisions. That's a big "but" for any of us who learned

that error-free writing comes first, but unless parents encourage change, teachers will be shackled to failed methods.

Even the most innovative Fairfax English teachers know
that students will not succeed in taking standardized tests
unless they are prepared to handle conventional, time-
limited writing tasks. Since Bonnie Geer had so much success with her students' October to May writing project, I was
curious to see how she would manage to confine the same
class to a fifty-minute writing exercise. I found that she not
only stayed within a single class session, but also found a way
of linking literature and writing. Ms. Geer began the period
by asking students for adjectives to describe scenes from *The
Pigman,* a book by Paul Zindel that they had just finished
reading. In five minutes or so, she elicited a torrent of
words—*defiant, realistic, extravagant, serious, lonely, sad,
carefree, rebellious.* Next Ms. Geer told the students to think
of characters who were important to the plot, and the class
talked about people who moved the story line along. This
prewriting probably consumed fifteen minutes or slightly
more.

"Now you're ready to write a paper about *The Pigman,"*
Ms. Geer told her students. Without hesitation twenty-six
ninth-graders began writing topic sentences that identified
the character they had decided was pivotal and singled out
the adjective that best described the individual. There was
no time for writing a first draft, a revision, and a second draft,
but, realistically, there will seldom be that kind of time
under testing conditions. Even so, Ms. Geer had managed to
save five minutes for a volunteer to read her paper to the
class. The bell rang before anyone had sufficient chance to
respond to the reading, but this much seemed clear: there
was no sense of "saved by the bell," no scraping of chairs,
and no sighs of relief.

Ms. Geer's concise techniques are practical and the innovations are not threatening. Parents tend to approve of class
periods of this sort, too, but Open School Night gives teach-

ers an opportunity to show why fifteen-minute blocks of time are insufficient for writers who view their work as a painstaking process. English teacher Lin McKay had her eleventh-grade students take home the results of a scant beginning: ten or fifteen minutes of uncorrected "free writing" that focused on positive feelings for family. One student recalled the time he was hospitalized and his mother remained at his bedside; many wrote about memorable family vacations; even the most rebellious of these adolescents remembered a treasured occasion. Lin McKay chose the topic, not as a means of restoring bonds, but as a means of making mothers and fathers more open to understanding how these students now approach writing.

"The draft that the kids bring home isn't intended to be well organized," she told me. "In fact, it's downright messy. The 'madman' phase, as we call it, is well named, because free writing is a time to give every idea a chance to be heard, not a time to worry about planning and organization. I just wanted parents to try to understand the first step that their sons and daughters take all the time." Master strategist Lin McKay then arranged to have the parents come to school for a demonstration—in which *they* spent ten or fifteen minutes doing their own madman writing, sharing special memories with their children. "Parents were excited by rapid writing," Lin said, "and they understood, often for the first time, that no one can produce a complete and correct piece in a short block of time."

"Madman" is the first phase of a four-part metaphor for teaching writing devised by Betty S. Flowers, associate dean of graduate studies and associate professor of English at the University of Texas. Students know that after the "madman" writes freely and gets group responses, the "architect" takes over and develops shape and structure—first by working individually and later in small groups. In time, the "architect," whose sweeping plans have, in all probability, overlooked the importance of details, gives way to the "carpenter," who goes over the piece word by word, line by line—a process that also may require both individual and small-group craftsmanship. Finally, the "judge" enters the picture, with a critical eye. Realizing that the madman-architect-carpenter-judge formulation may sound simplistic, a student in a gifted and talented class acknowledged, "It's such a concrete way of thinking about the basic steps in writing as a process that I can't blame anyone who thinks the headings belong in elementary school. And I certainly agree that they can be too linear." Then the honor student admitted somewhat sheepishly, "But you know something? Madman-architect-carpenter-judge sure helps me." It helps parents, too.

Focusing on the "judge" aspect of the writing process, ninth-grade teacher Susan DiMaina places great importance on students' working toward the goal of fashioning work that they consider worthy of being published. "High school freshmen can see themselves in print in small ways or in big ways," she points out. "Between our class book and our high school magazine, the county literary magazine and one contest after another, there's a whole range of opportunities." One of her students had just won a major prize and twelve other students had their writing published in the county magazine. Susan was so excited that she sounded as if she had won a prize.

Like hundreds of other Fairfax teachers, she knows that there has to be a better way to teach writing than to require that every student begin an essay with a formal outline. "That works for some people," she agrees, "and they should certainly stick with what works for them. But it never worked for me. When I was in school, I had to write my essay and then go back and figure out that dratted "preliminary" outline as an afterthought. And I *still* can't outline initially, because I never know where my writing will take me." But that no longer hinders Susan DiMaina; instead she plunges into the madman stage, knowing full well that her architect will organize and shape her "mess" when it is time. In fact, like other teachers who have completed a summer at one of the National Writing Project sites, Susan writes more than ever. "If teachers don't write," she reasons, "how can we possibly understand the processes that students need to experience when they write?"

Fairfax County teachers whom students often admire have had a clear impact. Ask Kiet, a high school junior who says, "I keep a pen in my hand when I read each night's history chapters; I guess it's my way of getting ready to write a response. Actually, writing helps me understand whatever I read—and reading helps me develop whatever I write." Or talk to Eric, who, like others in his ninth-grade English class, is required to write four pages a day in his journal. "At first I used wider margins and bigger letters to beat the system," he admits. "Then I realized that when I kept writing, even though I thought I had nothing left to say, unexpected ideas had a way of breaking through; but when I stopped too soon, they never emerged."

Kiet's and Eric's reactions were not unusual. In one way or another, many students gave the same message: kids in traditional classes hate to write. Given the negative attitudes, I wondered why old methods linger. "That's easy to understand," a senior with a particularly mature perspective explained. "Some teachers confuse 'process' with progressive education," Sara said, "and some with creative writing. The confusion scares them off. They worry that we won't learn to improve our writing, unless a teacher grades assignments after we've handed them in." Heads nodded in agreement.

"If these teachers saw writing as a process," Brian said, "they would understand why our writing *has* to improve. When you get a grade after it's too late to change anything, you can't find better ways to express yourself. But when you have conferences with teachers and other students as soon as you're ready to show them an early draft, you have time to work through one revision after another. That's what I call 'improvement'!"

JOURNALS

Mary Kollar, chair of Washington State's Woodinville High School English department, is a published writer, a teacher-writer, and a leader in the Washington State Association of Teachers of English. She doesn't know Brian, but she does know that he is correct: the process of planning, drafting, revising, and editing improves writing. She takes that position in her own school and in other districts where she serves as a teacher consultant. In fact, Mary Kollar teaches her own students to become part archaeologist, part historian, part psychologist, and part writer so that they can keep what she calls a "process paper" and delve into what helps or hinders their writing. "I find it helpful to keep an entire process journal myself," she explains, "but that much writing can be too demanding of high school students."

While Mary Kollar believes that writing is a process, she knows that the process doesn't necessarily function in quite the same way for any two people. Consequently, writers have to discover what works best for them. "The most effective way to make that discovery," she tells her students, "is to keep a process journal or even to write a process letter and describe what you thought about and what you did before you actually completed a piece of work." How wise Mary Kollar is. It wasn't until I had kept my own process journal for three months that I discovered I was more comfortable when I stopped trying to squeeze myself into the "madman-architect-carpenter-judge" format, because the judge in me didn't want to be pushed aside until the end; I needed to evaluate my work as I went along. Actually, I was most at ease when I bypassed the madman altogether.

I found that some of my discoveries were even more surprising. I always knew, for example, that I was a "morning person"; but I didn't know that I could create two mornings in a single day. After the first one, which usually began by 7:30 A.M. and extended to noon, I would take a brief walk and enjoy a light lunch. Then, with my answering machine safeguarding me from telephone calls, I settled down for an uninterrupted nap. When I awakened fully refreshed at 2:30 P.M., I was ready for another "morning" of work and was able to summon the muse back for another long session at my word processor. My process journal demonstrated, however, that no matter how hard I tried, I simply couldn't create a third morning. Since my metabolism refused to be deceived again, my evening writing was never as effective as I would have wished. Yet until my process journal clarified my working pattern, I was only partially aware of the picture that emerged. After I started keeping detailed observations, I understood the importance of this unique journal that says, in effect, "Writer, know thyself."

Curiously, while other journals of various sorts are widely discussed in educational circles from the elementary grades to the university, the expression "process journal" is not yet the school equivalent of a household word. Mary Kollar first encountered the term and technique when she spent five weeks under Anne Ruggles Gere's direction at NWP's Puget Sound Writing Project. "I was one of the early fellows to enroll in the summer institute," Mary recalls. "I wanted to understand strategies that other teachers have found effective, and I hoped to be able to contribute something of worth, too. But nothing I gave," she claims, "could have mattered to others as much as learning how to keep track of my own writing process has mattered to me."

Mary Kollar is convinced that this "keeping track" has resulted in her having become a more assured and more frequently published writer. She also thinks that documenting the way one's own process works provides a concrete way of responding to people who still question whether analyzing process can lead to an improved product. "Some writers may find they do most of their prewriting in their heads, while other writers may find that they think better on paper. Some writers may have to revise as they go along while others are more comfortable postponing judgments. The point is," she says, "when writers explore the process that is best for them, they produce superior products—and a process journal gives evidence of the exploration."

To get her students started, Mary Kollar eschewed an actual journal and, like Leslee Reed in California and Nancie Atwell in Maine, decided to use a letter-writing technique. "After we finish a piece of work," a student in her senior English class explained, "Ms. Kollar wants us to write down as much as we can remember about our writing habits from the moment we first thought of an idea until we finally typed 'The End.' She said she wants us to study ourselves as writers, to become historians of our own writing. And she said no thought was too unimportant to mention." This student reporter was frankly embarrassed. "Imagine telling the teacher whether we had rock music going full blast when we were supposed to be prewriting, or if we waited until the last minute before even beginning. Imagine telling her how we felt about what we were writing. After all, sometimes they were *her* assignments. But she even was interested in stuff like if we started and stopped a lot—maybe for something to eat or drink—or if we wrote in long stretches."

"She told us that the whole idea was for us to discover what gives us the most satisfaction and what causes the most frustration in the way we go about writing," a second student explained. "She really wasn't a sadist trying to make us relive moments of misery, but a colleague trying to help us find out how we write best. I remember Ms. Kollar said something like, 'I promise you, there is no one best way; there is only *your* best way.' "

Despite Ms. Kollar's convincing presentation, some students balked at having to write this letter version of a process journal. "Don't we have enough writing to do without that?" one senior demanded. "If a paper is finally finished, it's finished," he asserted—until Ms. Kollar told him that it was not finished until she got the accompanying process letter that was part of each assignment. Once students found that their good-natured teacher took these process letters seriously, the last grumbling about "not wanting to waste time" died down.

Students' own attitudes changed after Ms. Kollar's seniors started writing process letters. Some of the reluctant dragons acknowledged that they had begun to think differently. "I found out that I write best when I work under the pressure of mini-deadlines that I set for myself," a lanky redhead said. "I'll mark a date on the calendar and say to myself, 'Okay, Red, by a week from Tuesday your research should be finished,' or 'That's the time to have worked through a complete first draft—or whatever.'"

The student sitting next to Red objected to his plan. "That's weird; I found out the exact opposite. If there's one thing my letters to Ms. Kollar showed me, it's that pressure blocks my thinking." Red and his seatmate were each right, just as Jan was right in discovering that she held herself back by thinking she couldn't begin an assignment until she had her opening paragraph worked through, while Larry was right in finding that if he started to write too soon, he encountered one false start after another. "You know something," one of the most vehement protesters finally acknowledged, "these letters really work. We each have our hang-ups and our own best ways of writing. But we can't change what *doesn't* work until we know what it is."

There is a growing expectation that English teachers concern themselves with student journal writing, but it is a rare football coach who shares that concern. The head coach at Woodinville High School is such a rarity. Every Monday morning in season he has the members of the team write about the joy or dismay they felt after the previous Saturday's game and analyze why certain tactics either worked well or went awry. And football players discover, perhaps to their own amazement, that writing can be a catharsis for expressing their feelings and a technique for clarifying their thinking, even for improving their playing. Still stung by an overtime defeat at the hands of Bellevue High, one player wrote, "This loss burns inside of me," and a teammate admitted, "These two losses are barely sufferable," and a third concluded, "Our desire was there, fate wasn't." The captain summed up part of the team's problem when he wrote, "The offense sputtered." Clearly, students who are recognized for physical prowess can express themselves powerfully—provided they are writing about something that matters to them. It is that proviso that gives journal writing of every variety its great strength.

Journals serve many purposes. Some, like the entries by Woodinville's football team, foster writing by connecting primarily with the writer's feelings. Dick Friss, chair of the English department at Northgate High School in Walnut Creek, California, is a strong believer in the worth of this kind of journal. For the past fifteen years, his students have begun each class by writing a journal entry. I'm impressed by their range of interests," he told me, "and I am even more impressed by their growth as writers. But I marvel most at how many issues they handle: parents doing drugs, working parents, insufficient attention—you name it." In Dick Friss's view, journals encourage particularly fluent writing by giving students an outlet for their feelings. And journals serve a further purpose of helping him get to know his students in ways that would otherwise be impossible.

Journals of this sort may be worthwhile, but parents and teachers still wonder about the need for privacy. If teachers don't read confidential entries, how will they know if students' writing is improving? And if teachers do read such entries, are they not intruding on personal family matters? The Boston Writing Project *Newsletter* proposed a solution to what seems to be a catch-22 situation: students may clip together any pages they do not want read. If students don't abuse the practice by separating out too much off-limits writing, their individual privacy can be respected, yet teachers will still be able to seek evidence of improved writing and expanded interests. It is an imperfect solution, to be sure, since parents may view matters as private that students do not. However, before the days when journal writing became popular, my students used to tell me about troubling family problems, too: unhappy marriages, alcoholic parents, and family skeletons of all sorts.

Toby Fulwiler avoids most of the pitfalls I have been discussing by placing journals on a continuum between diaries and class notebooks. Diaries, he explains, capture personal thoughts and experiences, while class notebooks record other people's facts and ideas. The journal, like the diary, is written in the first person, but the journal, like the class notebook, should, in Fulwiler's view, concern academic subjects the writer would like to know more about. Although this continuum offers a useful way of thinking about journal writing, it is treacherous to speak of *the* journal, just as it is unwise to speak of *the* writing process, because both defy any single interpretation that applies to all situations.

Nonetheless, Fulwiler caught a common thread that runs through a number of journals. He wrote that each entry essentially asks, "How accurately can I describe or explain this idea? How far can I take it?" In Fulwiler's words, "The journal demands that students expand their awareness of what is happening, personally and academically, to them." Taking a different stance, however, many high school teachers believe that journals demand nothing more than student honesty, or student rigor in writing regularly. Since most secondary schools that are attempting to introduce even a minimal writing program now include some kind of journal writing, let's focus on those schools and school districts that are extending writing in a variety of other ways.

THE FIRST STEP
IS ALWAYS THE HARDEST

For eight years Tom Romano thought he was a misfit in Edgewood High School in Trenton, Ohio. Like other teachers, he had been taught in high school and college to place a heavy emphasis on outlining, correctness, and what Tom calls "due on Friday" assignments. But, unlike most teachers, he was determined not to repeat the misguided format that he had seen result in what used to be his own half-realized, slipshod writing. "Many of us never jotted down our ideas before writing," he recalls, "and we never talked about our ideas with teacher and peers before or during writing. The closer we got to each ominous Friday, the more intimidated we became. Revision, of course, was simply unknown. In fact, one of my buddies wrote his English papers during first period, European History. He handed them in second period. And," Tom concluded, "we simply prayed that there wouldn't be too many mechanical errors so we could chuck the returned paper in the wastebasket and not have to recopy it."

Tom Romano never forgot his negative experiences. Consequently, he began allowing students who needed the time anywhere from two to four days of thinking and planning before they even had to create a draft. "Many kids were unaccustomed to doing the kind of writing that had them stretching my assignments and finding their own places, their own topics, their own approaches," Tom explained. He knew he often needed to devote the better part of a week to exploring good examples of satire or poetry, persuasive writing, or any other genre he was asking students to create; he also needed to use the time to discuss ideas that they were beginning to generate. "Most of my students had just written their first drafts when students in other classes were expected to submit their 'due on Friday' assignments."

In another break with tradition, Romano decided that

writing in class was not only permissible but mandatory. "When students write during class," he explained, "teachers can be sure that everyone experiences the fulfillment and excitement that comes from sustained writing. No telephone calls. No interruptions. Just an opportunity to make blank sheets of paper come alive. Besides," he reasoned, "in other craft disciplines students use class time to make music, paintings, sculpture, clothing, and cabinets. In writing class they should make writing." Like other teachers, Tom sometimes objects to conversation in class—but for a different reason. "I'm not concerned about anyone's interrupting *me*, because I'm not lecturing when students are writing drafts; I just want them to be able to concentrate fully on their own efforts. Besides, there's lots of time for talk later when we discuss each other's work."

Recalling the chuck-it-in-the-basket mentality from his high school days, Tom Romano has long believed in the importance of revision. "Writing is not live television," he emphasizes, "so writers can see their words as often as they need to to reshape what they want to say." And Romano is convinced that a teacher can rarely decide how much time a student needs to rethink, reevaluate, and ultimately rewrite his revised work. "If a writer is really working hard on revision, a 'due on Friday' deadline can get in the way—which means there's no way of deducting a grade for every day a paper is late." Consequently, by the time Romano's students have reached the important step where they are correcting errors of spelling, grammar, usage, and punctuation, students in other classes may be finishing their second "paper" (Tom Romano would call it a "draft") or beginning their third. "It wasn't easy being out of step with traditional teaching, but I had to march to the beat of a different drummer, no matter how alone I was."

The drumbeat that maverick Romano heard grew louder in 1981 when he enrolled as a summer fellow in the Ohio Writing Project at Miami University, and discovered that some teacher-writers scattered throughout Ohio thought as he did—and still does. Discovering this group of colleagues was a turning point in Romano's life and, as events developed, in the lives of Edgewood students. "Once I found that other people in my profession respected my ideas, I decided to see what I could do to influence some teachers in my own school," he told me, never thinking that he would go on to write a book that would influence teachers all over the United States. "Half of the members of the English department at Edgewood High School have been through the Ohio Writing Project," he said when his impact began to be felt, "and even more—probably three out of four—see error-free writing as their final, not their first, goal." And the primary goal? "To keep our students writing." The "misfit" had already come a long way.

No one at Edgewood High School lays claim to a soft berth; English teachers have six classes a day, and in almost every class some students demonstrate an "I dare you" attitude. Yet Tom found time to write his book *Clearing the Way*, and if he had his druthers, he would rather teach students who were not grouped according to ability, or "tracked." "It may be easier to teach the motorcycle crowd and the college crew separately," he observed, "but when you sacrifice diversity, you sacrifice liveliness, too. Besides, I don't like misleading students about who is supposedly smart and who is not."

Dwayne, a student Tom Romano featured in *Clearing the Way*, was part of the motorcycle group. "Nobody's gonna get me to write nothing," he announced at the beginning of the year, fearing that his poor spelling and the teacher-assigned topics would be his downfall again. That was five drafts before he finished his first piece on motorcycles. When Dwayne compared later writing in his folder with that initial attempt, he concluded, "Why look at that, that ain't nothin'." But, convinced that it was essential for Dwayne to keep writing, Tom Romano helped him see something in each paper. True, the motorcycle composition had more than its share of mistakes, but they would be worked on during the year. More important, Dwayne had improved his writing with each revision and, acting on the suggestions of his classmates, had managed to remove an abrasive tone, while retaining his vigor:

> Well, this is for all you Honda riders. Before you say that Honda is the best, ride a Kawasaki (KX). Kawasaki has the best suspension, called Uni Track.
> When you ride a Kawasaki it is easy to go threw ruts and groves, just like flowing Water. They don't Bounce around and make it hard to control.
> It diffently has power. . . .

"If I accepted incorrect spelling and punctuation on a final copy," Tom Romano said, "Dwayne would be ill-served, because writing conventions matter. But if I had been too discouraging at first, Dwayne would still believe that he had nothing to say, and his writing would be skimpy, stilted, and probably incorrect in the bargain. What's true for Dwayne is true for every student."

During all the years that Tom Romano felt he was out there alone, he was edging toward writing as a process. In a suburb of Birmingham, Alabama, on the other hand, an English teacher named Peggy Swoger was somehow accommodating to the regulations of a conservative suburban school district where students' papers were automatically graded C if they had three minor errors and F if they had one major mistake. "You can imagine what that did to their desire to write, can't you?" she asked. "But we're changing." What she neglected to say is that she has coaxed, encouraged, wheedled, supported, and led that change every step of the way.

It all began in the summer of 1982 when Peggy Swoger enrolled as a summer intern in Alabama's Sun Belt Writing

Project at Auburn University, another NWP site. "Once I learned that there are far, far better ways to teach writing," she recalls, "it never occurred to me that it would take three years to begin to convince others. I should have known that change comes slowly," she says. "After all, I had been teaching for fourteen years and the first really innovative practice I had seen in all that time was viewing writing as the process it is."

Now, in her multiple roles as English teacher and department chair at Mountain Brook (Alabama) Junior High School, and one of ten members of the National Writing Project's advisory board, Peggy Swoger has a clearer picture of the impact one person can have on a school system. "When you create a well-informed team that begins at the superintendent level and includes principals from elementary school to senior high, plus a parent writing representative, you've got the makings of fine local support," she says.

Peggy is wise enough to know that change requires faculty commitment and is persuasive enough to have achieved it from the first. After working full days, twenty-nine teachers chose to spend four hours every Tuesday evening for ten weeks with Dick Graves, trying to learn what "process" is all about. (Dick Graves directs the Sun Belt Writing Project.) "Perhaps the most encouraging sign," Peggy Swoger notes, "occurred when I asked teachers in the first year of change what innovations they wanted to drop the next year. The answer? *None.*"

More encouragement followed. Since parents wanted a big push for a fuller use of the library, it was "a natural step," Peggy recalls, to develop a team of English, math, science, and social studies teachers who had expressed interested in writing. That step led to a deeper interest in discovering how thinking skills are incorporated in writing. "The more we learned, the more we saw that we didn't know enough about how people in other disciplines think," she said. The next "natural step" was to have the school district fund a one-week institute and arrange for two authorities to work with twenty-five teachers eight hours a day.

These teachers were paid to attend," Peggy Swoger says, "but another thirty-five teachers get no stipend for meeting regularly to discuss ways to develop writing workshops. Commitment like that is rare." True, but Peggy provides a role model. In addition to her work in the classroom, in the school district, and on NWP's advisory board, she serves as president-elect of the Alabama Council of Teachers of English, and on the board of directors of the National Board for Professional Teaching Standards. "That last item is a mouthful, isn't it?" she asks. "But you know we're trying to do important work when the presidents of the NEA [National Education Association] and the AFT [American Federation of Teachers] sit on the board, too."

CHARLOTTE-MECKLENBERG, NORTH CAROLINA

In 1985 Dr. Jay Robinson, then superintendent of schools in Charlotte-Mecklenberg, the largest school district in the two Carolinas combined, faced a quandary. He found the twenty-five teacher-consultants who completed the University of North Carolina/Charlotte Writing Project's summer institute each year to be outstanding, but he wanted to transform the thinking of 4,000 teachers and 76,000 students. To turn a system of that size around, Dr. Robinson needed to prepare hundreds of teachers to lead the way. Feeling the urgency of that need, iconoclast Jay Robinson decided to overrule those who caution educators to proceed slowly. Instead, he set out to chart his own course for the district.

In an attempt to produce quantity and quality, Superintendent Robinson, now a vice president of the University of North Carolina system, arranged for the school district to collaborate with the university and develop an abbreviated version of a summer institute. With too many teachers to turn into "team leaders" (400) and too little time (fifty hours condensed into two weeks), Charlotte-Mecklenberg's attempt at introducing writing process into the classroom "shouldn't" have worked—yet it has gotten off to a promising start. And with other teachers' being *required* to attend after-school training programs run by high-school-based neophyte team leaders the district's in-service training should have failed dismally. Yet Charlotte-Mecklenberg's writing across the curriculum can already serve as a national model.

At first it was hard to imagine how writing might apply to as unlikely a subject as algebra, but Myers Park High School mathematics teacher Beth Webb found classroom strategies, thanks to the summer program. In fact Beth Webb became so excited about the role of writing in teaching mathematics that she started what is known in Charlotte-Mecklenberg as an "action growth plan"; hers is entitled, "Using Writing to Learn in Algebra." Once students adjusted to the idea of writing in their math class, they weren't the least surprised to hear Ms. Webb begin a lesson by telling them, "Let's say that a new student has transferred to Myers Park, and he hasn't studied prime numbers before. Do you think you can write a clear explanation of them for him?" After about five minutes on the day that prime numbers were being reviewed in this way, a single voice broke through the sound of pencils scratching on paper. "Ma'am," a puzzled young man said, "I just found out that I can't explain prime numbers." He gulped. "I guess I don't really understand them myself. I thought I did, but I'm afraid I didn't get it."

"That's one of the reasons we write, Jim," his teacher reassured him. "It helps us find out what we know and what we don't. Remember when I asked all of you to write down everything you knew about factoring? Since we hadn't begun to study it, some of you simply wrote, 'I don't know anything.' And that was fair enough. Then, two weeks later, I said, 'Tell me everything you know about factoring now,' and you were able to see how much you had learned. If you check your learning log, Bob, you'll see that when we finally finished the entire unit, I asked you one last time to write everything you had learned about factoring—and most of you were amazed to see the difference among your three entries. If someone didn't see enough difference, it simply meant some more teaching and learning were in order. Writing to learn makes sense, doesn't it?"

For Beth Webb, teaching more effectively is a powerful reward, but gaining insight into her students' anxieties and accomplishments is also rewarding. "Keeping learning logs is a way my students and I see what they've learned," Beth Webb later explained, "and keeping journals is a way for students to express their feelings about learning math—or about being overwhelmed by concepts they couldn't grasp. Since logs and journals serve different purposes, my students write entries in both without a word of complaint, and I make discoveries in each." She found, for example, that students who have more trouble with algebra like keeping journals. "They feel they can show a little of what they *do* know, while tests only seem to ferret out what they *don't* know," she explained. "Once I learned this I knew I needed to give more thought to how I should construct tests."

History teacher Kay Nolan, a member of the writing team at Independence High School, Charlotte-Mecklenburg, is as committed to using writing in content areas as Beth Webb is. "If there's a better way to discover the way in which eleventh- and twelfth-graders' minds work, I have yet to find it," Kay said, as she introduced me to one of her favorite strategies for linking thinking, writing, and learning. "Take the time we studied the Revolution, and I wanted my students to look at political decisions from a number of different perspectives. To help them get beyond a simple us-and-them stance, and to help them appreciate the wealth of knowledge they have to draw upon when they write their next essay, I brought in different colored Murray cards." She explained that each "Murray card" stood for a different point of view. "One card represented a colonial merchant and one a British merchant, a third card spoke for a loyalist, a fourth for a revolutionary, and so on. Students began writing from one viewpoint, but every three minutes I changed to a different-colored Murray card, and they changed perspectives.

"This exercise," Kay Nolan continued, "is a form of brainstorming to generate ideas. By doing rapid 'free writing,' they're off and running. Later, they select the card that evoked their best thinking and decide upon the essay that each wants to write. No one faces the old 'I have no ideas' quandary, because everyone has had an amazing outpouring in three-minute spurts. I've taught the Revolutionary period many times before, but I've always felt I was telling my students what to think, really, what to memorize. This time their writing enabled them to reconstruct events for themselves and history came alive."

Adapting another activity from an idea that Independence High School's six-member writing team had developed for teachers in every department, Kay turned the so-called object lesson into a favorite project in social studies and writing. She told each student to bring an object to class that made a statement about contemporary society. "Some came with McDonald's boxes," she told me, "and a few students brought in floppy disks; this was one time when there were no missing homework assignments." But this was no kindergarten show-and-tell session. It was a mix of anthropology, sociology, history, and writing.

Students shared the objects and discussed what they implied about the United States in the late 1980s. After the class divided into groups and placed the assorted objects on tables, Kay Nolan threw out her challenge: "Suppose that society has been destroyed in some cataclysmic event, and this is all that remained. It is your job to write an account of the lost society, basing your conclusions on the objects before you." Clearly, the complex set of teaching objectives was geared for high school students. "What's really interesting," Kay Nolan later pointed out, "is that teachers can vary this lesson for classes as different as cosmetology and Latin, phys. ed. and chemistry."

Department by department, Charlotte-Mecklenburg's commitment to writing across the curriculum was apparent. Dean Johns, for example, was named Art Educator of the Year, in no small measure because of the connections he made between writing and other media, and, in my opinion, Betty Lowery deserved a comparable award in Business English. At least, I've never heard of Business English students who have written about the feelings they experienced when they donated blood, or, conversely, about their feelings when they decided not to give blood. "I don't want my students to be limited to taking dictation," their Garinger High School teacher explained, "and I don't want to turn out a bunch of robots with excellent keyboard skills and untapped brain power." Nor will she.

If there is a strategy for introducing writing across the curriculum, you may be certain that some Charlotte-Mecklenburg teachers are already trying it out. A wrestling champion is as likely to write a learning log about new holds he has learned as a Latin student is to discuss a lesson on English words that are derived from Latin roots. An industrial arts junior may plan a complex project he had begun to discuss in class, while an advanced science student may describe her reactions to the appearance and functions of the major organs of a guinea pig she has dissected. But a learning log is not a fancy description for taking notes or copying the teacher's outline. Students who keep a log put unfamiliar information in their own words and link it to what they already know. As one teacher put it, "Learning logs sneak up on writing. They bypass writer's anxiety." Before students know what is happening, they find themselves writing to learn—and learning to write.

A cautious admirer of writing in Charlotte-Mecklenberg says, "The jury is still out. Teachers are *saying* the right things; the question is, Are they *doing* the right things, too?" The same may be said of many innovative writing programs. But this much is certain: the jury has returned a guilty verdict on teaching methods that don't work.

Some new methods have begun to work exceptionally well in school districts in various parts of the state of Mississippi. These innovations stemmed from what had appeared to be an overly ambitious summer program in 1987. The goal of the Mississippi State Department of Education was to use a write-to-learn curriculum with sixteen- to twenty-one-year-old students and dropouts that would result in their achieving an eight-month gain in reading and math skills in an eight-week, half-day program. Instead, at summer's end, the combined reading and math test scores of 1,183 participants showed a gain of *three years and six months!*

"The fact that so large a gain was needed in the first place was an indictment of methods that schools rely on," observed Dr. Sandra Burkett, director of the NWP Writing/ Thinking Project at Mississippi State University, and designer of the writing-to-learn summer school program. The April-to-June planning time was certainly short, but Dr. Burkett thought through units that both remained close to students' interests and combined reading, writing, and math.

In responding to the first theme, "Who am I?," students who were already mothers wrote about that experience, dropouts who considered themselves failures wrote about their feelings, others discussed their roles as older sister, younger brother, foster child. Since authors often explore the question of identity, Dr. Burkett was also able to direct her students' interests to a variety of "Who am I?" books for this topic. And arithmetic became equally important when students started weighing and measuring themselves and using the results to plot graphs, add and subtract, multiply and divide, even to apply ratios and percentages to their findings.

Sandra Burkett was pleased when her subsequent themes, beginning with "Remembering People" and ending with "Mississippi Places," contributed to improved student skills, but she said she was actually troubled to find that some former dropouts had became so excited by learning that they said they might return to school. "I was afraid they would be returning to the very programs that had caused them to leave school in the first place," she explained. Sandra Burkett worries less now because the Mississippi State Department of Education has recommended the writing-to-learn curriculum to school districts throughout the state, and has required that interested teachers receive in-service training. To Dr. Burkett's satisfaction, that training is being provided by the Mississippi State University NWP project that she directs.

Anyone who remembers that primary school new math and high school new physics grabbed hold for a few years and then disappeared may wonder if reforms in the way we look at writing will last. Though not offering firm predictions, Harvard University's renowned professor Courtney Cazden says that no change in her memory has excited the imagination in the ways that writing has. "It is the only area I know of," she told me, "with so many lively ideas and so many excellent teachers who are also excellent writers and researchers." They are still not the majority, but teachers who have adopted new ways to encourage writing are not likely to revert to earlier methods. The enthusiasm in their classrooms supports more change, not less.

Nonetheless, parents and teachers who were raised on skill and drill understandably find it easier to stay with the familiar than to venture further. *The decision to change philosophies rests with us. To create a generation of writers, teachers need to give students opportunities to write and parents need to support these efforts.* Isn't that self-evident? Not always, unfortunately. But opportunities abound when students use journals and learning logs, when teachers embrace writing across the curriculum, and when parents and teachers understand that writing is a process that begins with struggle and works through to rich content and correct mechanics.

6

TESTING—GOOD
NEWS AND BAD

IRECTIONS: SELECT THE ANSWER THAT BEST COMPLETES EACH STATEMENT, AND WRITE THE LETTER BEFORE IT IN THE SPACE PROVIDED AT THE RIGHT.

1. An objective test consistently (A) asks fair and impartial questions (B) provides an inexpensive and accurate way of assessing student aptitude (C) combines speed and thoroughness (D) none of the above _____

2. When professional testers say a test is "reliable," they mean it (A) is valid (B) accomplishes its purpose (C) satisfies the standards applied by experts in measurement (D) none of the above _____

3. The primary purpose of a standardized test is (A) to set the ground rules for uniform questions (B) to give teachers and students feedback to improve instruction and learning (C) to foster a national curriculum (D) none of the above _____

4. Students will get higher scores if they (A) probe multiple-choice questions critically (B) avoid guessing (C) focus on the ambiguities embedded in some items (D) none of the above _____

5. A valid test (A) is reliable (B) deals with facts, rather than judgments (C) uses scientifically proven measurements (D) none of the above _____

6. A test that is objective, properly standardized, valid, and reliable will, by its very nature, be (A) thorough (B) accurate (C) desirable (D) none of the above _____

Many of the questions on the more than 100 million commercially developed tests that elementary and secondary school pupils have to take each year are as baffling as the six homemade items on the test that I designed. One major difference, however, is that you will find the right answers at the beginning of the next paragraph, whereas students never see the acceptable responses to conventional standardized tests. But the similarities between multiple-choice items on professionally designed tests and the above sample can outweigh the differences. Both give cause for grave concern. If you found yourself wanting to write marginal comments to qualify your answers ("but . . .," "except when . . .," "what if . . ."), you discovered that this format makes no allowances for such distinctions. Yet at best, the options posed are deceptive, for test developers design questions that confuse people with alternative answers (called distractors) that are plausible but not acceptable. At worst, the format does a serious disservice to education, for it rewards the right answer but ignores the value of underlying thinking.

If you happen to have answered each of the six questions with a (D) to indicate "none of the above," you got a perfect score—even if you got it for the wrong reason. But if you chose different answers through a process of elimination, your reasoning would be disregarded. And if you made the mistake of mulling over words as some of the brightest students do, you paid the price of deliberating too much. Test-wise students succeed on narrow assessments of achievement by steering away from too much thinking, and test-wise teachers resign themselves to drilling the answers to routine questions. Since the multiple-choice format prevents test developers from probing deeply, standardized tests that have been reduced to "covering" trivia are bad news, indeed.

The good news is that a movement is afoot to develop tests worth giving. Nowhere is this more evident than in assessments of writing. Instead of narrow tests that squelch this part of the curriculum, these innovative tests are supporting and enhancing it. Perhaps the most dramatic sign of change lies with the Educational Testing Service (ETS) in Princeton, New Jersey. A pioneer in the industry since the 1940s, ETS is probably best known for giving the traditional SAT, at the request of colleges and universities. To serve elementary and secondary schools, however, ETS is developing a vastly different generation of close-to-the-classroom tests.

Those who know ETS are familiar with its practice of inviting teachers to come to Princeton to review test questions and assess the answers. Now, however, some ETS test developers are going into classrooms to observe students' writing during the year. Teachers set the goals and collaborate with ETS researchers in developing assessments. Indeed, ETS research staff and local teachers in California, Maryland, Rhode Island, New York City, and Pittsburgh see themselves as partners who are seeking ways to link testing and instruction. These tests and others that are emerging in school districts—most notably, in Ann Arbor, Michigan, and in fifty-six schools that have formed a unique coalition—reflect a dramatic breakthrough.

The assessments I have seen are asking a key question that applies across the curriculum: Does the test show if students are learning what classroom teachers are teaching? "We've come to see that you can't talk about assessment without talking about instruction," Mary Fowles, examiner in test development at ETS, explained. "How schools teach writing and how they appraise it are intimately related. Instead of going along with a 'that's how testing has always been' viewpoint, the question that is gaining currency asks, 'How can we tell if you're talking about good teaching unless we see how students perform on good tests that reflect classroom practice?' "

To answer the question, innovative educators and evaluators have joined together to design "prompts" or writing tasks, administer them, score the responses in ways that satisfy measurement specialists, and return the results to the people who can use them to improve learning: teachers and students. This is no small accomplishment. By contrast, large-scale standardized tests are machine-graded and the scores of questionable worth are shipped to officials far from the classroom, who sort and rank the statewide and district-wide results. Their effect is to exclude some students from promotion and from high school graduation rather than to educate all students.

So much number crunching takes place in the name of assessment that American children may be, as some scholars contend, among the most frequently tested but the least thoughtfully evaluated students since the invention of machine grading. Teachers know this, but conventional standardized testing holds them in its grip, too. It fell to Albert Shanker, president of the American Federation of Teachers, to remind instructors who "teach to the test" and neglect other content that "Tolstoy didn't write skill sheets." But Tolstoy didn't live in an upside-down world of large-scale assessments so he had no need to fill in the blanks as a way of memorizing correct mechanics. The format of machine-graded, standardized tests didn't dictate the questions that could be asked. The questions didn't dictate the contents of textbooks. And neither tests nor texts dictated the curriculum. Now every subject suffers, but writing suffocates.

Taking time away from writing and revising, from reading and discussing, English and language arts teachers often spend hours, days, even weeks, coaching students in strategies for recognizing the "least worse" response to short-answer questions. And instructors of other subjects find themselves in a similar bind. To allow time for reviewing tricks that may stir sluggish memories into recalling dates, data, and formulas, teachers tend to skim the surface of some parts of the curriculum and crowd other parts out of the schedule altogether. The energy expended in helping students excel in narrow areas of learning seems pointless—until you realize that a few digits in large-scale test scores can brand the reputation of a school district from its classrooms and principals to its boardroom and superintendent.

Peter J. A. Evans leveled strong criticism at most assessments when serving as director-at-large and evaluator of the Canadian Council of Teachers of English. He compared the traditional use of blunt testing instruments to make fine measurements with a doctor's use of an ax instead of a scalpel. Unfortunately, as Evans pointed out, many teachers and administrators "believe somehow that these instruments are scientific, fair, and (blessedly) objective, and in that ignorance have convinced their local public that the school is really doing its job."

The fallout from false measurements is widely apparent. Some school systems use annual scores to determine a teacher's pay; others have dismissed their superintendents because neighboring districts achieved higher scores. At a time when every excess dollar is being squeezed out of the budget (and when "frills" such as librarians, remedial reading teachers, and writing specialist may be considered excessive), many school districts have put a full-time testing specialist on the payroll. A Colorado school district has set aside $450 in prize money for students with the highest or most improved scores; a Virginia district scheduled pretest rallies with teachers dressed as cheerleaders, and another district in the state had cheery yellow slogan buttons for all faculty members to wear during testing. All of this, of course, is added to the toll that skewed preparation has already exacted on learning.

To explain his concerns about the impact of standardized tests in Canada—an impact comparable to that in the fifty states—Hayden L. Leaman, professor of English education at the University of New Brunswick, recalled his boyhood in a Bay of Fundy village. Local fisherman, he said, were wary of the uniformly false weights and judgments that buyers used to "evaluate" different kinds of fish. "I have inherited the skepticism of these fishermen about assessment," Leaman observed, "but like them I do not reject the necessity, even the desirability, of assessing the product of the labor of a student, a teacher, or a school. *I simply ask that the measurer, the measure, and the method of measuring suit the fish* [emphasis added]." To that request, Professor Leaman added a corollary request: that "those who judge be aware of the effects of their judgments—the impact on teachers and their students."

Dr. Rexford Brown had eleven years of experience developing tests for the National Assessment of Educational Progress before he became director of communications and senior policy analyst for the Education Commission of the States. Immersed in the frustration of colleagues who are introducing the good news in testing writing, Brown recently explained:

> We want to develop writing tests, for instance, that honor the practice of writing sufficiently to require writing samples, that honor managers enough to give them their numbers, and that honor the needs of teachers to give them instructional advice. In doing so, we're constantly being criticized: we are not collecting *real* writing; we are not collecting *enough* writing; we aren't collecting *finished* writing; we're wasting money collecting *any writing at all.* . . .

Distressing reactions, yes; but the need for improved testing is so evident that these outcries have not slowed down the quest for new assessments. The public clearly needs tests that will inform—not misinform—parents and nonparents alike on what they are getting in return for spending up to $300 billion a year on their schools. Teachers and students need tests that will strengthen learning, especially tests that address the practice of writing. And policymakers need tests that will highlight promising practices that warrant further support. Conventional assessments that consume teaching time with drilling sessions are not the answer. But when real estate brokers, parents, and professional educators ask, "How do our school district's scores compare with ———'s?" you know they have the mistaken idea that these results provide a report card on the quality of a school system.

They do no such thing, and traditional writing achievement examinations do it least of all. Though excellent evaluations and excellent education are natural allies, excellent assessments are in short supply. And multiple-choice examinations are virtual enemies of any classroom whose teacher takes writing seriously. Yet one school district after another, indeed, one state legislature after another, has rushed to win civic approval by mandating the assessment of ill-defined skills through ill-considered tests.

The mandate won't work. Community leaders and public officials (many of whom are parents themselves) crave an uncomplicated score, but writing, thinking, and learning are too complicated to be treated casually. The most thoughtful innovators have found that assessments are complicated business—complicated and challenging because of the impact that evaluation and education have on each other. It is no accident that schools that hold conventional standardized test scores in high regard tend to take little note of thinking and reasoning. These subtle abilities defy measurement instruments that assume there is only one correct answer to every question posed.

The solution? Since conventional tests have encouraged the break between thinking and writing, there is reason to believe that a new kind of testing can undo the damage.

Reformers who accuse teachers of "teaching to the test" have objected to seeing tests drive the curriculum because they charge that education is demeaned by a focus on skill and drill. But "teaching to the test" would elevate education if it meant that assessments can encourage teachers to reunite higher-order thinking and writing.

Devising such tests has been a challenge. Throughout most of the 1970s, state writing achievement tests required—indeed, permitted—no student writing. As a result, replacing machine-graded A-B-C-or-none-of-the-above answer sheets with tests that sought some evidence of student writing achievement was considered a significant reform when Maryland led the way in 1978. By 1981, twenty-four states were conducting new assessments that included at least one writing sample, and by the mid-1980s twenty-seven states had taken their first significant steps forward—for a beginning. It is easy to find fault with tests that required students to produce a brief writing sample on what may have been an unfamiliar subject. But it is important to know that once writing was being assessed, however minimally, some teachers began to devote time to a part of the curriculum they had neglected.

Not every new state assessment of writing eliminated short-answer items, but some test reformers expressed serious reservations about "objective" questions that purport not to reveal the examiner's personal opinion. No matter how many times students may have heard a teacher announce an "objective test" on the causes of the Civil War, major events in Mozart's life, or vocabulary definitions, the fact remains *there is no such thing as an objective test.* The much-abused term refers to the method of scoring, not to the test itself. An objective test is simply one that can be scored by a machine or by individuals—even by children—who make no judgment about the acceptability of a response. The test developer has already done that, subjectively.

The "objective," multiple-choice tests can be riddled with shortcomings. As Mitchell Lazarus pointed out in 1976 in the journal *The National Elementary Principal,* they can be "ambiguous, wrong-headed, open to argument, even downright erroneous in the answers [counted] as correct." To drive the point home, Lazarus composed a nonsensical example that is free from bias—and free from common sense:

How tall was Macbeth?
a) 4 gallons
b) 3 pounds
c) 6 acres
d) 2 hours

No test maker would knowingly lampoon an item as Lazarus did, but, in the guise of objectivity, questions on a multiple-choice writing achievement test can include alternatives that, in their own way, are also irrelevant. Irrelevant, that is, when it comes to writing achievement, but right on target when it comes to conveying a message about spelling, punctuation, and curriculum content that test developers consider important. Responding to that message, schools emphasize or minimize whatever will be tested.

The concern (some say, overconcern) that measurement specialists have with "reliability" supports the use of multiple-choice tests. You and I would probably say that reliable tests determine whether students are competent readers, writers, mathematicians and such. But psychometricians define a reliable test as one that produces predictable outcomes whenever the same instrument is used. The key to reliability, in other words, is consistency—even if a test consistently provides inappropriate results. "If we have a yardstick measuring thirty-seven inches and use that yardstick repeatedly to measure a yard," Dr. Gertrude Conlon has explained in "'Objective' Measures of Writing Ability," a chapter in *Writing Assessment: Issues and Strategies,* "we have an exceedingly reliable measuring instrument in that we get the same results every time we use it: it always measures thirty-seven inches. It is not a *valid* instrument [emphasis added], however, since our goal is to measure a yard, which is thirty-six inches. A thirty-seven-inch yardstick is not measuring what it is supposed to measure."

Nor, common sense suggests, does a short-answer test of writing achievement measure what it is supposed to measure. Traditional writing achievement tests whose feedback resembles the thirty-seven-inch yardstick are reliable in psychometric terms but invalid nonetheless. Reforms in testing tell a different story—a story furthered by classroom teachers who also serve as test developers. To see an early example of teachers in this role look to South Carolina. In 1979 the state's Writing Committee was formed to devise a "T&T" ("teaching and testing") assessment. To make certain that teachers would play a role in evaluation just as evaluation plays a role in instruction, the Writing Committee included teachers from every grade level who worked with curriculum specialists, university faculty members, and State Department of Education staff. Teacher influence showed clearly when the committee rejected any attempts to develop multiple-choice items, contending that they would foster the classroom tendency to devote undue attention to grammar. Instead, teachers and their colleagues turned to writing as a process, and developed (and later revamped) the assessment that they first administered and scored in 1981.

The good news in testing has been advancing at such a clip that assessment in the entire state of California has been transformed. The California Assessment Program (CAP) had been administering annual tests of writing achievement since 1972. The old multiple-choice format had struck its advocates as heaven-sent for a large state with a growing population. Inexpensive to administer and quick to score, the assessment reassured many that neither time nor money would be wasted on evaluation. But when the National Assessment of Educational Progress reported in *Writing: Trends Across the Decade, 1974–1984,* that the performance of national samples of students it had been testing was distressingly poor, some California educators were shocked into realizing that they knew virtually nothing about the quality of their own students' writing.

The combined efforts of the members of a newly formed statewide Writing Assessment Advisory Committee resulted in almost 300,000 eighth-graders' taking a vastly different state writing assessment in the spring of 1987. Together, teachers, testers, curriculum specialists, and administrators produced another set of tests in December 1988 that CAP administered to some 250,000 high school seniors. By the spring of 1989, the entire sixth grade was also slated to experience the impact of new assessments, to be followed finally by the state's third-grade youngsters. Testing of this magnitude is no minor event. The combined enrollment of the four grades that will be tested in this new large-scale assessment exceeds the entire population of eleven states. Spurred on by size and scope, the designers of the new achievement tests expect to find out how well California students' writing reflects teaching practices that began with the Bay Area Writing Project and then spread to sixteen other writing project sites that comprise the California Writing Project.

The members of the Writing Assessment Advisory Committee agreed that they wanted students to submit substantial evidence of their ability to write. Believing that a test that allots as little as nine-minute segments for writing, as one prominent assessment was doing, was comparable to a math examination that asks only one question, California's Writing Assessment Advisory Committee chose to allocate a then-unheard-of forty-five minutes for writing and another fifteen minutes for going over the directions. (In 1988 the criticized test eliminated the nine-minute time slot and now allows at least fifteen minutes for writing.)

Agreeing again, the committee voted to have teachers

assume a pivotal role. As a result, fourteen members of the twenty-person team that designed the prompts or writing tasks and later conducted the summer readings of papers were teacher consultants who had developed advanced skills at the California Writing Project. Eighty-four other graduates conducted the initial field testing of proposed prompts. Well schooled in approaches that originated with BAWP and eager to introduce writing into social studies, science, and literature, teachers set clear criteria for the prompts they wanted to try out. "We had hundreds of tasks in mind at the beginning," said Mary Ann Smith, director of the Bay Area Writing Project, "but we wound up with handfuls."

Student scores were expected to reflect how well they understood classroom instruction, and, for the first time in their careers, teachers had an opportunity to be prepared to "teach to the test" in the best possible way. California's Department of Education sponsored two-day training workshops in which over half of the state's nearly fifteen thousand eighth-grade teachers enrolled. Their instructors? Fellow teachers, 380 of whom were graduates of the California Writing Project. At the workshops teachers learned that California was going to be concerned with maximum ability in eight types of writing:

1. autobiographical incident—narration of a specific occurrence in the writer's life
2. firsthand biography—characterization via incidents and description of a significant person in the writer's life
3. eyewitness memoir—recollection of a person, group, or event that was objectively observed
4. report of information—selection of data from observations and research to explain a concept
5. analysis—speculation about the effects of a specific event
6. problem solution—description and analysis of a specific problem, with proposal and argument for a solution
7. evaluation—judgment on the worth of a book, film,

piece of art. Writer must support the evaluation with reasons and evidence.

8. story—demonstration of a central conflict between characters or between a character and the environment. May be either third or first person, may include dialogue and description.

Not every student would be responding to every topic. Indeed, in a classroom of thirty or thirty-five test takers, no two writers would address the same prompt, although each student would compose a forty-five-minute essay. With large numbers of students throughout the state taking the test, this kind of "matrix sampling" provides a more complete achievement pattern than could emerge when everyone answers the same topic. The results would show whether students were more adept in reporting information, for example, in autobiographical writing, or in arguing for solutions to solve problems. (According to California researchers, this method is considered more statistically accurate than conventional assessments that have all students responding to identical writing tasks.)

Finally, in contrast to "writing" for a machine or for no one but the teacher, students would be instructed to direct their responses to a variety of hypothetical audiences: teachers, students in other classes, overseas pen pals, the PTA bulletin, the principal, family members, stockholders, friends, judges of a contest, the School Improvement Committee, a young people's magazine, the editor of their hometown newspaper, and at least half a dozen other readers. All told, the Writing Assessment Advisory Committee had devised ways of replacing multiple-choice tests with more substantive material.

There would be no directions telling students when to break the seal on their test booklets and lift their No. 2 pencil from the desk. Nor would teachers be keeping a watchful eye to prevent copied answers, for there would be no multiple-choice alternatives to copy. At the same time that one test taker might be following instructions to write a story about a character who does something that results in an unexpected ending, someone else might be writing a letter to a friend in 1774, describing events that have made many colonists want to revolt. And a third student might be recalling an autobiographical incident, using clues from the directions to help him focus on how the incident developed, and on how he became actively involved.

Consider the guidelines that enabled teachers to score more than 282,000 student essays without having to resort to personal opinions. The teachers who assembled at four regional sites in California (Los Angeles, Sacramento, San Diego, and Walnut Creek) scored each essay three times on a graduated scale. First, using a low of 1 and a high of 6, they evaluated rhetorical effectiveness, which simply means the extent to which the overall essay fulfilled a writer's purpose and met the reader's expectations. Using the same rating, they considered "general writing features," which include skills that are common to all types of writing. (Was the essay clear, lucid, coherent? Was the focus sharp? The elaboration interesting?) And to relieve the concerns of educators who wanted to be certain that writing mechanics were not overlooked, each essay was evaluated a third time (on a scale of 1 to 4) for correct conventions.

Does this mean that a well-trained team of teachers can always be as reliable as a computer? Not likely, even when evaluators have scoring guidelines that spell out the characteristics to look for before giving a paper a numerical rating. Not likely, in fact, when the guidelines are adjusted for every type of writing. But when carefully trained scorers consult well-defined criteria, the tests are statistically reliable. What's more, they are *valid* evaluations of writing—a claim that cannot be made for the multiple-choice format. A test of writing that bypasses the achievement in question is a contradiction in terms.

The following directions for evaluating rhetorical effectiveness illustrate how specific California Assessment Program instructions are. They spell out the criteria that an autobiographical incident would have to satisfy in order to qualify for the highest rating. Scorers are given equally concrete criteria in order to rate other levels of accomplishment and other kinds of writing (writing a report, telling a story, and such) and for six levels of accomplishment).

Writer narrates a coherent and engaging story that moves the narrative toward the central moment. The narrative tells readers what they need to know to understand what happened and to infer its significance to the writer. The writer of a 6 essay will use some of the following strategies:

- naming (specific names of people or objects, quantities, numbers)
- visual details of scene, objects, or people (size, colors, shapes, features, dreams)
- sounds or smells of the scene
- specific narrative action (movements, gestures, postures, expression)
- dialogue
- interior monologue
- expression of remembered feelings or insights at time of the incident
- slowing the pace to elaborate the central moment in the incident
- suspense or tension
- surprise
- comparison or contrast to other scenes or people

Using these guidelines, read the following with an eye toward rating this excerpt from an autobiographical incident, written by an eighth-grade student:

Frightened

One of the most frightening experiences I have ever had was the time I fell in the riverbed. I was so scared,

I will probably have a vivid memory of the incident in my mind for as long as I live.

. . . On this particular Friday, I chose to go over and visit my friend Ryan, who was my best friend in the fifth grade. My favorite hobby at the time was chasing and catching blue-belly and alligator lizards.

After school, we went to Ryan's house and got the supplies we would need. These supplies consisted mainly of brown paper lunch bags in which we held our captured lizards. We then rode our bikes roughly two miles before we came to the dried up Santa Ynez riverbed.

After the first twenty minutes, . . . we walked farther along the dusty riverbed. I came to the familiar four foot ledge that I had jumped from so many times before, but this time something went wrong.

Ryan was about ten feet ahead of me, had already jumped from the ledge, and was continuing along the bank. I was crouching on the ledge, holding my lizards and preparing to jump. I looked at the ground below me, then at Ryan. Suddenly I slipped and went sprawling head first to the ground. I smacked my head on a large rock and landed, breaking my fall with my wrist.

. . . Ryan began to run for help, and I told him to hurry. I sat down, afraid I might die from loss of blood before he returned. My wrist and forehead ached, and I began to cry. I tried to stand up and walk toward the bikes, but I was too weak. I just sat down and began to pray. . . .

After recalling the rest of his experience, the student ended:

Looking back on that incident, I sometimes shutter, thinking about how serious it could have been. "What if I was bit by a rattler?" I sometimes ask myself. I also realize how important a good friend is, in order to take away some of the fear.

It was important for the writer to have had ample time in which to write his three pages about an incident that still mattered to him, to have been unhurried as he changed the word "sitting" to "crouching," and to select other words, such as "smacked" and "sprawling." No multiple-choice test offers that opportunity. Indeed, no test that only allows time for a brief writing sample can appraise writing like this.

Breaking still more ground, the California Assessment Program first sends teachers an unpublished report of writing achievement test scores for their school as a whole. In addition to an overall writing grade, the report provides breakdowns of the results of tests of different kinds of writing ability (see below). The scores, which are never published, enable teachers to answer the question "How well did students in *my* school write?" Later, when statewide scores are reported in the press, teachers can compare their school-wide results with the statewide scores, thereby giving them an even clearer picture of where their own school's writing instruction needs strengthening.

Preliminary results show that most eighth-grade students submitted adequate or marginally adequate essays that received a score of 4 or 3. Thirteen percent of the students wrote impressively, achieving scores of 5 and 6; and 19 percent of the eighth grade (too large a group, in the opinion of the Writing Assessment Advisory Committee) wrote so poorly that they were limited to scores of 1 and 2.

Even more informative than overall scores are the breakdowns into specific kinds of writing. Early data indicate that over half of the state's eighth-graders scored 4 or higher in reporting information while less than half (46 percent) did as well in autobiographical writing. Forty-one percent achieved comparable scores when arguing for solutions to solve problems, but only 34 percent were as competent in supporting their judgments, or in their ability to think and compose coherently. And for every type of writing assessed, students scored higher in observing the rules that govern proper English than in thinking and writing.

Once teachers have feedback on the quality of student writing in their own school, they have grounds for devising new strategies to improve writing instruction and perform- ance. They may choose to change the instruction they offer and the homework they assign. They may want to use out- standing student achievement test essays as a teaching tool and arrange workshops with teachers across the curriculum. Decisions will vary, but for the first time statewide testing has set out to help teachers and students—and appears to be on the way toward accomplishing its purpose.

There is a striking similarity between innovative state- wide testing in California and Rhode Island. Since both states have introduced their changes with the help of Mary Fowles, a strong advocate of close-to-the-classroom testing at ETS, it is not surprising that Rhode Island teachers also par- ticipate directly in the assessment. Since Rhode Island is a small state, the committee that shapes the prompts that ETS develops has teacher representatives from every school dis- trict. When it comes to administering the tests and scoring them, moreover, *every* third-grade teacher has been a tester since the newly designed, annual writing assessment got under way in the spring of 1987.

While California's forty-five minutes of unbroken writing time is a striking innovation, Rhode Island's two-day testing goes even further toward answering critics of testing who complain that no assessment allows the process of writing to go through the steps that classroom teaching encourages. On the first day of Rhode Island's two-day assessment, third- grade teachers lead their students through a number of pre- writing exercises to encourage youngsters to think about a topic, jot down some notes about it, and begin writing their first draft. On the second day, test takers are expected to revise their drafts. When they have finished composing, their teachers guide them through a checklist with which students look at the clarity and organization of their writing as well as at correct grammar, spelling, punctuation, and capitalization. The contrast between Rhode Island's teacher-innovators and traditional teacher-monitors is as dramatic as the contrast between new writing assessments and conventional standardized tests.

To prepare for linking teaching and testing in the upper elementary school in 1989, Rhode Island's sixth-grade teachers have been working with third-grade teachers and with Mary Fowles of ETS on shaping test prompts, administering the test itself, and following carefully spelled-out guidelines for scoring the results. A similar two-day testing arrangement is also expected to be used with the state's eighth- and tenth-grade students, but that plan has not yet moved off the drawing board. What is already clear, however, is that assessments in junior and senior high school will also inform students and teachers that writing is expected to be taught as a process and evaluated in the same way. Also clear are the first results of Rhode Island's 1987 and 1988 two-day testing plan: third-grade students are producing better, longer, demonstrably superior writing now that they understand how to prewrite, draft, revise, and edit their work.

The evaluations that Rhode Island and California have introduced attempt to document writing achievements in new ways, but even the best efforts at focusing on what students have produced in a single- or a two-day assessment have inherent limitations. What a writer may not succeed in accomplishing at one time may be realized at a later time. To counteract limitations of the one-shot test, or, in Rhode Island's case, the two-shot test, the Maryland Writing Assessment has provided for even more drafts of writing in supervised settings. Taking another tack, other educators such as Peter Elbow, director, and Pat Belanoff, associate director, of the Writing Program at the State University of New York at Stony Brook, have students keep a portfolio of their writing over the course of a semester, much as an artist keeps a sampling of sketches. In this way, students have a chance to revise their efforts, even to put a piece of work aside for a while for revising—for real rethinking, in contrast to mere tinkering. What's more, Dr. Belanoff points out, the portfolio procedure prevents students from being penalized for poor initial skills if they wind up as strong writers. Progress, not one-shot writing, underlies portfolio assessments.

Stony Brook introduced this approach in the spring of 1983 with ninety-six students; two years later some thirteen hundred students were keeping portfolios. The examiners who are members of a four- or five-person reading group see the portfolio plan as a form of evaluation that goes beyond measurement in order to emphasize work and learning. Teachers come to believe in the ability of *all* of their students to improve their writing skills when they have time to plan their work, consult with instructors and peers, revise their first drafts, and copyedit in ways that a timed test does not permit. And students come to view their teachers as coaches who are there to be helpful, not as umpires whose function is to enforce rules and punish infractions.

Indeed, the portfolio system makes such good sense that secondary school teachers are now exploring a similar approach. In a small experiment under the guidance of ETS, twelve Rhode Island classrooms are participating in a study of student writing that teachers assemble in portfolios over time. The portfolio team plans to see how well writing that extends beyond two days correlates with state test scores. In a similar move, the California Writing Project is now collaborating with the Center for the Study of Writing on the Berkeley campus of The University of California to conduct a pilot portfolio assessment. And the New York City branch of the National Writing Project (NYCNWP) has developed a summer program to prepare junior high school teachers of different subjects to learn how, by beginning with their own writing, to assemble portfolios that reflect growth and change.

"Remember," the guidelines that NYCNWP prepared for

teachers begin, "you can feel free to include FIRST DRAFTS and REVISIONS in addition to FINAL products." The teacher-writers were also told to include an open letter to readers of the portfolios, describing what each contained and explaining the reason for selecting each piece. A social studies teacher with a strong interest in the environment, for example, used her portfolio to take readers through six drafts of her paper on ecology. The future essay began with a collection of sketchy notes that didn't pretend to have shape or form. Step by step, readers were caught up in the evolving piece of writing that began with the thesis that historically man has lived in fear of nature's "awesome forces"—until recently. "Today," the social studies teacher wrote, "it is nature who cries out to be rescued from the destructive powers of mankind." She ended the sixth and final draft with words almost certain to hold her students' interest: "Time goes on, and man, insulated in the comfort of his centrally heated home, engrossed in television's cinematic fantasies, sits oblivious to the planet crumbling underneath him."

A reader who assessed the first or second draft, or even the third, fourth, or fifth, could not have seen the progress that the full portfolio provided. The same applied to the assembled work of other teachers. True to his craft, a junior high school teacher of journalism included dated journal entries, documenting early summer confusion, false writing starts, gradual progress, and success. He also submitted initial drafts and completed revisions of an article about putting out a school newspaper, a travel article, and a piece of fiction, written first as a story and then, at the urging of his group, as a play. "I would never have thought to do it myself," he wrote in his covering letter, "and I'm still not sure it works better, but I'm happy to have had the experience."

Eager to further the portfolio approach, NYCNWP secured a grant of $375,000 from Chase Manhattan Bank. No longer without funds, the project was able to contract with ETS in order to develop portfolios that can satisfy the requirements that measurement specialists set for reliability and validity. "We don't want to create a top-down model of assessment, with ETS on top," development scientist Roberta Camp explained, "but neither do we want to see junior high school teachers collecting kids' writing—and missing a basis for forming judgments."

Whenever there is no one right answer, no machine-graded test, and no guarantee that teachers' judgments will always be the same, the same uneasy questions arise: how can student writing be judged consistently? And if evaluations are not consistent, how can students be treated fairly? Instead of dodging the challenge, ETS developed criteria for facing it head-on in California and in Rhode Island, and it is determined to come up with solutions before portfolio assessments moves beyond the pilot test phase. "Since advocates of the multiple-choice format have long believed that reliability is only assured when scoring leaves nothing to independent judgment," Roberta Camp said, "anyone who believes in the importance of essay writing is obliged to prove that trustworthy scoring methods are clearly possible. The burden of proof is on us."

The method of scoring that is gaining the most favor is called "holistic," which simply means that a whole piece of writing is greater than any of its parts. With the help of carefully spelled out criteria, scorers are expected to make a single quality judgment about the overall effectiveness of a student's writing. Surprising as it may sound, after relatively brief training in holistic scoring in order to minimize individual biases and establish accepted standards, experienced teachers agree with each other as often as 95 percent of the time. Also surprising, they can read and score thirty to forty papers an hour. Holistic scoring, therefore, appears to be rapid and efficient.

However, since the holistic approach purposely deals with the reader's total impression, it doesn't isolate and score specific features. To retain the value of scoring the total impression, while adding a method for focusing on particular aspects of writing that need improvement, the South Carolina Writing Committee designed a modified holistic approach. Students' essays are judged by at least two trained scorers. If they agree that the writer has earned a top rating of 3, 3.5, or 4, straightforward holistic scoring is sufficient. But if the writer has earned an inadequate score of 2, 1, or 0, raters use a modified holistic plan that identifies trouble spots for remediation; mechanics, word usage, sentence formation, and composition are classic causes of concern. And if one reader puts a score of 3 or 4 on an essay while the other reader rates it significantly lower, the opinion of a third reader is requested to resolve the difference.

The field of independent scoring and portfolio assessments has been changing at an astonishing rate. Only twenty years ago, the National Assessment of Educational Progress (NAEP) introduced the then radical idea of having students produce writing samples on the tests they were taking. Still in their infancy, the tests assigned topics that were well within the experience of many students, but not of all students. When some students are favored over others, a test cannot be valid, in psychometric terms or in everyday English. Yet this error in judgment still slips into tests occasionally.

Consider an assessment whose results were made public in December 1986. You are a nine-year-old, one of some 55,000 students in fourth, eighth, and eleventh grade whose writing was evaluated by the NAEP. You are given less than fifteen minutes in which to write a note to a friend, explaining how he or she should care for your pet while you are away on vacation. You may never have had a pet, much less have gone away on vacation, but you are supposed to tell the "pet sitter" how often to feed the animal, how much food to give it, and where to find the food in question.

Say you write a typical paragraph such as:

I would really appreciate it if you would take care of my dog while I'm gone. feed him and water him 1 time a day. The food is in the cabinet. let him loose every 2 days to get his exercise.

or

Hi! Could I ask you a favor. Could you feed my pets for two weeks. Here's how you do it. Give the dogs a panful each of fresh water everyday. Mix the dog food with warm water. I would appreciate it. Thank you. Could you also keep an eye on them. the neighbors dogs always fight our dogs.

You'll never see the way in which your answer was scored, but you might be astonished to discover that in both the above examples the rating was "minimal."

Why minimal? Not because of your occasional mistakes in spelling or punctuation, which were not even considered, but because your answer didn't include all the information necessary to make sure that your pet would be fed properly. You seemed to take it for granted that your friend would know how much or how often your pet should be fed or where the food was to be found. The readers who rated your response may have recognized that your voice rang clear or seen that your ideas were original, but these qualities didn't affect your score any more than mechanical mistakes did.

All writing samples were rated with just one purpose in mind: to determine the thoroughness with which you conveyed information about feeding a pet you may never have known. On the basis of this standard, NAEP scorers concluded that only *2 percent of your fellow fourth-graders wrote "adequate or better" responses to this question.* Although eighth-graders fared better in responding to the same prompt, they didn't fare well enough; only 19 percent of the answers earned a score of "adequate or better" As a result, decision makers at NAEP have decided that they will not use this prompt again. Nor will they use unduly restricted time limits that test reformers have criticized. A new writing test allows from fifteen to thirty minutes for replies to prompts.

Even if the press had been unaware of the test's flaws, however, reporters had reason to be troubled by some of NAEP's findings:

- Fewer than one-fourth of the eleventh-graders tested performed adequately on writing tasks involving skills required for success in academic studies, business, or the professions.
- Only 25 percent of the eleventh-graders, 18 percent of the eighth-graders, and 2 percent of the fourth-graders performed adequately when asked to compare and contrast, the easiest analytical task assigned.
- Fewer than one-third of the students were able to adequately back up their points of view in writing.
- Sixty-five percent of the eleventh-graders wrote adequately or better when writing about personal experiences for a job application. Fewer than 19 percent of the eighth-graders and 2 percent of the fourth-graders wrote adequate or better responses to a similar task.
- About half of the eleventh-graders and a third of the eighth graders wrote stories judged adequate or better. Less than 9 percent of the fourth-graders wrote adequate or better responses to the same task.
- Fifty-seven percent of the fourth-graders said they liked to write; the figure fell to 39 percent for those in eleventh grade.

A barrage of negative headlines and articles, however, resulted in virtual national hysteria about inferior student writing. A new Henny Penny had burst on the scene to alert anyone who would listen that the sky was falling in. So many journalists took heed of her dire warning that the press discovered the "writing crisis" all over again. "Johnny Can't Write Either, Survey Finds," *The Washington Post* announced. Speaking of the same "Johnny," a headline over a column by the nationally syndicated newspaperman James J. Kilpatrick exclaimed, "Can't Read, Can't Write." In a more restrained style, *The New York Times* said, "Study Finds Poor Writing Skills in Schoolchildren." It was hard to find a newspaper that did not caution its readers about students' depressing writing achievement.

However ballyhooed in the press and dismissed in the schools, NAEP's findings were important, for writing is a serious problem in American education. But it is not easy for testers to come up with a prompt that is fair to every student: the rural child and the city dweller, a native American and a suburban youngster. Their diversity may get the better of many educators, but not of Theodore Sizer. Benefiting from his extraordinary experience at Harvard, Phillips Academy, and Brown University, Sizer seems to have found the key to universal feelings. Discarding prompts, he calls the stimulation he uses to evoke writing "provocations."

In his new role as chair of the Coalition of Essential Schools, Sizer needed to arouse students' thinking and feeling, no matter how diverse their backgrounds. The Coalition, which extends to fifty-six schools in twenty states and a province of Canada, includes students from low-income, minority families; from affluent, suburban homes; and from a wide range of ethnic, religious, and socioeconomic backgrounds. "Despite these differences I have yet to meet anyone who doesn't know what fear is," Sizer said. "So when we tell students to write their own definition, they're not baffled by the provocation."

Like fear, "hunger" is another word that students can define. To stimulate their thinking, Sizer suggests two meanings: "You hunger after the girl at the next desk" and "You hunger when your belly is empty." Defining a word at a school that is a member of the Coalition requires different skills from those expected in conventional schools. There's nothing wrong with using pencil and paper to define a word, assuming students express themselves well—and correctly. But writing a definition is only part of the assessment in a coalition school. In fact, teachers don't talk much about assessment. They speak instead of "exhibitions."

An "exhibition" may also include both oral and visual presentations. When students define "fear" or "hunger," for example, they are expected to define the word in three media, only one of which is necessarily done with pencil and paper. Painting, sculpture, drama, and dance are other forms of communication that are appreciated. With more complex exhibitions, students are expected to synthesize what they have learned and make critical judgments—again in various media. When Dr. Sizer described these "exhibitions," I thought of an experience I had in England in 1968, talking with Sir Alec Clegg, who was chief education officer of the West Riding, Yorkshire. After listening to Sir Alec discuss the way in which some young students learned to read and write (no basal readers, no workbooks, no ditto sheets), I asked him if he could show me these youngsters' test scores.

"Certainly," he said, as he opened the straps of a large old black valise. Instead of finding the scores I sought, I saw silk-embroidered tapestries and sensitively written poetry; collages of items collected on nature walks—complete with explanations about a variety of leaves in their different seasons; write-ups of scientific experiments, stories, biographies, photographs, paintings, and sculpture. Sir Alec's evident pride in the materials in his valise and Ted Sizer's later program to synthesize the listening ear, the thoughtful mind, the written word, and the sensitive eye seem to have much in common.

Since the school-based methods of evaluation that the Coalition of Essential Schools employs run counter to state-imposed tests, Coalition members have already had to seek waivers from state or district boards and local teachers' unions in order to implement their concept of assessment. Even when legislation requires that students take a statewide writing assessment, there is nothing to prevent local schools from also designing more personal evaluations of students' growth. Nothing, that is to say, except teacher time and energy, student inclination to take a voluntary test seriously, and administrators' expressions of interest. Nonetheless, local testing is possible. Witness the experience of the Ann Arbor, Michigan, school district, where fifty-two English teachers instruct more than fifteen hundred students in two large high schools and in an alternative school. To encourage the teaching of writing, the Ann Arbor school board took the unusual step of approving a reduced teaching load for English teachers. And to find out if the policy produced results, the board requested an assessment of students' writing in 1983. The administration complied—but neglected to consult teachers about the content or the conduct of the process. And the teachers who were bypassed in this manner did not take kindly to their lack of involvement.

Fortunately, Richard Stock, then director of secondary education, and Lee Hansen, the associate superintendent for curriculum and instruction, listened to the teachers' complaints and suggested that they might want to design an assessment that better served their needs. As a result, five high school English teachers, the school district's coordinator of instruction in the language arts, and four University of Michigan faculty members joined together as a research team to assess the writing of some one thousand eleventh-grade students. In the process, the group became convinced of the value of local assessments conducted by teachers.

The distaste for long-distance testing was easy to understand. California and Rhode Island had not yet begun to prove that statewide assessments do not have to be removed from the way that teaching and learning take place in particular classrooms. It seemed that the larger the population being tested, the more out of touch with students' interests the examination would be. Certainly, the remoteness of mass testing yielded gross findings that neither identified the needs of individual students nor assisted teachers in developing specific strategies. Even the acclaimed home-grown tests that the Portland, Oregon, public school system designed with a view toward evaluating teaching and learning, has had to consider the needs of 51,000 students in eighty-nine schools with a staff of 2,500 certified teachers. By comparison, Ann Arbor's locally developed measures of students' writing provided an opportunity to meld the teaching program that high school juniors experience with the evaluation process itself.

The advantage of teachers' formulating and conducting the assessment goes hand in hand with the underlying argument the Ann Arbor research group made for local assessment. Assessments that are designed to serve the needs of administrators and policymakers have one major goal: to demonstrate that learning is or is not taking place. That objective is basically intended to serve management purposes, not to address more complex educational issues. English teachers need to know why their students' writing skills are developing in the manner they are and what kinds of instruction can serve to stimulate their students' writing skills further.

Ann Arbor's involvement of its English teachers throughout the assessment process was unusual but not unique. Seeking the advice and criticism of high school students, however, and encouraging their participation were virtually unheard-of. Yet teacher and student involvement heightened learning for both. Two classes, for example, tried to devise their own prompts, but found that their efforts resulted in scanty responses. Through this experience students discovered the difficulty of planning a topic and their teachers came to appreciate the extent to which a writing assignment shapes the finished product. Thus challenged, eight teachers piloted a range of prompts, which their students often evaluated, and prompt selection developed into a shared effort.

The writing assessment they finally developed in 1985 differed markedly from the 1983 administratively mandated one, which had intruded on class time without providing teachers or students with new learning opportunities. Indeed, the newly assessed students saw the 1985 instrument so differently that they put their names on their essays for the first time, knowing that the papers would be returned after local teachers evaluated them. And as part of the link that has joined the writing assessment that Ann Arbor students helped design with their classroom instruction in writing, the testing procedure included a day of prewriting.

These tests are part of the good news; they are worth teaching to. But in the best of all possible worlds, gifted educators don't need to teach *to* any test. They decide what should take place in the classroom. Feedback from good tests may assist in their decision making, but it does not dictate their judgment; they are more likely, in fact, to seek suggestions from fellow teachers. The data that guide teachers on the staff of the Prospect School in North Bennington, Vermont, are the biweekly narrative records they write for every youngster—accounts that affirm the potential of each student, while remaining blessedly free of jargon, clinical terminology, even of test scores. The observations and examples that portray a child's school experiences are shared with other teachers during a two-hour Tuesday "staff review," and their combined input links the connections of any one student's experience from year to year.

Patricia Carini, cofounder of the Prospect School and its archive collection, which forms the basis for both education and research, believes that schools have not given the idea of evaluation based on description rather than measurement a real try. "As a result," she notes, "the unique set of circumstances and aptitudes of each individual tend to go unappreciated." They are not unappreciated at the Prospect School, where there is ample opportunity to consider students' writing as well as teacher narratives. When I last spoke to her, Dr. Carini said that a six-year collection of Pamela's writing and artworks included some twelve hundred pieces—not counting, of course, the pieces that she had taken home. Nor is this unusual. In fact, the school's archives house 300,000 specimens of students' writing and other kinds of learning.

Pamela was ten years old, when she wrote the following poem during a regularly scheduled writing period. Neither the dialogue form nor the subject matter was assigned, and the form, punctuation, and spelling were used by the writer, who, her teacher observed, "resembled many of her peers":

The conversation between Now and Past

"Hello, Now," said Past.
"Hello, Then," said Now.
"I wish that I had such great inventions
like you." said Past.
"Well, my People have made something to destroy
both of us. So . . . I wish my People were like your
People."
"Well, what is this something."
"This something is a nuclear bomb."
"How much power does this bomb have."
"Enough to blow up half the world and
kill what is left of it and also kill us."
"How can we stop this."
"I'm afraid we can't."
"Are you sure."
"Yes. I am."
"You mean the only way for this to stop
is for the People to not want war."
"Yes."
"That's not fair."

"I know, but there is nothing for us to do."
"Good-bye."
"Good-bye."

Prospect is a private school, but the student body repli-
cates one that you could meet in virtually any Vermont
public school, and Prospect's budget is comparable to whatever public school in the state you might name. Nor is the
narrative-descriptive form of evaluation and staff review
that Pat Carini pioneered limited to a private school faculty.
In fact, it has found its way into public schools outside of
Vermont. Children who entered the Ithaca City (New York)
school district's prekindergarten program, for example,
have already graduated from high school, with Pat Carini's
descriptive approach to evaluation and Ithaca's locally designed quantitative assessments supporting their learning all
the way.

The staff review is considered so significant, that the
Ithaca student whose work is being discussed is invited to
meet with the faculty. The student's parents are invited as
well because as Ann Gunning, the recently retired director
of curriculum explains, "Parents are the most important
teachers of all. We are pleased when they gain insights into
their own child through the way we look at his or her work."
The work that receives the most attention is usually the
individual's writing, with teachers going over a piece of
work line by line. "Our object," Ann Gunning emphasizes,
"is to get the *meaning* of what a student is thinking and
feeling, not to critique it."

No one values the qualitative tone of the staff review more
than Kenneth Pickens, chair of the English Department, but
no one is more committed to quantitative evaluation, either.
"If you can't measure writing," he asks, "how can you teach
it? And if you don't measure it, how can you keep writing at
the forefront?" Answering his own question, Ken Pickens
has been responsible for the Ithaca assessment with its

twenty-three prompts. Students from kindergarten through twelfth grade learn to become skillful first with personal narratives and then with descriptive, informational, and evaluative writing. Not surprisingly, given the emphasis on writing from age five to age eighteen, Ithaca quietly acknowledges a huge difference between the number of competent writers in its school district and the number in the national sample in the NAEP assessment. But it's a rare school district whose teachers have insisted on getting state tests back. Retrieving tests takes time and determination but Ithaca proves that it is worth the effort.

Even when the leadership of a school district takes a more traditional view of assessment, a cluster of forward-looking teachers can show that there are other ways to evaluate children and describe their progress. The two dozen or more members of the Philadelphia Teachers Learning Cooperative (PTLC) have done precisely that at the staff review that they attend voluntarily each week. Small in number, they have made such an impact that the University of Pennsylvania Graduate School of Education includes staff review in its curriculum, and the North Dakota Study Group on Evaluation publishes material written by PTLC members.

The clearest indication that these teachers are highly regarded can be found in some of Philadelphia's public school classrooms. So many parents want their children to be taught by a PTLC teacher who understands her students through keen observation of what they are saying and doing that the requests exceed the available space. Teacher Rhoda Kanevsky described a typical conference with a mother. "Your child may not have done so well in standardized tests," she might say, "but let me show you his progress since September." With that, Ms. Kanevsky would go to a cupboard and take out a folder holding months' worth of the child's writing. Instead of talking about scores, she would talk about learning—about a growing ability to use a fine-tuned vocabulary to capture exciting events, to depict tender moments, to portray colorful characters.

I began this chapter by asking six questions that I had designed. I'll close by asking one: Do you know how *your* school is testing writing? If you do, you also have some idea of how it teaches it.

7

"BUT WHAT CAN I DO?": A PARENT'S MANUAL

When you kiss your children good-by as they leave for their first day of school, you may think that their education is about to begin. But education begins at birth, when you are the primary teachers in your newborn's world. Even as those days expand into the preschool years, mothers—and occasionally fathers—will still be the most important teachers in a child's growing universe. You, more than anyone else—more than other family members, more than day-care workers, more than nursery school teachers—are the most significant educators of babies, toddlers, and preschoolers, for you introduce them to the world of words. And by now you know that language is a child's most important intellectual achievement.

If I had a single wish, therefore, I would like to ban the expression "I'm only a parent." Researchers know that mothers and fathers who believe they are insignificant underestimate the importance of the groundwork they have laid for listening, talking, reading, and writing—accomplishments that underlie more advanced learning, thinking, and reasoning. Professor Benjamin Bloom, well-known scholar of education, has found that by age four children have developed 50 percent of the intelligence they will have upon reaching maturity. In fact, Bloom says, the most rapid period of learning ends at just about the time that you might think it begins: when children enter first grade. "Some parents make good use of the early years," he notes, "but others don't. The net result is that some students are far ahead of others before the school bell rings."

Some parents also make good use of the school years, but others may not realize that they still have a major role to play long after that school bell rings. Understandably parents, who have no formal credentials, often don't see themselves as teachers. How many mothers and fathers are likely to realize that by the end of eighth grade, their child has probably spent 9,000 hours in school—but 95,000 hours outside of school? Despite this skewed distribution of time, one generation of parents after another has succumbed to the myth that without a teaching license it would be presumptuous for mothers and fathers to see themselves as educators. To dispel that viewpoint and change parent practice, the U.S. Office of Education has coined the expression "curriculum of the home" to accompany "curriculum of the school." Reinforcing the new emphasis, former secretary of education William J. Bennett observed, "Not all teachers are parents, but all parents are teachers."

Despite this new stance, you may still have trouble thinking of yourself as an educator with genuine expertise. "Who, me? You've got the wrong person. I wasn't a particularly good student. I've never taken an education course, and I certainly couldn't teach *writing*, of all things! Grammar was always my worst subject." Since your language arts and English teachers probably assumed that writing was nothing more than correct grammar, your equating the two is understandable. And your distaste for "writing" was—and is—usually shared by the very people who are supposed to teach it.

But the writing I'm talking about starts with words, not

rules, and you know you don't have to be a specialist in language development to help your children learn to talk. Under your guidance, babies who enter life not knowing what language means will have mastered complicated sentence structure before they enter school. "I don't understand how it happened," parents often say. Scholars don't fully understand the phenomenon, either. After analyzing masses of data, they can answer "when" questions: between their first and second birthdays, toddlers are likely to speak three hundred words; the biggest language explosion usually occurs between thirty and thirty-six months. By the time preschoolers are four and half years old, they often have a vocabulary of two thousand words. But scholars don't agree on the answer to the all-important "why" question: Why does talking occur as it does? "There is ultimately no way to examine how what goes on inside the brain is related to the words that appear outside whether we write or speak," acknowledges Frank Smith, recently retired professor of education at the universities of Toronto and Victoria, who is known for his books and lectures about writing.

There are ways, however to consider how the words your children speak, and later the words they write, are affected by your influence as parent-educators. Think of the advantages parents have over teachers who tack a weekly vocabulary lesson onto their lesson plans. Several years before school begins (and long after), you can read stories to your child that he or she—not an entire class of children—wants to hear. You can expand on discussions that address your child's individual interests rather follow the teacher style of whole-class instruction, and you can encourage conversation, in contrast to school rules that reward student silence. You can, in other words, improve on school practice, instead of having to imitate it. Informal language development may strike you as haphazard, and therefore less worthwhile, than formal vocabulary building in school, but research findings show otherwise.

Gordon Wells began his renowned ten-year study in England by analyzing 1,280 recordings of casual, unplanned conversation in the homes of preschoolers from every socioeconomic level in the city of Bristol. To complete his investigation, he followed a representative sample of these children through their early school years. His conclusion? Regardless of parents' own educational attainments or socioeconomic levels, homes were consistently more effective than schools in providing richer opportunities for learning through talk with an adult. Indeed, for no child—not even for those who were supposed to be learning disabled— was the language experience of the schools that Wells's researchers observed comparable to the experience of the home.

Now, translate Bristol, England, to your community and think of the distinct opportunities that you can enjoy. Without having to keep a classroom of students reasonably quiet, you can encourage your child's conversation. Without having to follow a lesson plan, you can follow your youngster's interests. You can read the books that he wants to hear, go to places that she wants to see. In sum, you can collaborate with your child as a partner in learning and discover how much more rewarding that is than being laden with the obligation of whole group, deliberate instruction. I don't know a teacher anywhere who wouldn't like a class of one or two or even three children.

You needn't be concerned about lack of time, either, despite the whirlwind world in which modern American families live. Granted, with at least one mother in two working outside of the home and single-parent households becoming almost commonplace, spare minutes are a precious commodity. But being a parent-educator who focuses on language, writing, and reading doesn't require carving out an extra chunk of time. For the most part, it simply means looking at possibilities for teaching and learning that are already embedded in everyday activities. You'll find that some opportunities you may take for granted hold the key to being a parent-educator.

If the opportunities seem to be insignificant, consider the findings in the U.S. Department of Education's recent report, *What Works: Research About Teaching and Learning.* To offer the most informed conclusions, the editors consulted with some two hundred educators. The advice they received? Begin the report with a key section on the *home,* not the classroom or the school. Consequently, *What Works* states emphatically: *"Parents are their children's first and most influential teachers. What parents do to help their children learn is more important to academic success than how well-off the family is."*

The statement is not hedged by the level of family education. It makes no reference to the fact that half of today's marriages end in divorce and that the proportion of children being raised by teenagers is rising. The point is that, regardless of circumstances, parent-educators can affect whether their child is advantaged or disadvantaged. Youngsters who are encouraged to join in the give and take of conversation, to share new experiences, to ask their full share of questions, and to know the pleasure of hearing family anecdotes recalled, are likely to escape the hallmarks of thwarted childhoods: smaller vocabularies, shorter sentences, a briefer attention span. On the other hand, researchers have found that youngsters who are raised by distracted parents or by care*takers* (not care *givers*) who may be irritated by childish questions and chatter learn to observe less in the world about them and to say nothing that may annoy the adults in charge. Their "good" behavior is anything but good, for it takes a toll on thinking, writing, and learning over the years that is not easily overcome.

One research study after another suggests ways for improving aspects of school achievement, although writing, the stepchild of American education, is rarely mentioned. What's more, the suggestions that are offered usually apply after the school bell has rung. My advice is different: Don't wait until then! Don't even wait until kitchen table conversation begins. Communication needs to start in the cradle, on the changing table, in your infant's bath. Outlandish? Not at all. Babies are ready to begin learning language immediately after birth, and to respond to different kinds of teaching as they go through different stages of childhood.

IN THE BEGINNING: THE EARLY ACQUISITION OF LANGUAGE

The word *infant* is derived from the Latin *infans*, which means "speechless," but language begins to emerge during early speechless days—and nights. And *emerging* well describes the way language develops. The beginning of speech is a gradual process.

It's also a fascinating one. While parents thrill to the sounds of cooing they hear when their very young infant lies on her back and later delight to the purposeful jabber of babbling, scientists have conducted studies of infant repertoire. And they have found that babies produce sounds that are heard in any language, not just in the infants' native language—until, little by little, babies choose the sounds of their parents, their sisters and brothers, and others who spend time talking to them. Gradually, international babblers lose the easy capacity of producing sounds of other tongues and becomes proficient only in the sounds of their own language.

To introduce an understanding of language, Dr. Ira Gordon, the late, renowned early childhood educator, used to urge parents to envelop their babies in what he called a "language envelope" and talk freely to them in the course of performing everyday parenting acts. You may feel self-conscious at first when you chat with your infant son as you undress him, and wash and powder his tiny body, or as you change your daughter's diapers and put her in clean clothes—size three months. Or you may enjoy talking to your baby from the outset. But in time, well before your infants know *what* you are saying, they are likely to form some early ideas about communication. And the words that were part of the early "language envelope" will become part of the oral and written language that you have transmitted to your child.

Some of your teaching is likely to be unplanned, but quite effective. When your infant daughter raises her head high enough to crane her neck and look around the room for the first time, can you imagine yourself watching her achievement without saying a word? When you are convinced that your six-week-old son has started smiling real smiles that are clearly not just gas, do you think you'd be likely to exclaim, "Good for you, Billy. Wait 'til I tell Daddy!"—or would you stand silently by? As the smiles become more frequent and physical coordination becomes sturdier, you will probably find yourself marveling spontaneously at each accomplishment. The words you speak as you observe growth and development, the excitement you express, the delight and wonder in your voice will contribute to your baby's language development.

Of course, you will not always be admiring your baby. If she keeps throwing toys out of the crib and crying until you retrieve them, you may scold her. And if you have to change diapers three times in an hour, you may express real or mock annoyance. Interaction takes many forms. Your major role in an infant's early months will probably be to serve as a caretaker and a source of comfort. Regardless of whether you are admiring, scolding, or comforting, however, you will find yourself interacting with words as well as body language.

But you don't have to do all the talking in these early months. Well before your baby is able to form recognizable words, you can actually begin having two-way conversations. In fact, as soon as your infant is able to make baby sounds, you may want to try your hand at what Dr. Diane Brackett, director of communication therapy at the New York League for the Hard of Hearing, describes as "volleys." This kind of preverbal exchange is simply repeating back to babies the sounds that they have made in the first place. If babies repeat the sound a second time, a "volley" has taken place, and language begins to become a social tool.

Dr. Paula Menyuk, director of the language behavior program at Boston University's School of Education, has found that talking *with* babies, not *at* them, is a better way to nurture early language development than is the typical tactic of providing young children with a steady flow of one-way conversation. Dr. Menyuk arrived at her conclusion after she and her coworkers made monthly visits to fifty-six families with new babies until the children were three and a half years old. During each visit the Menyuk team made audio and video recordings, which they later analyzed. At the end of their study the group was able to say that the frequent parental method of talking a lot to children—but not conversing with them—is an ineffective way of stimulating early language skills. Instead, she demonstrated that parents who listened to their infants "talk" and who responded to them made a greater impact on their language skills.

In explaining the talk-response approach, Dr. Menyuk suggested, for example, that parents might say, "Hi, baby," and pause before asking, "How are you?" Next, the mother or father would do well to pause again. By giving your baby a chance to reply with a smile or a coo, you can teach even young infants that conversation is a dialogue, not a monologue. When you talk with your infant, use short, simple sentences, exaggerate key words ("Do you want some *apple juice?*") to hold a limited attention span.

Perhaps the most important early language lesson you can teach your baby is, in Dr. Menyuk's words, "that people listen to you and care about what you are saying." By asking short questions such as, "Are you sleepy?" and listening to responses, and then giving further feedback, you are establishing a model pattern of conversation that will hold you and your child in good stead well past the first year of life.

Jim Trelease, author of *The Read-Aloud Handbook,* supplies another model when he says you may want to begin to read to your infant on her first day home from the hospital. Certainly, he says, you can begin by six months of age. One mother was observed reading nursery rhymes to her six-week-old infant. When the mother came to a rhyme she had sung to the baby since birth, he wiggled and grinned. Seemingly he recognized the familiar rhyme at only six weeks of age.

But a child's "understanding" of what you are reading, Jim Trelease points out, is not the key issue. Conditioning your baby to your voice and to books is the central point of early reading. It is the comforting warmth of your body as you cuddle your infant, the familiar sound of your voice, the colorful pictures, and the pattern of your reading a story each day before naptime and bedtime that will prepare your babies to respond to language and to books. Indeed, before they can talk, babies may indicate the favorite stories that they want to hear you read. Perhaps certain rhymes appeal to them; perhaps they enjoy the repetitions that are built into the tale. This kind of devotion to books can start at a *very* young age—and last a lifetime.

To lay other foundations for rich and early language, parents are often told to use real words, not baby talk, even when talking with a tiny pink or blue bundle. But no one explains why. You're also advised to speak clearly and distinctly from the outset. Again, no one explains why, but the reason is straightforward: both good and bad language habits are copied so quickly that in the first three months of life your infant has already begun watching your lips move. Individual and creative as babies are, they are also great imitators. The same is true, incidentally, of toddlers and preschoolers. And you don't have to worry about using slightly advanced words once in a while, for language learners understand more than they can say. Bit by bit, they may absorb some of your more mature conversation and stretch their own vocabularies, too.

As your baby nears her first birthday, you may wonder whether the *ma-ma-ma* sound you have been hearing really means "mother," whether it stands for any woman, or whether it is not yet really a word. The same is true for "da-da-da." But you won't have to wonder long. Just as cooing gave way to babbling during your baby's first year, so babbling is likely to give way to words during the second year.

TODDLERS LEARN TO TALK: AGES ONE TO TWO YEARS

When your toddler begins to talk two things happen: she starts expressing herself in exciting new ways, and you start rejoicing over her charming mistakes. So what if Diana skipped over verbs and dropped letters she couldn't say? You knew that *Am* was her dog Sam and *mook* meant "milk." So what if she said "Baby want" instead of "I want"? You knew what she was trying to say. All you had to do was fill in the gaps, or, at times, make her language part of your family folklore. If the closest she could get to saying "Grandma" and "Grandpa" was "Ma" and "Pa," her naming was applauded, not corrected. You probably hugged your fledgling talker to show your admiration and gave her your broadest smile—but you certainly didn't try to make her talk differently. Thoroughly relaxed, you knew in time she would learn to fine-tune her speech and pick up her own revisions.

Children will do the same later as beginning writers, if given the chance. But there is a mystery: Why is the chance that awaits children who are learning how to talk, denied children who are learning how to write?

Consider the story of twenty-month-old Peter, who followed his mother's every move as she unloaded the marketing they had done together. He saw her put canned goods in a cupboard, detergent near the washing machine, and cleaning products in the broom closet. No comment from Peter. When his mother opened the refrigerator door, however, and put a dozen eggs in the egg tray, Peter broke his silence. "Mommy!" he exclaimed. "Baseballs!" Parent-educator that she was, Peter's mother was intrigued by the similarities in shape that her toddler saw and by the connections he made. "Yes, the eggs do look like baseballs, don't they?" she replied, expanding on his language but not correcting him. Without formal instruction, Peter has gradually come to understand the difference between round and oval, breakable and solid, perishable and lasting, edible and not. "He's becoming an independent learner, if ever there was one," his mother said.

But what will happen if Peter writes about "BASEBALZ" and "EGZ" when he is in kindergarten or first grade? His teacher's response will depend on the extent to which she prizes correct spelling. If Peter reverses the *E* or mixes capital letters with lower case, he may be raising another issue for his teacher to cope with. Fortunately, Peter's mother and father are parent-educators. The characteristics of the "Yes, they do look like eggs" response are likely to continue as he again tries to make sense of the unfamiliar.

Before he reaches that stage, however, Peter will have been surrounded by a language-rich environment. Most children aren't. Recent research has found that some children experience one-tenth the amount of talking as others. And they pay a price for limited experience, for the sheer quantity of conversation proves to be important in learning language. Yet American mothers on average spend less than half an hour a day talking, explaining, or reading with their children and fathers spend less than fifteen minutes. While it is not easy to combine a career and parenting, with a little imagination and a lot of commitment it can be done.

Perhaps you are a single parent and the only way you can find time to do your laundry is to take your fourteen-month-old with you when you go down to the laundry room of your apartment building at night. The room is not brightly lit, and the only books and toys are the ones you put in your laundry basket. What is really important, however, is that the one-to-one time you have with your toddler gives him a chance to try out new words and gives you a chance to make sure that you understand what he is trying to say before you respond. In this way conversation becomes a real partnership.

Lest evenings in the laundry room or the supermarket leave you feeling somewhat guilty, don't worry. Reliable research has found that the toddler who frequently accompanies a parent on errands and trips is likely to engage in *more* conversation than the child whose parents choose to leave her home. What you do with the time together in a car or in a checkout line at the market is far more important than where you do it. If you see it as an opportunity to build on your toddler's first words, you can be a parent-educator in the laundry room. You can respond thoughtfully to what your language learner is trying to say and you can concentrate on following the lead rather than dominating the conversation. To help you understand the unclear thoughts that your toddler is trying to convey, it's a good idea to repeat and paraphrase what you think he has been saying. And it's always a good idea to talk about topics that are familiar to your toddler.

You may be surprised at how quickly he expands his language when you include him as you go about doing chores that are routine for you but that are new experiences for your youngster. In the grown-up world of mothers and fathers, your toddler will pick up words that are associated with cleaning, doing the laundry, shopping, and cooking; with taking out the garbage, clearing snow, gardening, and making house repairs. Going on errands in the car can provide another informal language lesson, as the vocabulary of the shoe repair shop, the bakery, the library, and the bank become part of your child's "dictionary."

In his ten-year research study of early language, Gordon Wells compared one-to-one talking with throwing and catching a ball. First you have to make sure that your child is ready, with hands cupped, to catch the ball. Then you throw the ball gently and accurately so that it will land in the waiting hands. And when it is your child's turn to return the throw, you will need to be prepared to run to wherever the ball goes and bring it back to where your child really intended it to go. "Such is the collaboration required in conversation," Wells said, with "the adult doing a great deal of supportive work to enable the ball to be kept in play."

Just as talking becomes increasingly important between your toddler's first and second birthdays, books also take on a new meaning. Not yet able to express more than a fraction of what they are thinking, children are already developing the ability to understand some of the content of the carefully selected stories you read to them. Soon one story before naptime or bedtime will not be enough, and as soon as you have finished the first book, your toddlers may go to their little collection—and *every* child should have both library books and inexpensive paperback books—in order to bring you another request. You'll find that certain choices may reappear with great frequency, but if you think you can speed matters a bit by skipping a verse here and a page there in any of the most favored tales, you may find yourself caught in the act.

OLDER TODDLERS AND PRESCHOOLERS: AGES TWO TO FIVE YEARS

There are always differences among children, many of them traceable to the early exposure to language their parents provided. Still, by and large, researchers observe that it is not unusual for once-speechless infants to compose quite complex sentences by age four and a half. Skilled communicators often connect clauses with words such as "and," "because," "so," "if," "when," "but," "before," and "after." At that age children have also begun to understand relationships such as tall/short and big/small. These accomplishments are all the more reason to encourage ongoing language development. It's important to carry over with children aged two to five many of the attitudes and activities that you brought into play with infants and toddlers. The first rule of thumb, therefore, is to continue your earlier emphasis on conversation and on reading. And to remember the importance of a talk-response pattern of communication.

Some parents, and I include myself, forget our natural ability to expand on our children's interests; instead, we try to assume the role of schoolteacher, whose lesson plan dictates what *we* stress at home. How we organize a trip to the zoo is a case in point. *We* select the variety of animals for them to see, instead of being guided by their interests. *We* introduce the patter we want our children to hear (but not necessarily to listen to) about what they have seen, heard, smelled, tasted, and touched. Meaning well, we have exposed our children to experiences outside the home—and overloaded them with information in the name of being model mothers and fathers.

In my early years of motherhood, I was an example of how not to develop language. After reading a number of *Curious George* books to my firstborn, for example, I took him to the zoo, intent on his going to the monkey cage. The adventure, I was quite convinced, would provide an ideal opportunity to introduce new words and phrases, such as "jumping from branch to branch" and "hanging upside down." But we never got past the entrance to the zoo! David insisted on remaining on the outskirts so that he could feed the pigeons.

Nothing could convince him to budge, but he did acquire some new words that *he* wanted: "beak," "wings," and, his favorite, "pidgin poop."

My husband, who was an ardent reader of *Babar* stories, took our third son to see the elephants at the zoo. When Jeff returned home, it was clear that he was not the least interested in the size of these real *Babars*, in their floppy ears, or in their lumbering gait. There was only one thing he wanted to talk about, because it was so funny. "Elephant ate my boon," he giggled. It seems the elephant ignored the food Jeff had wanted to feed him and used his trunk instead to suction our son's big pink balloon. Jeff had never seen what was, in effect, a living vacuum cleaner and he was not about to forget the sight. Instead of talking about the "boon," however, I'm ashamed to say, I asked, "What else did he eat?" Jeff could not have cared less.

It takes a while to overcome anxiety about being a "good" first teacher, but there are some basic dos and don'ts for parent-educators:

- *Don't* underestimate the importance of the casual, almost instinctive ways with which you foster language development in the course of daily activities.
- *Don't* assume that your natural approach is inherently inferior to the deliberate methods of vocabulary building that professional educators are prone to use.
- *Do* allow for the now well-established probability that even teachers with advanced preparation in speech and language are likely to benefit from paying less attention to their own formal instruction and more to the techniques that parents like you seem comfortable using.

Gordon Wells cites a brief conversation between a mother and her two-year-old that illustrates one such technique. Mark has just drawn his mother's attention to the "jubs" in the garden. At times Mark is able to say "birds" and at other times he still calls them "jubs" but his mother understands her bilingual little boy.

> "Birds, Mummy," Mark says.
> His mother affirms, "Mm."
> "Jubs," Mark says.
> "What are they doing?" his mother asks, beginning by picking up what Mark had said.
> "Jubs bread."
> "Oh, look," Mark's mother expands on the word "bread." "They're eating berries, aren't they?"
> "Yeah," he agrees.
> "That's their food," Mark's mother adds further knowledge. "They have berries for dinner," she says.
> "Oh."

Without making a conscious effort to teach, Mark's mother has accepted his calling her attention to birds ("jubs"), added the words *berries, food,* and *dinner* to her son's vocabulary, and expanded his information. In other words, she taught by listening and by building on what her two-year-old already knew. Chances are, you have had conversations like this a dozen times a day without even stopping to think about the significance of what you were saying.

Every mother and father can help their child develop strong language skills. You won't want to stint on reading, of course, because, children benefit from both good literature and from the conversation that usually accompanies reading aloud. Even when you still have a sinkful of pots and pans to scrub and your three-year-old is beginning to rub his eyes, you'll find his bedtime ritual is incomplete unless you both talk about the book you're reading together. If you don't ask questions, he will. With a little encouragement, your child will relate an episode in the story to an everyday event. And with no encouragement he'll probably fetch another book and ask for "just one more story."

Reading aloud is all the more important when you consider two of Jim Trelease's findings:

- The average television set is on for six and one-quarter hours a day.
- The average kindergarten graduate has already seen more than five thousand hours of television. That is more time than it takes to obtain a college degree!

But as Trelease points out, a television set can't hug a child. Caring parent-educators, therefore, can compete with the electronic tube—and win. By selecting books thoughtfully and presenting them with a change of expressions (you don't want Peter Rabbit, his sisters and brothers, and Mr. MacGregor to sound alike, do you?), you can instill a love of reading, a delight in language.

Without minimizing the importance of reading, try not to stint on writing, either. By the time your child is two years old, and certainly before age three, you can begin to make writing an essential part of her world. When you do, you will be giving a lifelong gift that contributes to clear thinking and learning, a gift that enables child, youth, and adult to make a permanent record of ideas and feelings. Some people think that writing is the way we express what we have in mind to say, but the opposite is closer to the case: writing is the way we discover what we mean. And what's true for an adult is true for a small child.

The toddler who learned to talk by hearing you talk will learn to write by seeing you write. Jimmy's mother doesn't wait for him to go to sleep before she writes to her family in Holland. Instead, mother and son sit at the kitchen table together, corresponding overseas. One writes, the other makes marks and wiggles, which are his ways of writing. Mary uses similar techniques when she adds her own signature to the holiday, birthday, and get-well notes her mother sends. Nor is the young scribe's writing limited to being part of her mother's correspondence. When she sees her baby-sitter taking messages, she writes messages, too. When her father makes notes of the errands he needs to run on Saturday, Mary puts her own list together. And she colors a marketing list to parallel her mother's black-and-white one. This not-quite-three-year-old has already begun to see that writing serves practical and social purposes.

Most busy parents will recognize that part of writing instruction is less deliberately educational than purely practical, but distractions that appear to be mere busy work actually seem to give children a head start in using the printed word before schooling begins. Indeed, years of research have persuaded professors Jerome Harste, Virginia Woodward, and Carolyn Burke that three-, four-, five-, and six-year-old children learn a great deal about written language at home. So if you find yourself making time to concentrate on the day's mail by giving your Mary "Occupant" mail to open and read, you have not merely devised a temporary diversion. An activity like this can contribute to the knowledge about writing that your underfoot toddler or preschool child absorbs.

Don't discount the importance of scribbling, either. Indeed, when Harste, Woodward, and Burke analyzed the advanced scribbling of a four-year-old American, an Israeli, and a Saudi Arabian child, they found that the shapes the children used looked like the written words of their respective native languages. Dawn wrote a series of wavy lines going from left to right, while Ofer's series of shapes, all bearing an uncanny resemblance to Hebrew letters, went from right to left. When Ofer made a mistake and scribbled from left to right, his grandmother said that he wrote backwards. (An American grandmother could say the same if her grandchild's scribbling went from right to left.) And Najeeba imitated the Arabic she didn't yet know by scribbling intricate curlicues with a great many dots. Then, as the researchers reported in their book *Language Stories and Literacy*

Lessons, Najeeba explained that they wouldn't be able to read her paper because she wrote it in Arabic where "we use a lot more dots than you do in English." These international comparisons of scribbling added to the scholars' conviction that young children begin to use written language well before school.

But the very parents who admire and repeat their children's early speech, complete with mistakes that become part of the family's vocabulary for years to come, make the mistake of dismissing the worth of scribbling and later may carp over the correctness of their children's writing as well. Try to remember how much you appreciated your baby's first efforts at talking so that you will be able to appreciate your preschooler's early efforts at writing, too. In its own way, scribbling is comparable to the sounds you heard when your eight-month-old had yet to speak a recognizable word. Talking and writing, in other words, both go through developmental stages that respond to observation, practice, and informal feedback ("Yes, they do look like baseballs, don't they?"). But unless you are careful, there is likely to be a difference in the ways that talking and writing develop. The early stages of one are greeted with praise, while the early stages of the other may be downplayed.

You would do well, therefore, to begin to help your young scribbler with the viewpoint with which Donald Graves starts his landmark book, *Writing: Teachers and Children at Work.* "Children want to write," Graves says. "Before they went to school they marked up walls, pavements, newspapers with crayons, chalk, pens or pencils . . . anything that makes a mark. The child's marks say, 'I am.' " Encourage and respect your child's scribbles; with practice, they will develop through recognizable stages that become less random, and in time the scribbles will include more of the distinctive qualities of letters. Regardless of whether your toddler's efforts are primitive or more advanced, display them on the refrigerator door or on a special bulletin board that you can also use for drawings, paintings, and actual writing; research shows that your interest and acceptance are critically important. Indeed, one researcher has commented that the industriousness of youngsters whose efforts are appreciated, "violates the child labor laws."

To encourage writing, you'll find that drawing, painting, and clay modeling are important. So are dramatic play, music, and dance. The more media that your children use to express their ideas, the more their related language will expand. You don't have to be part of all this activity, of course. You can watch from the sidelines, offering no more than an occasional question or observation to stimulate thinking and learning. There's no harm in looking at your children's artwork and asking, "Who are the two little girls in the picture you just drew?" or "Can you tell me what your picture is about?" So long as you are showing genuine interest and not demeaning your youngsters' efforts, you don't have to worry about hurting their feelings. In fact, your questions can encourage language-rich explanations that are a starting point for later writing.

To further demonstrate your interest, it's a good idea to mix a tempting variety of tools of the trade with the toys that are part of every day play. You probably already have crayons and different kinds of paper, ranging from napkins and a spiral pad to the cardboard some laundries use to pack shirts and old, out-of-date stationery. Chalk and a chalkboard are inexpensive and easy to acquire. Since vibrant-colored felt-tipped pens are both enticing and comfortable for young fingers that are still gaining control over small muscles, you may want to buy a few—but to avoid disaster be sure to select the water-soluble kind.

The activities that stem from your homemade media center are preliminary to what a teacher may call "real" writing. In fact, scribbling and drawing *are* real writing for young children. By the time your preschooler shows an interest in letters, however, a new question arises: What can a parent do to encourage writing words and sentences?

At the very least, seize the opportunity that your child gives you when she asks you to write a few words on a picture she has drawn ("my house," "a bird," "trees"). Better yet, encourage her to write words of her own. Make sure your children know that you won't worry about the correctness of spelling, and that no one expects them to write every letter perfectly. In fact, you can expect a backward *E*, a *P* that looks like a *Q* or an *M* with one too many peaks. Show your pleasure at the overall effort by displaying the art and writing for others to enjoy. You don't want to stint on praise even if some letters are wide of the mark, but you can offer to print a difficult word on another piece of paper so your child has a model to copy. *But don't write on your youngster's paper unless you get permission to do so!* There's no more certain way to discourage writing before it gets under way than to put *your* mark on your child's work.

The media center that you developed to encourage early interest in drawing and scribbling can now be enlarged. You may want to add a thoroughly modern motivator: an inexpensive electric pencil sharpener. As your preschoolers develop an interest in letters and words they may want to use a label maker to stamp out simple messages. As a result a Paul Bissex–style sign may caution you not to intrude on their privacy: DO NAT DSTRB GNYS AT WRK. And an ink-splattered shirt may greet you after your youngster has begun spelling out sentence fragments with a rubber stamp and a well-inked pad. The basic idea is to be as practical as possible while selecting equipment for your children's writing center that is appropriate to their age and needs and to your income.

Dr. Harvey S. Wiener, author of *Any Child Can Write*, cited an unusual addition to his toddler's writing supplies. Ever since Melissa began crawling into her dad's study in order to watch and imitate a writer at work, she wanted to have her own pencil and paper. Soon after she could talk, she asked for her own typewriter, too. For her second birthday, therefore, Melissa's parents gave her a red plastic children's typewriter that she continued to use for several years. Not every father is an author, of course, and not every child is as precocious as Melissa, but without great expertise or expense every parent can support an interest in writing long before school begins. Simple writing supplies and ongoing commitment on the part of parent-educators can accomplish the same purpose.

Of course, writing tools are only as good or as bad as the use they get. Some of the ideas that Melissa's parents came up with had to wait until she was in school. Traditional notes to the teacher that parents write, for example, were written by Melissa and cosigned by her mother or father. But other note writing became a frequent activity while Melissa was still a preschooler. An easel in Melissa's room made it possible for Mrs. Wiener to leave little notes at night that Melissa responded to the next day. But the equipment would have served no purpose if mother and daughter had not engaged in a more mature version of the "volleys" that Dr. Diane Brackett described for young infants and parents.

Before he reached Melissa's level of skill, our youngest son used to write the same three words over and over again: "I LOVE CRUSH." For the longest time neither my husband nor I could figure out the meaning of this strange grouping of words. The answer that we finally learned taught us another lesson in how to encourage writing. It seems that Steve had copied the words "I LOVE" from birthday cards he received and the word "CRUSH" from packing cartons that came with a large red-and-white sticker reading, "DO NOT CRUSH." Growing up in a family of writers and readers, our four-year-old shared our interest in words and relied on his own resources to put together a unique combination. Now that manufacturers have produced alphabet blocks on soft materials that can be hurled without hurting an innocent bystander, families can give young children a complete set of letters so that even rambunctious preschoolers are less restricted.

Steve reached his fifth birthday before the value of invented spelling had begun to be recognized. As a result, he limited himself to dictating brief picture titles that someone spelled (correctly) for him. But he decided to join his brothers in writing (dictating) a dedication to put in a scrapbook that was to contain reviews of his father's first book, *Crisis in Black and White*. Who could question the power of words upon reading:

> Dear Daddy,
>   I hope you got a good day with peace and quiet, and you don't get no yelling no more and no screaming. I hope that book is finished.
>
> Love,
Steven

I had not realized how many times I had insisted on "peace and quiet" until Steve captured my expression, nor had I appreciated the neglect he had felt for eighteen months; the power of his writing left no doubt about the impact of words. Steve's ability to convey ideas and attitudes in writing has held him in good stead: he is now a journalist. Yet he went through school from kindergarten through high school with only one teacher showing interest in writing; all the rest focused on mechanics. Although more schools now claim to be concerned about communication, one way to be certain that your children can convey their thoughts and feelings on paper is for *you* to recognize that their future ability begins with you.

Writing can actually become a childhood game. Perhaps another anecdote that is enshrined in the *Crisis in Black and White* scrapbook may establish the point. This time the writer was seven-and-a-half-year-old Jeff, who sent a memo to his five-year-old brother. This is how it looked:

TO   FROM
Mr. Steven   Mr. Jeffrey

My Dad Chalse
Rote a book called Crisse in Black
and white.
He is in the best seller
List he is nineth.
You are a good man.
Your friend

The date, August 20, 1964, and an arrow that circled the memo from the "M" that began "Mr. Jeffrey to the "d" that ended "friend" completed the play memo.

Intrigued by the sound of my children's voices on paper (I recognized the personalities of both Jeff and Steve), I became particularly interested in research in which students of language have been exploring the relationship between talking and writing. Although they concluded that writing is not simply speech on paper, they found that a child's skill in speaking is, as University of Georgia professor Kenneth Kantor has succinctly put it, "a key that can unlock the front door of the writing house, even though it may not unlock all doors within the house."

When you encourage your children's oral language, therefore, you are giving words an importance you won't regret. Informal conversations that you may take for granted are actually the building blocks of literacy. So when your preschooler bursts into the house shouting, "Guess what happened to Nancy!" or "I just saw a man walking *ten* dogs," it's a good time for you to ask questions and talk about the answers.

"Who was with Nancy when the truck went into a skid?" Listen to the answer.

"Why was she crossing the street by herself?" Listen again.

"That could have been serious. Was anyone hurt?" Similarly, your preschooler's eyewitness report of dog-walking lends itself to your entering into a discussion about how one person managed to handle so many pets simultaneously.

Not all children are equally verbal, however, and some shrink from a question-and-answer give-and-take. If that happens, you will need to take a different approach. You don't want to turn into an inquisitor, of course, lest your child avoid conversation still further, but neither do you want to see a nonverbal youngster grow more silent for lack of appropriate stimulation. One possible solution is for you to recount events that cropped up during the course of your own day. Have you ever stood in line at a supermarket, for example, and while you were waiting to have your wagonful of food checked out discovered you had left your wallet home? Tell your child about it. "I turned the contents of my pocketbook upside down, spilling everything on the floor," you might say, "and I *still* couldn't find my wallet. I didn't know what to do next. Do you think I should have put all the food back on the shelves?" At this point your nonverbal child may enter into the tale.

If she doesn't, be alert to other opportunities where she can pick up on something you said without forcing the issue. Under different circumstances it is the parent who expands on something a child said in order to develop it further, but you'll need to reverse the procedure when you have a child who doesn't initiate conversation. "I really didn't want to return the strawberries to the fruit and vegetable section," you might continue, "because I had picked out the most beautiful berries I could find just for you. So I wondered if I should ask the store manager to put my wagon aside while I went home for my money—but I didn't know where I'd find my wallet. You know I'm always putting things away for safekeeping and forgetting where I put them." Perhaps your daughter will chime in, "Like your keys" or "Your glasses."

Bit by bit as you gain skill in recounting the color and

tension that underlie commonplace occurrences (you saw the perfect sweater for your new plaid skirt; you didn't recognize a former neighbor who greeted you by name), you may find that your untalkative child will begin to view "unimportant" experiences in her world as occasions to share. If you can help transform a "nothing happened" youngster who has little to say or write about into a "Guess what happened!" child you will have earned your laurels as a parent-educator.

THE SCHOOL BELL RINGS

By the time children begin school, many parent-educators have done an outstanding job of teaching babies, toddlers, and preschoolers to listen, follow directions, and converse. The best parent-educators have also raised children who are eager to learn to read and who have already begun to write. But research demonstrates that more work lies ahead.

Professor Denny Taylor spent three years studying literacy activities in the homes of six families whose school-age children were becoming exceedingly adept in developing writing ability and reading skills. What were these families doing that produced such clear results in school? In the course of her fieldwork, Dr. Taylor found that in each household writing and reading were natural outgrowths of the everyday life of parents and children. Since reading is a rather common experience, while writing is more unusual for most families, consider some of her findings on the family-based writing that children and parents produce regularly.

The message that these mothers and fathers convey so effectively is that writing is an important means of communication. As a result, six-year-old Carol Simms keeps the names of her friends and their telephone numbers near the telephone in the kitchen. Similarly, seven-year-old Ellie Dawson records the dates of important events such as ballet lessons and birthday parties on the calendar in her room. Ken Langdon, another six-year-old, has a large loose-leaf folder in which he jots down his homework assignments and draws the tanks, destroyers, and spaceships of his battles on Venus and Mars. And Sandy Lindell, following the pattern of busy adults, writes memos to herself. Once, for example, when Sandy had forgotten to take home a birthday invitation, she wrote on a torn piece of paper, "Sandy take home Vicki's card." She placed this note on the top of her desk at school where she would see it when it was time to go home. Bonnie King also writes notes to herself and pins them on her notice board so that she will remember to take things to school. Although the literate beginnings of these school-age children jam cupboards and desks in the basement and family room, they wind up spilling over further from there.

Parents in the Taylor study proved to be examples for their family when they wrote messages to one another and to their children to convey information that could not be delivered directly. When Dan Dawson was called away on business after his wife had left for work, he left a note on the kitchen table, telling her where he was going and how long he would be gone. And he added a P.S. saying that he had found some missing clothes in the dryer. Another father left a note for his wife that might seem disjointed if you didn't know the family context, but that made perfect sense:

> Laura—I ate pizza—rest on stove. Margaret called again—wants to talk to you. Dog gone when I got home. Put him on chain if he arrives before you go out again. See you at 6:30. Will jog first. Barry

Parents' notes to children were also brief, but showed the importance of written communication. One mother taped a note on the front door politely asking her seven-year-old and her four-year-old daughters to be quiet because the baby was sleeping. Brief as the message was, it included the words "please" and "thank you." As children get older, so much is happening in their busy schedules that the family may use notes to keep on top of their busy lives. A perfect example, written to an eleven-year-old twin: "Beth—Don't forget your violin Friday—take a small hand towel for a chin rest." Some notes are intended for all the children in a family, such as one banning morning showers because children were leaving for school with wet heads or another, reading, "Please do not slam this door."

Denny Taylor found that these messages were not intended to be a conscious way of teaching writing. They did serve, however, to fill each home with an abundance of words and clearly expressed messages. Consequently, children in these six families also learned to write notes to their parents. They wrote thank-you notes, I-love-you notes, I-hate-you notes, get-well notes, and notes that defy classification. A favorite of mine:

> Dear Mummy and Daddy, I hate to be a tattletale But I just couldn't help it! BENJAMIN put Aim tooth past on the off white Rug in the hall. . . . people will step on it! It is one in. and 3 senameters! I almost stepped in it. It felt gwee! It is near the green rugs. You daughter Louise Taylor.

School-age children also integrated writing in the clubs they formed: the Ghost Club, the Preteen Sweethearts Club, Kathy Farley's Style Place (a beauty salon), a restaurant. Writing was important because members listed the names of people who were "in" and those who had violated the tenets and were "out." Club members also wrote job descriptions (e.g. "Watering the grass every day and change the [furniture] inside"), prepared menus ("Drinks: milk, milkshake, Pepsi, Lemonade and Sandwiches [ham]"), and decreed the rules that would guide acceptable behavior. The most inventive entrepreneurs tried to sell ice-cold water, which they promoted as being "Very Good For You. Doesn't Rot Teeth Like Lemonade."

In sum, regardless of whether writing was a part of play or a way that family members communicated with each other, it promoted natural connections among children and adults. Founded on the needs of children as they develop and on parental activities, the writing at home that Dr. Taylor collected bore little resemblance to artificial school assignments that are built into lesson plans. Writing and reading are lifted out of context in schools, while they are inseparable from family life at home. Having identified these linkages, Denny Taylor was not surprised to find that children in the households she studied excelled in reading and writing in school. Clearly, parents' lack of professional licenses did not prevent them from remaining "real" teachers at home.

"The single best way to improve elementary education," the U.S. Department of Education's volume *First Lessons* points out, "is to strengthen parents' role in it, both by reinforcing their relationship with the school and by helping and encouraging them in their own critical job of teaching the young." Emphasizing the point, the report says, "Parents belong at the center of a young child's education." Some of the activities to keep in mind as your child grows are an extension of what you did during your earlier years. It is still important to continue your previous emphasis on reading, for example, though appropriate books will be different. Your child may prefer fairy tales and fables or she may lean to children's classic stories such as *Charlotte's Web* and *Winnie the Pooh*. Just-turned-seven-year-old Matthew spent an hour sitting on the floor of a bookstore before he chose the stack of books he wanted for his birthday presents. "The trouble is I really want fourteen, but I don't think I should get more than seven. E. B. White is my new favorite author," he went on to say, "but I still like Dr. Seuss a lot. I even like these books better than television."

That's quite a statement. A telling study of fifth-graders' reading habits revealed that 90 percent of the children surveyed read books only four minutes a day or less. The same children may watch television an average of three and a half hours a day.

Parent-educators may think that once children can read to themselves, there is no need for mothers and fathers to read stories to them as they once did. Not so. The tradition of reading books aloud that initially served the purpose of helping very young children develop language skills and acquire an early attraction to books can be dispelled by graded readers and assorted textbooks. (As California teacher Jo Gusman said, "No one ever gave a child a textbook for Christmas.") To continue to encourage an ongoing love of *good* books and to enhance reading skills that go along with school success, parent-educators need to continue to read to school-age children.

Equally important, the family that reads together forges strong bonds that are not easily developed these days. You may protest that your six-year-old wants to demonstrate that he is grown up by reading to you. Fair enough, but you can combine your child's reading with your own. Reading is slow going at first for a youngster who is just learning to recognize words or to sound them out. As a result, your young reader may tire easily and lose interest in the story before completing it. If this happens, a six- or seven-year-old might become indifferent to books or bored by them. To avoid that turn of events, you might alternate reading the pages of a book or even the sentences with your young reader so that he doesn't weary of the story. An added advantage of taking turns is that you can model reading so that your child learns to pause at commas, stop at periods, and show excitement when a sentence ends with an exclamation point. If he mispronounces a word, you can simply pronounce it correctly when you encounter it during your turn.

Up-to-the-minute parent-educators also know that young

readers enjoy listening to tapes of a story and following along in books. More and more local libraries lend such cassette-book combinations. While this innovation can be a boon to busy parents and increasingly independent young children, it should be used to supplement family read aloud times, not replace them. Nor should older readers be deprived of hearing chapters of a book read. When different dialects and inflections need to be captured and characters' personalities interpreted, read-aloud sessions are first-rate entertainment. The major point for parent-educators to keep in mind is that just as reading aloud should begin well before a baby understands the story, so should it continue well after a reader can handle books independently. Speaking as an adult who can't turn out the light and go to sleep until I have read at least a few pages of the book I keep next to my bed, I know that a love of reading can last a lifetime.

And reading and writing are Siamese twins. Or they should be and will be once your children see that writing serves a purpose in their parents' lives just as reading does. To link the two and get the family started on listening to each other's writing, someone has to take the first step. A father I know told his daughters, "I've been reading letters to the editor in *The Daily Press* for years, but I didn't realize until today that it would be a good idea for me to write one, too. So I'm drafting a letter to say that a traffic light needs to be put on the corner of Main and Oak streets. Did you know there have been six accidents this year and one death! But," he continued, "before I go further, it would help me to hear what you think of what I've written so far." When children see that they are on an equal footing with their parents, they may risk asking for responses to their writing, too. But don't be surprised if it takes more than one such request for their opinion before listening sessions become comfortable.

As your children move into the upper grades your job as parent-educators changes again. *What Works,* a U.S. Department of Education report, advises parent-educators to continue reading, talking, playing games, and sharing hobbies with older children. That's good advice, but you'll need to devise activities on a higher plane than before. Are you devoted to crossword puzzles? Do you play chess or bridge? Do you follow football or baseball in the daily paper? How about hockey or basketball? Seeing who in the family first gets to read the sports section in the newspaper can become something of a contest. The news and feature sections offer other opportunities for reading and talking about timely events and prominent people.

If you're going to buy a car, a camera, a television set, ask your children's opinion about which to get. Reading *Consumer Reports* is one way to narrow down choices. Comparing these reports with promotional brochures is also instructive, for you can help your sons and daughters detect ways that words can color presentations and style can evoke interest. Ask your children to go with you to showrooms and discount appliance stores so you can discuss your reactions with each other. If you wind up feeling the salesperson misled you or the service department didn't meet its obligations, why not put your heads together and write letters of complaint to the dealer, the manufacturer, the Better Business Bureau? If your state has a consumer protection agency or if the legislature has passed a so-called lemon law, your letter-writing protests have just begun. But don't do all the writing yourself. Since the entire family uses appliances and automobiles, include your older children in the letter writing. Everyone old enough to contribute to the letter writing needs to be represented.

What Works proposes some monitoring obligations that are less fun but that have proven to be important for children of all ages. Parent-educators need to observe routines for meals, bedtime, and homework, for example, and to keep an eye on the amount of time spent watching TV. Since well-chosen special events and news programs can offer

quality time, sensible amounts of this kind of television viewing are desirable. But remember, just as your toddler
learned to imitate your speech and your young child developed attitudes about writing that reflect yours, your older
child's television viewing may mimic yours.

If possible, try to provide a special place as well as a special
time for studying, and, if you can, equip the place with books
and supplies. A picture dictionary with simple sentence explanations was useful when your children were beginning
readers and writers, for example, but as they progress
through lower elementary school an illustrated dictionary
with more words—say, 10,000—is more likely to fit their
needs. By upper elementary school something like *The Har-
court Brace School Dictionary* with its 50,000 words
becomes more appropriate. Once your children move to the
secondary level, a more advanced dictionary is again in
order. Regardless of whether or not you can afford to buy
these books, however, you *can* engage in activities that cost
nothing: talk about school problems and successes, help your
children meet deadlines, and discuss school events.

A thesaurus is an excellent tool for expanding a teenager's
vocabulary. Suppose, for example, that your eighth-grader
told you that the football coach is "nice," the girl who sits
across the aisle in math is "nice," the movie they saw together was "nice," and the used car his brother wants to buy
is "nice." Treading carefully on adolescent feelings, you
might say, "Tim, I told some friends from out of town that
you liked the film, but when they asked me what you had
said about it, I didn't know what to say. Do you think you
could come up with any other word except 'nice'?" If Tim
was in a particularly good mood, he could go to the thesaurus
you gave him, where he would find over one hundred ap-
proximate synonyms. He'd probably discard most of them
because they would strike him as too fancy or phony. Nonetheless, he might tell you that the movie was "subtle" and
"clever" or he might say it was "tender," "delicate," and

"warmhearted"—all more descriptive words than "nice." And if he got into the spirit of word hunting in the thesaurus, he might come up with precise adjectives to tell you more about his coach, the girl in his math class, and the used car.

Your son or daughter will be most likely to get into the spirit if writing is an integral part of your family life. My husband and I have written letters to our sons on important occasions: birthdays, graduations, bar mitzvahs, engagements, marriages—no store-bought cards for our family. We have composed prayers to retain the religious traditions that we value, yet to make them more contemporary. Our sons have seen us write notes of appreciation that are not routine matters (and I write a note in response to receiving cards as well as presents); they have seen me struggle to find words of sympathy when words do not come readily. Writing is sometimes hard, but they see that it is worth the effort. As a result, our sons have responded in kind and from time to time a friend or relative tells us, "We received such a wonderful note from Steve [or Rick, or Jeff, or David]."

Even if you've not stressed writing in your child's early years, there is still a job you can do. To begin with, try viewing the drafts that your children bring home from school as early attempts. There will be errors; ignore them. There will be confusing transitions—so what. A draft is not a finished product, it is a preliminary attempt. But so long as you go error hunting, so long as you look for premature perfection, so long as you are more concerned with basic skills than with basic ideas, you will communicate the message that writing is a *product*, not a process that requires drafts, revisions, and editing before it is ready to see the light of day. In other words, you will get in the way of good writing instruction.

By now you know that if you haven't been an influential educator during the years between giving birth and sending your child off to school, you have already fallen behind. And if you haven't gotten involved during the elementary school years, you have lost further opportunities as a parent-educator. Junior high and senior high are late in the day, but not too late to make a difference—especially if you accept the role of parent-advocate and work closely with your child's school.

8

STRATEGIES FOR CHANGE: PARENT INVOLVEMENT AND PARENT ADVOCACY

A chain of command is already fixed in most school districts: Policies are decided on by the school board and conveyed to superintendents, who relay them to administrators, who pass them on to teachers for implementation. The established structure, like that of a large corporation, defines roles and responsibilities, and parents, like small stockholders, are usually expected to go along with the status quo. Under such circumstances, "parent involvement," a widely used expression in educational circles these days, often means becoming involved with business as usual, and parent advocacy of curriculum reform is seldom taken seriously. But it doesn't have to be that way. Parent involvement can now take you into the classroom as a teaching partner and parent advocacy offers a way to influence schools to redirect teaching and learning. Both strategies for change are needed to give writing a central place in the curriculum.

Chic labels, however, are often attached to old activities. Long before anyone spoke of parent involvement, for example, you probably tried to make certain that your children did their homework and you helped them over the hard parts. You went to parent-teacher conferences, ran pot-luck suppers, chaperoned field trips, and attended open school nights to be informed of educational plans that had already been made. All of these traditional activities and a good many more are now considered a part of "parent involvement." But parents are usually kept so distant from *real* involvement that when an educational journal recently devoted an entire issue to ways of improving our schools, it proposed new roles for students, teachers, and administrators—but didn't mention parents.

The omission was not surprising when you consider how differently most parents and professional educators view parent involvement. The differences became particularly clear after Dr. David L. Williams Jr. and a team of researchers from the Southwest Educational Development Laboratory surveyed the attitudes of three thousand parents and four thousand educators in six states. At the outset of the study, all of the participants had agreed that they valued parent involvement. When the five-year study ended, however, the findings revealed that parents and the education community weren't always talking about the same thing, even though they used the same expression. At times, in fact, they had sharply different priorities.

Most teachers, principals, and parents were comfortable with traditional roles and expectations. It was, they agreed, very important for parents to collect tickets for school activities and to be in the audience for various programs. But disagreement became apparent when respondents to the study questionnaires thought about new kinds of parent involvement. Administrators and faculty members objected to parents' questioning educational policy and administrative decisions. Most parents, however, felt they should be able to exercise judgment on children's learning and on the people entrusted with it. Many mothers and fathers wanted to meet with the school board or other officials to seek changes in rules or practices in the school, even in the entire school system. Parents also stated strong interest in serving on an advisory board, a school committee, or a governing board. At the very least, they wanted to give their opinions to members of these boards or committees.

Given the attitudes of most educators, it is understandable when parents hesitate to take on new roles, lest district-wide advocacy be seen as trouble-making and involvement in the classroom be misconstrued as interfering. "I'd hate to be seen as a teacher's adversary instead of her partner," an Ohio mother said, "and I certainly don't want to tread on her toes. But I don't want to be look foolish or be rebuffed, either. And I'd feel terrible if my child felt any reprisal."

The relationship that one parent developed with teachers and curriculum specialists in Montgomery County, Maryland, however, shows that parents can play a new role in the classroom, indeed, in the school system. It all began in 1983 when the Litt family lived in Brooklyn, New York, and Rebecca, a kindergartener in P.S. 230, discovered the excitement of expressing herself in writing. She didn't just have a tea party, she wrote invitations and made place cards. She didn't just build with blocks, she made signs to caution about the danger of her construction. For weeks the Litts' living room was dominated by a large, irregular edifice that bore Rebecca's warning: DON'T COME INTO THE THING THAT HAS BIG RECT AINGALS [RECTANGLES] AND 8 SCINY [SKINNY] SMA [SMALL] RECT AINGAL IT IS A TRAP. When Rebecca was five years and three months old, she wrote instructions for her grandparents who were taking care of her and her baby sister, Miriam:

MIRIAMS MEDASIN ND MI MEDASIN ARE IN THE RE-FRIGARADR WE HAVE THE MEDASIN A HOUR BOFOR MELS I GO TO BED AT 03:7 MIRIAM GOS TO BED WEN SHES TIRD
    LOVE   REBECCA

Rebecca's mother, Debby, herself a product of conventional fill-in-the-blank writing, decided to visit her daughter's kindergarten to find out what miracle was producing a five-year-old author with several books to her credit. (A work that clearly expressed Rebecca's feelings was called *My Sister Is a Mess.*) One school visit led to another, as Rebecca's mother became an enthralled observer of what Lucy McCormick Calkins terms a "writing workshop" and Rebecca called "Writing Land." The Columbia University professor had observed that when children spend extended periods of time (an hour a day, four days a week) drawing, printing signs, and planning projects, the process of writing is no miracle. It becomes second nature to youngsters like Rebecca.

Although Debby Litt began her kindergarten visits as an observer, she found herself being drawn into the role of active participant. Encouraged by Rebecca's teacher and sought after by children, Debby Litt couldn't resist responding to young writers who asked, "What do you think of this?" In fact, the entire idea of linking a writing workshop with writing process was so intriguing that she went on to become a student in Lucy Calkins's summer institute.

Looking for a way to introduce a writing workshop into a school after the family moved to Maryland, Debby brought samples of work from Rebecca's kindergarten class to a meeting of NWP's Capital Area branch in Washington, D.C. "Of course, NWP teachers didn't need any convincing about the merits of writing as a process," Debby said, "but some wondered how they could find time to encourage the amount of writing that Rebecca's teacher had done. Kindergarten, they seemed to think, was one thing, but they had to concentrate on a curriculum. When I heard that, I knew I had found the perfect place to arouse interest in the writing workshop!" The NWP meeting proved to be so perfect that one teacher asked Debby if she could volunteer a little classroom time to develop such a workshop. That fall (1984), Debby gave three mornings a week. Unaccustomed to having a parent-partner, the teacher decided to keep most of the second grade for reading, while Debby formed a writing workshop with a handful of children.

The outpouring of writing that resulted from the work of one parent volunteer in one classroom was just a beginning. By December, Debby Litt was developing writing workshops with the entire second grade, the kindergarten, and the fourth grade of the school. But her work didn't stop there. Using her own money, she took a 6:00 A.M. bus to New York City to enroll in Lucy McCormick Calkins's Saturday institutes to learn more about the writing workshop. While some Maryland teachers whom Debby Lift had stimulated also made (and paid for) the day-long trip, they had to return to their classrooms on Monday morning. Debby, on the other hand, had the time to become an educational consultant in Montgomery County. In five years' time, Debby Litt's expertise in writing process and writing workshops made her a familiar figure, admired by teachers who choose to attend her workshops and welcomed by children who discovered the magic of writing with her.

Debby Litt's expertise is essential to her success, of course, but she is also succeeding because of her clearly focused sense of balance. She knows that advocacy is destined to fail if parents are too domineering for teachers' comfort—or too retiring for their voices to be heard.

One mother who was uncomfortable with her daughter's compositions told me she was even more uncomfortable about overstepping the limits of what she regarded as a parent's proper role. "How would you like it if your child's teacher criticized the way you keep house or your skill as a cook?" she asked. "How would you feel if she had something negative to say about the car you drive, or about your taste in clothes or furniture? . . . The point is, that your personal decisions are really no one else's affair."

This mother is quite right in wanting to avoid criticism that may be taken personally. She is correct, too, in feeling that parents and teachers should not infringe on each other's prerogatives. There are times, however, when walls between "a teacher's business" and "a parent's business" have to turn into bridges. What if a child habitually dozes off in school—from an acknowledged lack of sleep (or because of an unacknowledged drug problem?) What if a child is not handing in carefully prepared homework on time? What if a child has been trading the lunch he has brought from home for cake or cookies? What if a child squints when she reads what's on the blackboard, or appears to have a hearing problem? In such instances the teacher *should* "interfere" at home. By the same token, if you think your child's writing leaves room for improvement, if you are concerned about content or mechanics, you should "interfere" at school. Teacher and parent share legitimate concerns about a youngster's performance that are separate from personal matters. With sensible and sensitive involvement, home and school can support each other's best efforts.

Though Debby Litt is unusually well equipped to provide effective parent involvement, she is careful to avoid behavior that might be viewed as parent dictatorship. "My role is to share ideas and help teachers with new methods, if they care to have that help. But I'd feel terrible if I thought a teacher's response to seeing me coming was, 'Uh-oh, here comes that Litt woman. I wish she wouldn't come barging in here, telling me how to run my classroom.' " Any parent, no matter what contribution she hopes to make, would be wise to develop similar thoughtfulness. Even parents who are only going into a classroom to cut and paste may be surprised to find that they can appear to be threatening.

"*Me*, threatening?" An Iowa mother was astonished by my words. "I was shaking in my boots when I offered to help out. How could *I* make a teacher feel insecure? Surely Ms. S. couldn't think that I would try to take over her classroom." Like parents, however, teachers can be insecure. They may feel uncomfortable being observed and they may, indeed, fear parent takeover. Fortunately, there are as many kinds of parental involvement as there are parents and teachers. The role that you select will depend on your own background, your personality (are you shy or outgoing?), the amount of time you can offer, and the receptivity your child's teacher shows.

In her four years in the classroom, Kym Zanmiller has learned to become adept in building partnerships with parents. Trained at the University of Wyoming, where faculty parents viewed the Lab School as a second home, Kym had to devise ways to encourage parents in a regular public school to feel comfortable spending time in her combined first- and second-grade classroom. "Since parents worry about 'incorrect' spelling, I always invite them to spend time in September, so they can become acquainted with invented spelling and see how children's spelling lists grow out of the stories they write. When I take time to explain what I'm doing," Ms. Zanmiller said, "I can help parents respond to their children's work at home—and they can help me in school."

Two months after school begins Kym sends a flier home asking parents who would like to assist in the classroom to let her know what would be the most convenient time for them. "Some parents do, more don't; but I've never had the enthusiastic response I got from Christopher's mother. It wasn't until we had gotten to know each other over the course of many Monday afternoons that I learned she had been teaching in her church since she was fifteen years old, but she had been frozen out of Christopher's first grade in another school. She was afraid to say anything about helping me until she received an invitation." Had Kym Zanmiller not been so welcoming, she would have missed the services of a mother who was a licensed teacher's aide.

As things worked out, parent and teacher helped each other in unexpected ways. Christopher, it seems, had to complete forty skill sheets a night in first grade in an effort to perfect poor penmanship. His mother thought that was an extreme measure, but she found the messy stories that Ms. Zanmiller accepted extreme in another way. "Christopher is a messy kid," his teacher agreed, "but any time I couldn't read what he had to say, he wrote it over. That didn't happen very often. What *did* happen was an outpouring of wonderful ideas. Christopher is a marvelous boy and I wanted to make sure his mother appreciated him. Once she saw the adventure stories he wrote, no one had to convince her that her son was amazing."

Instead of being at loggerheads with a concerned parent, Kym worked out a teaching partnership with Christopher's mother. "I couldn't be everywhere at once, but my aide sat at the side of young writers and coached them one-on-one. She saw for herself that helping them form ideas was more important than helping them form letters. And I saw once again that parent volunteers don't have to be consigned to the ditto machine. Children could listen to good books and have more support as they wrote their own stories. Parents and teachers are a natural combination.

Christopher is in another grade this year, but his teacher hasn't requested help from parents and his mother shrinks from volunteering, lest she be rejected. "Maybe," she mused, "I'll go back to Ms. Zanmiller—if she'll have me again." Such is the delicate relationship that can prevent even parents who are experienced teachers from offering their services.

Lois Brandts, a first-grade teacher at the Hollister School in Goleta, California, received parent support of another kind. "I don't know what you're doing differently now," a mother critiqued, "but Lisa is writing about thoughts and feelings in a way that Ronnie never did." (Ronnie, now a fourth-grader, had been in Ms. Brandts's first-grade class.) "The note from home caused me to think through precisely how my writing instruction has changed," Lois Brandts said. "I realized that I'm starting writing the first day of school now, and I'm encouraging what kids want to say, instead of a urging them to write a 'Dear Grandma, thank you for the present' note."

"It's exciting to be included in Lisa's life," the note from home concluded. "If she weren't able to write about private feelings, I would never have known that my six-year-old wasn't being lazy when she resisted taking out the garbage at night. She was too embarrassed to tell me the real reason, but her sealed letter said it all: I DONT LIK TO GO OUT BECAWZ I AM AFRAD OF WOLVSES."

Other "wolvses" can intimidate adults. Parent-teacher conferences, for example, are sometimes a dreaded encounter. You may worry about what you're going to hear, and teachers may worry about what you're going to say. In fact, mutual tension is such a widespread phenomenon that the magazine *PTA Today* recently featured a pair of articles on the subject. The first, "Advice for Teachers," provides suggestions for teachers to follow in order to reduce *their* anxiety; a companion piece, "Advice for Parents" does the same for mothers and fathers.

The cause of this trepidation on both sides of the desk is often little more than poor communication. No where is this more evident than in writing instruction. Your child's teacher may be emphasizing his poor punctuation, grammar, and usage, demonstrated in her sheaf of ditto pages, at a time when you want to focus on his good ideas, demonstrated in your collection of stories that he has written. Conversely, his teacher may want to stress his imagination when you are concerned about his overly imaginative spelling. Regardless of who is the reformer and who the traditionalist (roles where no one has a monopoly), you and the teacher may have one thing in common: a single-mindedness that ignores the other's concerns.

Since millions of parents and teachers face the same problems, it's a good idea to look beyond your own experience. If a teacher, any teacher, is not ready to give up the props on which she has been leaning, she will feel put upon if she thinks parents want her to replace rules with what she considers anarchy. Likewise, parents, any parents, who are not ready to see correct mechanics taught through actual writing will resist a process approach. By its very nature, change is unsettling, and change that is misunderstood leads to heated opposition. For innovations in writing instruction to take hold, therefore, reformers need to explain their reasons for seeking change and discuss the programs they have in mind. Discussion, of course, is a dialogue, not a monologue. Consequently, reformers also need to appreciate the real concerns that opponents to change will raise.

To acknowledge that there can be real differences of opinion, however, is not to suggest that such differences are inevitable. Quite the contrary. A particularly notable illustration of parent-teacher collegiality has developed between Rick Monroe, eighth-grade English teacher in Washington state's Woodinville High School, and sixteen parents whose help he enlisted to sustain an innovative writing program. It's hard to know who derives more satisfaction from their combined efforts, Monroe or the parents. This much is certain, however: Together, teacher and parents have discovered how *real* parent involvement can solve what would otherwise have been a Catch-22 bind.

Rick's commitment to teaching writing was so unusual that he found himself needing to respond to more drafts and revisions than he could handle. As a result, he faced two alternatives: either discourage his students' outpouring of ideas because the paperwork was overwhelming or respond to them in an untimely, limited fashion. Neither solution satisfied him. Now Rick sends papers with covering letters to sixteen parent-readers. He explains the assignment and indicates how far into the drafting stage the papers are. Monroe always tells parents that he does not want them to grade the papers, because grading is his responsibility, but he doesn't fret over sharing other aspects of his role. Indeed, he wonders how he ever managed without the help of his parent-readers.

Instead of feeling dislodged, he appreciates their willingness to respond fully to the content. "If you feel compelled to, go ahead and correct the spelling, usage, and punctuation," he said in the first letter he sent to parent-readers, "but more importantly, I'd like you to listen to what the student has to say and then respond to the ideas you have read." He suggested that parents might want to write a letter to the student, and he raised more than half a dozen points that parents might address. (Is the writing vague? If it lacks detail, rewrite a section, demonstrating how clear and concrete writing is done. Is the piece informative? Is there a main idea that holds the writing together? Does each sentence prepare you for the next, each paragraph for the next? Is there a beginning, a middle, and an end?)

Rick Monroe's guidelines conveyed his own standards—standards so high that he feared parents might find them overwhelming. Instead, they were heartened to see the improvement between drafts that *they* had initiated. "I think I learned more from reading these papers," one parent wrote Rick Monroe, "than the kids did from writing them." Another parent thanked him for letting her read the papers, and concluded modestly, "I hope I was able to help." Letters like these show some of the rewards of a genuine educational partnership.

After being included in teaching and learning for the first time, parents saw how the process of writing works. They understood how students's drafting, getting responses along the way, and revising writing improves the final product. And they found they no longer felt compelled to correct spelling, usage, and punctuation at the beginning, even though Rick Monroe had freed them to do so if they felt the need. Focusing on ideas the drafts contained proved more intriguing and they knew that postponing concern about mechanics did not mean neglecting them.

Students benefited from having parent-readers, too, for they reported that they liked writing for an audience other than their teacher or their peers. And Rick Monroe found that parents taught him an important lesson, for he discovered that their encouraging responses to students' efforts were more productive than his more critical ones. "They didn't slough over key issues," Rick observed, "but they didn't stint on praise, either." For parent involvement to make the kind of headway it has at Woodinville High School, it was important for both parents and teachers to realize that neither party is the enemy, and that either party can assist the other, if given the chance.

That kind of understanding pervades Illinois's Lincolnshire-Prairie View School District 103. Sixteen times a year, administrators, teachers, and subject specialists attend Parent Information Sessions where common concerns are discussed. The anxiety that some parents had first expressed to classroom teachers about the schools' seeming to neglect basic skills while teaching writing as a process went on to become a topic that parents and educators discussed together. "When it became clear that we *all* needed a firmer grasp of writing instruction," school superintendent Oscar Bedrosian told me, "the school board provided funds to hire Robert Gundlach, director of writing programs at Northwestern University." True to the cooperative spirit of the district, Gundlach did not neglect parents in the course of working with teachers and principals. Instead, he offered them six 2½-hour sessions on writing as a process. Some 250 parents attended and explored topics such as: how writing is learned, what the school curriculum does to show its support of writing, and how parents can evaluate what their children are learning.

Involved parents in a number of model schools in Vermont also were motivated to find out more about writing. The reason? Their children's enthusiasm. Paul Escholz and Alfred Rosa, then codirectors of the Vermont Writing Program, were invited to attend parent meetings in schools in six different communities (South Burlington, Middlebury,

Milton, Stowe, Westford, and Tunbridge) where parent attendance was about triple the usual turnout. "Parents told us they had to see what was making their children so excited about school," Paul Escholz said. "The kids were coming home talking about writing and talking about school in a way that parents had never heard before, and they wanted to know why."

The same parent interest showed itself in P.S. 148 in East Elmhurst, New York, where five hundred parents (in a school of nine hundred children) crowded the cafeteria, the classrooms, the hallways on Authors' Night. "I really saw the power of writing last spring," the president of the PTA told me, "when I saw how it helped my son Patrick handle his sadness after his grandfather died. No one seemed able to help Pat—not his father, not I, not even our priest. But Patrick found his own solution. He wrote a story that spoke of his loneliness and his memories. And he ended it by saying that he knew Grandpa was in heaven now. Imagine! My third-grader could write the words he was too choked up to speak."

Indeed, Patrick was such a busy writer that his sister Erin began following his example before she entered kindergarten. When Erin's mother said she would help her little girl with a Christmas letter to Santa Claus "tomorrow," Erin decided to proceed independently and compose her own DER SANTA note. Erin wrote her own letter. Her mother was elated. "Parents at P.S. 148 who attend our winter workshop on writing process—and we get a large turnout for this meeting—have learned that spelling is one of our last concerns. Ideas come first. Erin had so many ideas that if we were going to worry about anything, it would probably have been whether Christmas was going to break the bank!"

Parents in Richmond, Virginia, and the surrounding area presented another picture. There, unlike P.S. 148, the schools had typically bypassed writing, but a number of parents were curious about the neglected second R. In fact, almost one hundred mothers and fathers applied to be selected for eight slots in a unique Summer Institute for Parents, sponsored by the Capital Writing Project (a branch of the National Writing Project). All told, the institute managed to stretch the slots fourteen ways, and the participants later found ways to reach hundreds of teachers, parents, and children during the school year.

After her summer experience, one mother offered to begin a Friday writing group for the lowest achieving third- and fourth-grade children. Not surprisingly, her overture was gratefully accepted. "It wasn't the writing that mattered to the classroom teacher, at first," the parent volunteer acknowledged. "I think I would have received the same gratitude if I had offered to take these kids to shell peanuts. But in a while the writing itself really bowled teachers over."

A second mother received the same kind of appreciation when she offered to undertake a writing program for another population with special needs: learning disabled children. A third parent held a book-binding workshop for Girl Scouts who wanted to write and "publish" their own material, and a fourth reached parents with children in a day-care center. It would be hard to think of activities less threatening than these. When praise of various gentle efforts filtered back to the school, it was clear that the resistance toward writing was beginning to break down. Some secondary English teachers asked to have their own parent-led writing workshop. Next, a school-wide writing workshop attracted members of the larger faculty. Indeed, several parents went on to lead workshops for teachers attending five Richmond Area Reading Council regional conferences. The multiplier effect led to PTA groups' scheduling workshops and to schools' asking parents to staff booths on parent-conference days. Perhaps the most unexpected reaction came from Richmond bookstores that decided to sponsor writing sessions for parents and children.

When you take a look at what took place during the weeklong training session, you can understand how fourteen parents were motivated to have the impact they did. On the morning of the first day, the same piece of writing was distributed to groups of three readers. The first person was told to respond as though the writing had been prepared by a best friend, the second to play the role of editor, and the third to be a teacher. Automatically, when the "teacher" surfaced, the participants' first reaction was to mark errors or correct them, instead of attending to the meaning in print. The traditional teacher was present in every parent at the outset, both parents who were dissatisfied with a school or a teacher and parents who had no complaints. The first night of the training session was equally revealing. Parents were to ask their children to fill out a questionnaire about the process they go through when they compose a piece of writing. A seven-year-old was so afraid of being "wrong" that he failed to write anything on the questionnaire, and an eight-year-old wept because he believed that his work was not neat enough to turn in and his mother didn't have a second copy of the form. In less than twenty-four hours, parents learned that even first- and second-grade children suffered from writing panic.

Another surprise: parents found themselves unable to remember the grammar they had been taught in formal lessons only a few years ago. But as they started to do their own writing each day, parents discovered that the process of writing offered a tool for learning in many areas, including grammar. Knowing the effort *they* put into writing, they also discovered how important it is to encourage a young writer who works hard to put down honest feelings. Yet shared horror stories made it clear that those earnest efforts are typically rewarded with comments about insufficient margins or sloppy handwriting. Parents-turned-writers acknowledged that they had the same "margins mentality" until they saw the more pressing need for reactions to work in progress. By week's end, program participants were turning into advocates who viewed writing in entirely new ways.

Even though the National Writing Project was formed to help teachers, many, perhaps most, of its chapters might find the idea of staffing a mini-institute for parents appealing. Unfortunately, few, if any, have the funds that this modest project would require. NWP offshoots may be able to answer requests for information, however, and suggest ideas for a workshop you could create in your own school. A listing of the regional offices of the NWP can be found on pages 265–267.

As you learn about the impact that a new approach to teaching writing has already had in some innovative districts, you will probably want to encourage reform in your own schools. But you will be in a better position to advocate change when you find out how writing is being taught outside of your child's classroom. Correct mechanics are probably emphasized with monotonous regularity. But what about the connection between writing, thinking, and learning? What about the awareness of writing as a process? What about writing in math and science, social studies and foreign languages? In other words, what about writing that extends beyond language arts and English; what about writing across the curriculum?

To answer these questions you'll want to visit a wide range of classrooms (with the principals' permission, of course). Since no one person can take on such a Herculean task, you're going to need the help of other parents who have the time and commitment to offer. It's a good idea to develop an observation checklist for everyone to use while visiting classrooms. In that way you won't have parents emphasizing the frequency of writing, the amount, or the nature of teachers' comments. The guidelines that follow will give you some ideas, though they are not meant to be followed slavishly. You will find that preparing your own classroom observation checklist will make you sensitive to what your ears hear, your eyes see, your feelings sense, and your minds question.

	Always	Seldom	Never

TOPICS

1. Are assignments chosen by the teacher?
    or
    Are they chosen by students?

2. Is writing limited to English and language arts?
    or
    Is writing used to teach *all* subjects?

3. If students find their initial idea is not working out, are they required to stay with it?
    or
    May they change plans, so long as they do not keep flitting about aimlessly?

4. Must students all begin their work at the same time and complete it at the same time as well?
    or
    May they adjust the process to fit their needs?

COMPOSING

5. Do students write as many drafts as they need, within limits, to satisfy *themselves* as writers?

	Always	Seldom	Never

6. Do you hear questions that focus on satisfying the *teacher:* "How long do you want it to be?" "Does spelling count?" "Will you take off points if the paper is late?"

7. When writers are ready for feedback, do they read their work to classmates?

8. Have students learned to offer encouraging, specific, and honest responses? Are they able to ask helpful questions to guide the writer toward his next draft?

9. Do teachers wait to provide comments until students have completed their work?
   or
   Do they have ongoing student conferences throughout the composing process?

10. Is *revision* at the heart of student writing just as it is central to professional writing?
   or
   Do students mistake *re-vision* (looking at something in a new way) for copying over, which they see as punishment for not having written something in the teacher's way?

	Always	Seldom	Never

OTHER PRIORITIES

11. Do teachers also compose in class? Do they seek student responses? Do they revise one draft after another? In sum, do they serve as role models?

12. Is there a clear, ongoing connection between reading and writing?

13. Does frequent writing have an impact on students' grasp of grammar, usage, punctuation, and spelling?

14. Is copyediting for writing conventions a close-to-final step that student writers and editors do together, with each bearing responsibility for correctness?
    or
    Does the teacher's search for errors begin at the earliest possible moment?

15. Is writing directed only at the teacher who is reader, editor, and grader?
    or
    Do students publish stories and articles for the class or the school library, for the local newspaper or PTA bulletin, for the school literary magazine—and write for their teacher, too?

	Always	Seldom	Never

16. Is the sound of a student's voice on paper considered important?

17. Are tables or desks clustered together so that students can share ideas with each other?
    or
    Are desks lined up one behind the other?

18. Is writing an important part of the day, consuming at least a half an hour for in-class writing?

19. Do you hear the hum of *purposeful* activity and see the signs of growing accomplishment?
    or
    Is the classroom a silent place, where writing is a solitary chore?

20. Does teaching accommodate innovative instruction, yet respect the importance of correct conventions?

Before your group has collated its findings, you will already have made major strides toward developing an overview of the writing curriculum in your school or your school district—an exceedingly rare accomplishment for any parent group. To complete the picture, you may also want to collect report cards that are used so that you will know how writing is assessed, if, indeed, it is. You'll undoubtedly find, as Chapter 6 indicated, that the nature of statewide, school-district, and local-school assessments (short answer, essay, portfolio, or some combination of these approaches) affects how writing is taught. And if there is no assessment, in contrast to the frequent evaluation of reading, for example, the very absence is illuminating. Under those circumstances it is hard to fault teachers for getting the message that writing isn't considered terribly important.

Having read *Growing Up Writing*, you will know the answer to the question a prominent educator recently asked: "How would *parents* know how writing should be taught?" In fact, you'll probably know more about desirable writing practices than do many professional educators. And having delved into your local writing program as much as time permitted, you probably know more than the superintendent about the district's approach to writing instruction. But if you are troubled by the teaching you have observed, a question remains: who can help you make sure that children receive improved writing instruction?

The qualities of sensitivity that are important for parent activists are more important than ever. You could, for example, take your findings directly to people at the top of your school district's organization chart: board members, the superintendent, and assistant superintendents. They, presumably, are in the best position to use their influence to support a training program for teachers. But the people with the most power have the least contact with the life of the classroom. Well-intentioned as they may be, they can undermine a program before it even gets started. Indeed, any approach that begins by circumventing teachers runs that risk.

You will find that although teachers have very little power or influence in the hierarchy of a school system (the only groups with less are the student body—and parents), no one can make change work except teachers themselves. And they probably won't make writing reform work if it is imposed on them. Begin your advocacy, therefore, by developing a cadre of parents who recognize teachers for the important people they are. Nancie Atwell, director of Bread Loaf's Writing to Learn project, suggests that some parents who want to encourage writing as a process invite a few teachers to weekend or after-school writing groups. It will take courage to get a group started and more courage for parents and teachers to trust each other enough to overcome the embarrassment of sharing drafts and revisions of their own writing. In time, however, the walls can come tumbling down. When that happens, teachers and parents will be able to talk about applying their own group experience to the classroom.

When secure teachers and committed parents put their heads together, children usually benefit. Eleanor Kron, recently retired from the Mount Vernon, New York, public school system, says that her third-grade writing program would not have taken shape without parent help. And I know that I would not have offered that help had it not been for her openness.

Ms. Kron had already made language the centerpiece of her lively classroom. Knowing that most eight-year-olds come to school with experiences to share, she encouraged them to talk about their ideas and feelings. Children who are able to talk freely, she believed, want to write about what is on their minds and read about what is on someone else's. Strongly committed to the connection between spoken and written language, Ms. Kron was troubled to find that the worthwhile reading and writing she had expected didn't materialize. "I couldn't figure out why kids who lingered over children's classics at home zipped through Little Golden Books or their equivalent in school," she recalls. "My principal probably would have said that there was too much buzzing in the room for concentration, but I had seen these kids concentrate so deeply that they didn't hear the bell ring."

With a little outside perspective, the mystery did not seem hard to solve. A weekly book report that looked like a way to encourage reading and writing actually discouraged both because children can't savor a book in a week's time and write a polished report that explores their feelings about what they have read. And having children submit their reports on four-by-six filing cards probably seemed to be a way to establish a record-keeping system, but the cards were likely to have inhibited writing. Good readers usually are eager writers who have a lot to say.

Ms. Kron was satisfied with the sleuthing. "You've found the culprits!" she exclaimed. "But it's one thing to know what *not* to do, and another to put a good writing program together. Do you have any ideas?" Teachers don't usually ask parents this kind of question, but Ms. Kron was an unusual teacher and I was fortunate to have an unusual background. As senior research associate on the staff that was compiling material for my husband's book, *Crisis in the Classroom*, I had just finished visiting some pioneering British infant schools where third-grade children were enrolled, so I was able to tell Eleanor Kron about the variety of writing that permeated the schools I had seen. She seemed so interested that I gave her a copy of the report I had written of my experience abroad. "I thought this might interest you," I said mildly, not wanting to be unduly intrusive. *"Interest me!"* she exclaimed the next day. "I stayed up until two in the morning; I simply couldn't put your report down!" When I asked her what she had found so engrossing, Eleanor Kron said, *"I found the teacher that I meant to be, the teacher who got lost along the way."* And I found that there is almost no limit to the ways in which parents and teachers can work together.

Very rarely, a parent's offer to help teach writing may be accepted. Debby Litt is such a parent. Joyce Vining Morgan is another. Donald Graves and Virginia Stuart describe Ms. Morgan's experience in their book, *Write from the Start.* This mother had experience teaching composition at a university but had never taught second grade. Lack of experience didn't stop her from volunteering to assist in her daughter's classroom, however. "You don't need elementary school credentials," Joyce Vining Morgan said, "to know that writing is not likely to flourish in a room where students sit in rows working on the same assignment at the same time—and the teacher scolds children ahead of time to make sure they don't get out of line." The teacher's I-dare-you-to-succeed attitude was reflected in her response to the offer of volunteer help. The time she selected was Friday afternoons—typically the most difficult stretch of the week for any teacher, and particularly so for this stern taskmaster, whose students couldn't wait to escape from her clutches.

On the first day Ms. Morgan brought to class nineteen pages of drafts that a local poet had gone through before he was able to reduce his effort to eight lines. Eight lines that, despite the many revisions, were not accepted for publication. The children were fascinated that a "real" writer could erase some words, cross out others, and squeeze new thoughts in the margin, just as they did. After the children had written a piece on the movie *E.T.*, a topic their teacher had assigned, Ms. Morgan and another parent volunteer who was working in the school system each took six children at a time and tried to form response groups where writers would read their work to classmates; they in turn would learn how to offer helpful ideas and ask the kind of questions that might spur the writer on to the next draft. Instead, youngsters who had never been taught to work cooperatively turned the groups into competitions, with each student asking the others, "How many questions did *you* get?" The number, not the substance, was what mattered most. Equally discouraging to Ms. Morgan and her colleague, the children wanted to correct punctuation and spelling on pieces that were not yet ready to become free from errors.

The solution? A two-stage process. Although Morgan was convinced that it was premature to move on to copy editing, the teacher was most concerned that the children learn mechanics. Together they decided that Morgan would work with small groups of children on content questions in early drafts. When the writers were ready to edit, they would go to their teacher. As time passed, the veteran classroom teacher was impressed by what her students had succeeded in doing. To her surprise she found that they were able to select their own topics. Even more surprising, they were able to work together without direct supervision. "I never would have believed that this boisterous class could maintain order," she acknowledged. In fact she was so impressed that she came up with ideas for seeking more volunteers to lend a hand with classroom writing instruction.

Parents who want to help free teachers from the security—and dullness—of ditto sheets don't have to be amateur writers, much less college instructors with the advanced skills of a Joyce Vining Morgan. If you can type, for example, you can do what many mothers are doing in the younger grades from New York to Indiana to California: transform children's final handwritten product into a copy to be published for the class or school library. To complete the transformation, you can learn to bind the writing in handsome wallpaper-coated cardboard covers. You'll find that when teachers know that parents will free them from having to labor over the final production, writing is likely to take on a life of its own. And before you know what has happened, you'll also find that your time in the classroom isn't limited to this final stage because children come to view every adult as another resource person. ("Do you have any ideas about what I can read about inventors?" "Do you like the way my story begins?")

Teachers and parents in kindergarten and the first two grades of elementary school are clearly the most receptive to change, but other heartening examples of parent advocacy certainly exist. Joanie Chancer, who now directs a reading-writing workshop in the intermediate division of La Colinas School in Camarillo, California, experienced the kind of parental support that cheers a teacher. Parents of her fifth-graders wrote principal William Lamp to ask if he could arrange for children to stay with her when she moved up to sixth grade, where intermediate classes begin. These parents recognized the importance of Ms. Chancer's combined curriculum, and they wanted to see their children's remarkable growth continue. Never before had Amy chosen to write poetry or to read one book after another. Never before had Brian realized that he didn't have to stop thinking in order to be cool. And never before had so many parents said that a teacher could count on their continuing to read every draft and revision their children wrote.

Most parents who get involved in their child's education tend to be mothers (unless disciplinary issues are at stake), but Jim Lenfestey experienced the gratification of working with young children when he responded to a Minneapolis kindergarten teacher's call for volunteers to help her children write weekly journals. "I thought I'd be ill at ease as the only adult male in the room, but I was so fascinated helping five-year-olds discover what they could do as writers that I lost all self-consciousness." Upon asking around, Jim found that the principal and other teachers wanted more volunteers.

Clearly parents can play a worthwhile role, but you already know that parents are not always the initiators of change and teachers are not always reluctant dragons. Both parents and teachers tend to cling to a system that hasn't changed in over a century but, by and large, you'll find that educators are more likely than parents to understand the place that writing can occupy in thinking and learning, for they have a support system that parents lack.

Part of that support is tucked away in a little house on Court Street in Portsmouth, New Hampshire, where publishers unfamiliar to the general public, Heinemann Educational Books, Inc., and its division for secondary and college teaching, Boynton Cook Publishers, produce a treasury of books that outstanding teachers have written for other teachers who want to explore new ways of thinking about writing. (See Recommended Reading.) The publishers' leading authors—people like Donald Graves and Lucy McCormick Calkins, Nancie Atwell and Tom Romano—are key figures in a writing revolution.

Teachers seeking to change the way they teach writing can also fill their library with affordable books and journals published by the National Council of Teachers of English. In addition, they can exchange ideas and practices with thousands of their colleagues who travel great distances at their own expense to attend NCTE conventions and workshops and still other teachers who make comparable trips to meet with NWP colleagues. But teachers' best instincts can be thwarted by administrators who issue mandates on "correct teaching" without considering the connection between language and ideas, or by test developers who address narrow skills. As a result, teachers need to be able to count on parent approval rather than disparagement, parent help rather than obstruction.

To gain the political sophistication needed to advance advocacy in a school system, you can turn to the two major national organizations that came into being in 1973 in order to foster an expanded role for parents or citizens. The National Committee for Citizens in Education (NCCE) in Columbia, Maryland, is a national advocate group that is committed to promoting local action to transform schools from what they are to what parents want them to be. The title of its recent book, *Beyond the Bake Sale: An Educator's Guide to Working with Parents,* is a close-to-ideal summary of the organization's three statements of purpose:

- To help parents improve education for their children.
- To train parents, educators, and citizens to work constructively for better schools in their community.
- To provide information and resources parents, educators,

and community members need to improve the quality of public schools.

"It doesn't make any sense, does it," NCCE senior staff associate Carl Marburger asks, "to have people who never see students decide what they should learn? But that's how most schools operate. People who have the least to do with the life of the classroom have the most to say about teaching and learning. I'd call that top-down mismanagement." Undeterred by the fact that superintendents, assistant superintendents, and board members have exercised this power as long as he can remember, Carl Marburger has set out to bring decision-making power to parents, community leaders, teachers, and administrators who are close to the classroom. "These are the people who should design programs and figure out how much time is needed for successful learning."

There are many examples of schools that are being transformed by those most directly affected by what happens in the classroom. You'll find them in school districts all over California, in many parts of Florida, New Jersey, South Carolina—indeed, in almost every state—as well as in major cities and small school districts. Consider what's happening in Hammond, Indiana, where ten-to-fifteen-person "design teams" of parents, teachers, administrators, and students form one core team per school, with teachers making up a majority. Early results are promising. The central office, for example, had nothing to do with Kenwood Elementary School's restructuring its schedule to allow a ninety-minute block of uninterrupted time for reading instruction. And no one at Lafayette Elementary School had to ask the superintendent's permission for a team of teachers and administrators to work closely with parents on designing programs and selecting textbooks.

The other well-established advocacy organization, the Institute for Responsive Education (I.R.E.) is housed in Boston

University's School of Education. Founder and president Don Davies explains that the term *responsive education* is meant to signal the need for better two-way communication between schools and families or communities. "Under some circumstances," Davies says, " 'communication' " can be a vague term, but we're talking specifically about communication that results in informed citizens participating in educational decision making."

A recent I.R.E. publication, *Consumer's Guide to Schools of Choice . . . For Parents and Other Educators,* fosters that goal by showing parents who are in the enviable position of being able to select a public school what kinds of learning are supposed to lie behind various labels. For a fortunate few, parent values and a school program mesh. More likely, parents will have to put advocacy skills to work to bring about change. Another publication, *Parents and Schools: Partnership or Politics,* takes the mechanisms parents have used to question and oppose school policies in special education and extends it to other areas where unequal opportunities exist. And I.R.E.'s quarterly, *Equity and Choice,* is a forum for provocative ideas that are not found elsewhere. It is not unusual, for example, for education journals to note that "acquiring literacy skills" (that's jargon for "reading and writing") is the joint concern of home and school. But it is unusual for such an article to propose that shared concern lead to parent evaluation of the teacher-of-teachers, the school principal.

A mother or father who has asked, "But what can *I* do? I'm only a parent," can look to the success of Gerry Moriarty and Cindy Baran that was featured in the I.R.E. article "When Parents Do Their Homework" three years ago. The two young women had a clear-cut goal: to revitalize a flagging parent commitment to public education in Holyoke, Massachusetts, in order to restore quality schools. Since they didn't have an equally clear hold on how best to proceed, Moriarty and Baran did their own homework, researching success stories of stimulating parent participation from Providence to Atlanta (and learning from others' mistakes as well as from their accomplishments). Motivating Holyoke's diverse ethnic and economic population took persistence, persuasiveness, dedication, and know-how—the same qualities that parents advocating any change need in order to achieve results.

Refusing to be discouraged by the resistance they encountered, Moriarty and Baran worked out a new partnership between the city and a vigorous network of parent organizations. Indeed, Gerry and Cindy are "only parents" whose impact caused an admirer from the central office to say, "My experience in schools is that change does not come traditionally from those in power. Change is effected by people who demand change, and sometimes you need a person perceived as an outsider to say, 'Wait a minute, let's try something different, it's time for a change.' "

Developing a worthwhile writing program begins with the same viewpoint as Baran's and Moriarity's. "We just figured that if we didn't do it," Cindy said, "we couldn't sit back and expect other parents to roll up their sleeves." For these parent activists, "it" meant developing a lasting way for parents to have a say and improve education for their own kids and others in Holyoke. For you, "it" means showing thoughtful concern about the school's failure to make writing central to thinking and learning. At first Cindy and Gerry had no one to turn to but each other in shaping a new plan. You are not so limited, because branches of BAWP and NWP and fired-up teachers from Bread Loaf, New Hampshire, and other writing programs are eager to make an impact on school programs.

Most of the activities that Baran and Moriarty undertook related to their specific goal, of course, but part of their philosophy is universal. "These are *our* schools," Gerry Moriarty said, "and we have a right to voice our opinion about what happens there." Phrasing the same idea somewhat differently, Cindy Baran designed red buttons for the children that read, "I am the future of Holyoke." The schools in your community are also yours—and your children are the future. For them to have the future that is rightfully theirs, remember that you need to wear a button, too. Invisible as it may be, the five words on it should read, "I am my child's advocate."

The most exciting discovery I made while wending my way through outstanding classrooms around the country was that Johnny and Jane *can* write when they are well taught. And teachers *can* teach well when *they* are well taught. The genius of gifted teachers needs to be heralded. And the accomplishments of so-called ordinary children need to be celebrated—celebrated, and used to realize that wonderful possibilities lie before us.

▪APPENDIX

NAMES AND ADDRESSES OF NATIONAL WRITING PROJECT REGIONAL DIRECTORS AND THE STATES IN EACH REGION

Northeast Region

Connecticut
Maine
Massachusetts

New York
Rhode Island
Vermont

Directors:

Joseph Check
Institute for Learning
    and Teaching
University of Massachu-
    setts, Harbor Campus
Dorchester, MA 02125

Richard Sterling
Herbert H. Lehman College
    (CUNY)
Bedford Park Blvd.
Bronx, NY 10463

Mid-Atlantic Region

Delaware
District of Columbia
Maryland
New Jersey

Pennsylvania
Virginia
West Virginia

Director:

Robert Weiss
West Chester University
West Chester, PA 19383

Southeast Region

Alabama
Florida
Georgia

Mississippi
North Carolina
South Carolina

Director:

Samuel Watson
Department of English
University of North Carolina
Charlotte, NC 28223

Mideast Region

Illinois
Indiana
Kentucky

Michigan
Ohio
Wisconsin

Director:

B. J. Wagner
English Department
National College of Education
Evanston, IL 60201

North-Central Region

Iowa
Manitoba, Canada
Minnesota

North Dakota
South Dakota

Director:

Keith Tandy
English Department
Moorhead State University
Moorhead, MN 56560

Mid-Central Region

Colorado
Kansas

Missouri
Nebraska

Director: Michael Vivion
English Department
University of Missouri
Kansas City, MO 64110

South-Central Region

Arkansas   Oklahoma
Louisiana   Texas
New Mexico

Director: David A. England
223 Peabody Hall
Louisiana State University
Baton Rouge, LA 70803

Pacific Region

Arizona   Hawaii
California   Nevada

Director: Sheridan Blau
Graduate School of Education
University of California
Santa Barbara, CA 93106

Northwest Region

Alaska   Utah
Idaho   Washington
Montana   Wyoming
Oregon

Director: William Strong
Secondary Education
Utah State University
Logan, UT 84322

■RECOMMENDED READING

Here are some of the books I found helpful, listed by subject:

Preschool Through Elementary Grades

Bissex, Glenda L. *Gnys at Wrk*. Cambridge: Harvard University Press, 1980.

Calkins, Lucy McCormick. *Lessons from a Child*. Portsmouth, N.H.: Heinemann Educational Books, 1983.

———. *The Art of Teaching Writing*. Portsmouth, N.H.: Heinemann Educational Books, 1986. (This book goes beyond sixth grade but the emphasis is on the elementary level.)

Clay, Marie. *Writing Begins at Home*. Portsmouth, N.H.: Heinemann Educational Books, 1987.

Graves, Donald H. *Writing: Teachers and Children at Work*. Portsmouth, N.H.: Heinemann Educational Books, 1983.

Graves, Donald H., and Stuart, Virginia. *Write from the Start*. New York: E. P. Dutton, 1985.

Hansen, Jane, Newkirk, Thomas, and Graves, Donald, eds. *Breaking Ground: Teachers Relate Reading and Writing in the Elementary School*. Portsmouth, N.H.: Heinemann Educational Books, 1985.

Harste, Jerome C., Woodward, Virginia A., and Burke, Carolyn L. *Language Stories and Literacy Lessons*. Portsmouth, N.H.: Heinemann Educational Books, 1984.

Newkirk, Thomas, and Atwell, Nancie, eds. *Understanding Writing*. Chelmsford, Mass.: Northeast Regional Exchange, 1982.

Pinnell, Gay Su, ed., *Discovering Language with Children*.

Urbana, Ill.: National Council of Teachers of English, 1980.

Taylor, Denny. *Family Literacy: Young Children Learning to Read and Write*. Portsmouth, N.H.: Heinemann Educational Books, 1983.

Trelease, Jim. *The Read-Aloud Handbook*. New York: Penguin Books, 1982.

Wells, Gordon. *The Meaning Makers: Children Learning Language and Using Language to Learn*. Portsmouth, N.H.: Heinemann Educational Books, 1986.

Wiener, Harvey S. *Any Child Can Write*. New York: McGraw-Hill, 1978.

Secondary School and Beyond

Atwell, Nancie. "Writing and Reading from the Inside Out," in Hansen, Jane, Newkirk, Thomas, and Graves, Donald, eds. *Breaking Ground*, Portsmouth, N.H.: Heinemann Educational Book, 1985.

Atwell, Nancie. *In the Middle: Writing, Reading, and Learning with Adolescents*. Portsmouth, N.H.: Boynton Cook, 1987.

Boyer, Ernest L. *High School*. New York: Harper Colophon, 1983.

Murray, Donald. *Writing to Learn*. New York: Holt, Rinehart and Winston, 1984.

———. *Read to Write: A Writing Process Reader*. New York: Holt, Rinehart and Winston, 1986.

Perrone, Vito and Associates. *Portraits of High Schools*. Princeton, N.J.: Carnegie Foundation for the Advancement of Teaching/Princeton University Press, 1985.

Romano, Tom. *Clearing the Way: Working with Teenage Writers*. Portsmouth, N.H.: Heinemann Educational Books, 1987.

Shaughnessy, Mina P. *Errors & Expectations*. New York: Oxford University Press, 1977.

Sizer, Theodore R. *Horace's Compromise: The Dilemma of*

the American High School. Boston: Houghton Mifflin, 1984.

Wigginton, Eliot. *Sometimes a Shining Moment: The Foxfire Experience, Twenty Years Teaching in a High School Classroom.* New York: Anchor Press/Doubleday, 1985.

Writing Across the Curriculum (Writing to Learn)

Gere, Anne Ruggles, ed. *Roots in the Sawdust: Writing to Learn Across the Disciplines.* Urbana, Ill.: National Council of Teachers of English, 1985.

Martin, Nancy, et al. *Learning & Writing Across the Curriculum, 11–16.* London: Ward Lock Educational, 1976. Reprinted, Portsmouth, N.H.: Boynton Cook, 1976.

Mayher, John S., Lester, Nancy B., and Pradl, Gordon M. *Learning to Write/Writing to Learn.* Portsmouth, N.H.: Boynton Cook, 1983.

Moffett, James. *Active Voice: A Writing Program Across the Curriculum.* Portsmouth, N.H.: Boynton Cook, 1981.

Stock, Patricia L., ed. *FFORUM: Essays on Theory and Practice in the Teaching of Writing.* Portsmouth, N.H.: Boynton Cook, 1983. See:

    Bailey, Richard W., "Writing Across the Curriculum: The British Approach."

    Baker, Sheridan, "Writing as Learning."

    Britton, James, "Language and Learning Across the Curriculum."

    Fulwiler, Toby, "Why We Teach Writing in the First Place."

    Odell, Lee, "How English Teachers Can Help Their Colleagues Teach Writing."

Thaiss, Christopher. *Language Across the Curriculum in the Elementary Grades.* Urbana, Ill.: National Council of Teachers of English, 1986.

Zinsser, William. *Writing to Learn.* New York: Harper & Row, 1988.

Testing

Applebee, Arthur N., Langer, Judith A., Mullis, Ina V. S. *Writing: Trends Across the Decade, 1974–1984.* Princeton, N.J.: National Assessment of Educational Progress/Educational Testing Service, 1984.

———. *The Writing Report Card.* Princeton, N.J.: National Assessment of Educational Progress at Educational Testing Service, 1986.

Evans, Peter J.A., ed. *Directions and Misdirections in English Evaluation.* Canada: Canadian Council of Teachers of English, 1985.

Greenberg, Karen L., Wiener, Harvey S., and Donovan, Richard A. *Writing Assessment: Issues and Strategies.* White Plains, N.Y.: Longman, 1986.

Houts, Paul L., ed. *The National Elementary Principal,* Volume 54. Number 6. Reston, Va.: The National Association of Elementary School Principals (July/August 1975).

Hoffmann, Banesh. *The Tyranny of Testing.* New York: Collier, 1962.

Owen, David. *None of the Above: Beyond the Myth of Scholastic Aptitude.* Boston: Houghton Mifflin, 1985.

White, Edward M. *Teaching and Assessing Writing.* San Francisco: Jossey-Bass, 1985.

Parent Involvement/Advocacy

Davies, Don, ed. *Schools Where Parents Make a Difference.* Boston: Institute for Responsive Education, 1976.

Equity and Choice. Boston: Institute for Responsive Education, a quarterly publication.

Henderson, Anne T., Marburger, Carl L., Ooms, Theodora. *Beyond the Bake Sale.* Columbia, Md.: National Committee for Citizens in Education, 1986.

Marburger, Carl L. *One School at a Time: School Based Management, A Process for Change.* Columbia, Md.: National Committee for Citizens in Education, 1985.

Teacher Training and the Teaching of Writing

Carnegie Forum on Education and the Economy. *A Nation Prepared: Teachers for the 21st Century.* New York: Carnegie Corporation, 1986.

Elbow, Peter. *Writing with Power.* New York: Oxford University Press, 1983.

————. *Embracing Contraries: Explorations in Learning and Teaching.* New York: Oxford University Press, 1986.

Knoblauch, C. H., and Brannon, Lil. *Rhetorical Traditions and the Teaching of Writing.* Portsmouth, N.H.: Boynton Cook, 1984.

Perl, Sondra and Wilson, Nancy. *Through Teachers' Eyes: Portraits of Writing Teachers at Work.* Portsmouth, N.H.: Heinemann Educational Books, 1986.

Smith, Frank. *Writing and the Writer.* New York: Holt, Rinehart and Winston, 1982.

————. *Joining the Literacy Club.* Portsmouth, N.H.: Heinemann Educational Books, 1988.

▪INDEX